HOW TO SAFELY BUY REAL ESTATE IN THAILAND
(Second Edition)

By

Rene-Philippe R. Dubout[1]

Thai Edition
Published by: DoingBusinessAsia.Com (HK) Ltd.,
Hong Kong

International Edition
Published by RealTime Publishing
Limerick, Ireland

---

[1] This book as the 1st edition was edited by Sam Fraser of Thaienglish.com and Illya Garger.

Remark: Second Edition. The first edition was published in March 2009 under the title *"How to Purchase Real Estate Offshore: The Case of Thailand"*

For information: Rene Philippe & Partners Ltd, 82/9 Soi Langsuan 10330 Bangkok Thailand.
www.renephilippe.com
www.doingbusinessthailand.com

Disclaimer: The author has exercised his best endeavors in preparing and writing this book, including research, study and review of the information contained herein with Thai lawyers, but cannot warrant that the information contained herein is error-free[2]. This book is intended as general information on the subject of purchasing real estate offshore and in Thailand only, and is not an exhaustive treatment of the subject. The contents of this book are not intended to constitute legal, accounting, tax, investment or other professional advice or services. The information is not intended to be relied upon as the sole basis for any decision that may affect you or your investment.

Last Updated: This guide was last updated as of 15 January 2010.

Comments: If you have any comments about this book, or want to share your experiences with the author, please contact him at:
contact@renephilippe.com

Thai Edition
ISBN: 978-974-613-509-2
Published by: DoingBusinessAsia.Com (HK) Ltd,
Hong Kong

International Edition
ISBN: 978-1-906806-83-5
Published by RealTime Publishing
Limerick, Ireland

---

[2] Errare humanum est

ABOUT THE AUTHOR

In addition to his expertise as an authority in real estate, Rene Philippe Dubout, is also an accomplished Swiss attorney with a background in international business, transactional law and arbitration. As an expatriate living and working in Thailand for more than 10 years, he founded Rene Philippe & Partners Ltd in 2002.

A leader in his field, Rene Philippe has been recognized as *"the real-estate veteran"* (Bangkok Post 29.05.09) and *"real estate finance expert and author"* (Herald Sun [Australia] 28.06.09). He is also a member of the JFCCT[3] Property Meeting and is actively trying to improve the rights of foreign buyers in Thailand.

As a lecturer on international private law in the Asia Institute of Technology master degree program, Rene is an accomplished speaker who has been invited to many events in Bangkok, Singapore and Hong Kong. He has also published many articles in local magazines.

His books include the must-have and well-received *How to Safely Buy Real Estate in Thailand*, nominated for the USA Book News National Best Book Award category in business/real estate and well received by the Thai press and numerous readers. He is currently working on his next book, *"How to Safely Invest in Thailand"* to be published in October of 2010.

His email address is: **contact@renephilippe.com**

Follow the author's blog **www.doingbusinessthailand.com**

---

[3] The **Joint Foreign Chambers of Commerce in Thailand (JFCCT)** is the umbrella body for the various Thai-foreign chambers or business associations operating in Thailand

ABOUT THE RENE PHILIPPE GROUP

The Rene Philippe Group is the merging of a *Law Firm* and a *Consulting Company* and includes both *Rene Philippe & Partners Limited* providing legal services and *Rene Philippe Consulting Services Limited* offering a comprehensive business advisory platform, including legal and business consultation, accounting and tax services and other professional services.

In Thailand: Our team provides a full range of professional services to investors looking to establish and conduct business or purchase real estate in Thailand as follows:

> *Legal Services*
> *Real Estate Services*
> *Consulting Services*
> *Accounting & Audit Services*

Overseas: We have more than 10 years' experience in assisting our clients with establishing offshore companies and opening bank accounts with suitable offshore banks. We only use the services of well-known international commercial banks. Our services include:

> *Offshore Company Formation*
> *Offshore Bank Account Opening*

RealEstate: To safely purchase your property in Thailand contact our sister company ThailandBestProperties Ltd
www.thailandbestproperties.com

Contact us:
Rene Philippe & Partners Limited;
82/9 Lang Suan Road, Lumpini, Pathumwan, Bangkok 10330, THAILAND
Tel: +66 (0) 2651 9560 - Fax: +66 (0) 2251 5625
Email: contact@renephilippe.com
Website: www.renephilippe.com

ABOUT DOINGBUSINESSTHAILAND

DoingBusinessThailand is Rene Philippe's latest venture aiming to:

"Provide potential investors with a comprehensive and up-to-date source of information on how to do business or purchase real estate in Thailand"

Follow Rene-Philippe on:

DoingBusinessThailand Blog

Visit our blog: **www.doingbusinessthailand.com**

DoingBusinessThailand Group on FaceBook

Join our Group http://www.facebook.com/group.php?gid=219126990634

DoingBusinessThailand iPhone Application

Download the DBT (DoingBusinessThailand) iPhone application from iTunes stores and receive and read the DoingBusinessThailand blog on your iPhone

FOREWORD TO THE SECOND EDITION

So, what's new other than the change of title? Firstly, let me tell you that no one was more surprised by the reception of the first edition than I was. Quite honestly, I never anticipated I would have to print a second edition only six months after the initial launching of the book. This being said, let's move onto the second edition.

As in the first edition, the second edition has been broken down into two books. What's new is my division of the first Book into two parts. The first part is called "The Dos and Don'ts for Buyers of Offshore Real Estate" and contains 16 chapters taking readers through all of the issues to be considered before buying property in a foreign country. Why are they buying? What do they aim to achieve? Is success always a given when buying property in a foreign country? What happens to those who fail? Are all developers the same? Is there a particular type of developer to be avoided? How can buyers know how to trust a developer? Should I be wary of my agent? Does the rental guarantee offer such a good deal? And the list goes on... The purpose of this first part is to take potential buyers through the buying process step-by-step while helping them avoid the pitfalls and potential minefields.

The second part of the first book is divided into seven chapters dealing with the practical issues pertaining to the purchasing process. Although it is all very well to buy property in a foreign country, offshore purchases require a few additional considerations. First, you will need a bank account. Then you will need to transfer foreign currency into that account. If you decide to buy your property, you will eventually need to transfer foreign currency out of the account. Are foreigners permitted to do all of those things in Thailand? If so, how? I will explain these "how-to's" in two new chapters. Then, you will be purchasing a real estate asset with a purchase price in foreign currency. What are the risks? Finally, should you finance the purchase of your real estate property through a loan or in cash? Once the purchase of your property has been completed, there will be another question to consider: How will you be able to live in your dream property? Is there any preferential visa status applicable to property buyers? I completely rewrote this chapter and provided ample explanation on the two main types of visas that may apply to property buyers in Thailand.

The second book is devoted to Thailand's property market and legal issues arising from ownership. This book is unchanged for the most part, except for one new chapter and some modifications brought to a few chapters updated in the end of October of 2009. For example, I inserted a chapter on my proposition on how to deal with the current 49% foreign ratio for condominium purchases. I also restructured the book by separating the issues pertaining to the purchase of land and house in one part and all issues pertaining to the purchase of a condominium in another part. Like in the first edition, this second book covers issues such as land tenures and relevant regulations, buyers' rights, immovable property rights and tax issues, all of which are directly related to purchases in Thailand. While I'm aware that this part of the book is not easily digested in terms of general reading, I have tried my best to discuss those issues in layman terms. Furthermore, if you are a potential or current purchaser, you really need to have an understanding of the issues dealt with in this second book. Finally I added a content table listing all the summary tables inserted in this book.

I hope you will find this second edition of "How to Safely Buy Real Estate in Thailand" useful and that it will help you complete a safe purchase.

Finally, if there are any issues I have not dealt with in this book that you would like to see in a subsequent edition, please do not hesitate to contact me at contact@renephilippe.com

Rene Philippe
Bangkok, 15 January 2010

TABLE OF CONTENTS

INDEX OF SUMMARY TABLES

BOOK I

ISSUES TO CONSIDER WHEN PURCHASING OFFSHORE REAL

ESTATE

PART 1

THE DOS AND DON'TS FOR BUYERS OF OFFSHORE REAL

ESTATE

Chapter 1   Why Do People Purchase Real Estate Overseas?

Each year, about a million people purchase properties outside their home countries. They purchase real estate overseas for two reasons. The first reason is purely emotional; buyers travel to a foreign country for the holidays and are seduced by the landscape, inhabitants, and climate, so they impulsively decide that this country is as good a place as they'll ever find to spend future vacations or their retirement. This type of buyer will often decide on the spot to purchase their dream property without any legal advice or taking any kind of precaution.

The second reason is investment. In most Western countries, the return you can expect from owning and renting out real estate is lower than it used to be, and a large part of the rental income will inevitably end up in the pocket of the taxman. Furthermore, property laws have become more and more complicated, and so lenient toward tenants that renting out a property has become risky business, because you might end up with a bankrupt tenant you're unable to evict without lengthy legal proceedings. As a result, many investors interested in real estate are discouraged from purchasing in their own countries and turn offshore for their real estate investments.

Buyers of offshore real estate firmly believe that purchasing real estate in a foreign country such as Thailand will not only be easier, but yield them higher rental returns than at home.

Is it really easier to purchase offshore real estate? In a country like Thailand, the formalities of transferring a property at the Land Department (the cadastral registrar) are indeed straightforward and the transaction takes only a few hours to complete. Furthermore, the officers of the Land Department are very accommodating in helping the parties file the required documents.

On one hand, the transaction seems very easy indeed – but that's only the case if you're Thai. On the other hand, several critical issues will enter into the consideration if you're a foreign buyer, and this will make the transaction far more complicated. One of the paradoxes of offshore real estate is that many of the countries becoming favorite destinations for buyers, such as Thailand, have legal systems that prohibit or limit the rights of foreign buyers in purchasing real estate. So, while purchasing real estate in Thailand might seem to be a straightforward and easy transaction at first glance, my personal experience has shown this to not always be the case, because there are other factors entering into the consideration and muddying the process, even if the actual formalities are often easy.

For example, a buyer who purchases property in his home country faces fewer risks than a buyer who purchases in a foreign country because the buyer is better informed. Even if the buyer is not a professional, he will have a minimum understanding of his country's titling system, zoning regulations, building control laws, individual rights and market prices. Finally, buyers purchasing in their home countries will be familiar with reliable developers there. In other words, the buyers will be able to protect themselves.

Most offshore buyers have no clue about the legal system in their destination country, do not often read or understand the local language and are frequently unfamiliar with the reliable developers in the local market.

In larger countries like the US, it often happens that a buyer living on the east coast can purchase a property on the west coast based on pictures only. This kind of purchase is referred to as a "blind" purchase. In the matter of the offshore real estate business, most purchases are blind, not because the buyer doesn't see the property, but because 99% of the cases involve buyers who actually purchase without taking any precautions at all and without any knowledge of the multiple traps awaiting them.

In France, we say of a person who is acting carelessly or recklessly, *"He's bought himself a rope to hang by"*. Unfortunately, this is exactly what too many buyers purchasing offshore real estate do in Thailand.

Does offshore real estate yield more income than real estate in your home country? Here again, this is a double-edged sword. Most real estate products in Thailand yield an average return of only 5% to 8%[4] on investments per year. That is only if you purchase a normal property (and by this I mean any property such as a condominium or house) to be rented out on a monthly or yearly basis. From a Thai investor's point of view, and with banks offering average interest rates between 2% and 3% on deposits, a gross rental return of 5% or 8% is very satisfying.

This is especially so when coupled with the capital gain property owners will make after a few years of ownership, which is no more or less than they could get in their own countries. Most of the properties sold offshore with the promise of an annual return of 10% to 25% are extremely specific products, such as apartments or houses located in resort areas that will be rented out on a daily or weekly basis, mostly to other foreigners vacationing there.

Therefore, while it is true that real estate may yield a larger offshore income than in your own country, this is generally correct

---

[4] Please see chapter 21 for the average rental yield in Bangkok

only in relation to very specific types of properties. What buyers fail to recognize is that while niche market properties may yield more income than ordinary properties, they are more likely to be affected by unpredictable events, because the promised return will depend entirely upon the tourist market in the offshore destination. Political crisis, bird flu, SARS or a tsunami are all events that will affect the influx of short-term tourists and impact the income buyers will earn from their properties.

I am not saying that buying offshore real estate is extremely complicated or dangerous, or that it is not a good investment. On the contrary, there are many people who have earned a lot of money this way. My point is that, contrary to what brokers or developers who specialize in offshore real estate would have you believe, success is not always a given. Furthermore, there are many legal issues to consider and many traps awaiting unwary buyers.

This book is divided into two parts. In the first part, I will present critical issues requiring consideration before purchasing offshore real estate. Not all of the issues discussed here will arise in every country (as they do in Thailand), but awareness of the issues will prompt you to ask good questions. In the second part, I will discuss the example of Thailand.

Even if you aren't interested in purchasing real estate in Thailand you would still benefiting from reading this book because, as previously mentioned, most of the issues I've addressed here are relevant to purchases in other countries. Read it as you would read one of those books containing hundreds of house blueprints, a source of examples and ideas.

Chapter 2   Fortunate vs. Unfortunate Buyers

There are several methods for categorizing buyers of offshore real estate. Users versus non-users, apartment buyers versus house buyers, or low-end buyers versus high-end buyers are just a few of the categorizations available.

At the end of the day, experience tells us that only one classification matters: fortunate buyers versus unfortunate buyers.

The fortunate buyers are those who actually acquire the property they paid for. The unfortunate ones are those who will end up losing part or all of their money while attempting to purchase offshore real estate, or those who purchase a lemon of a property. While the fortunate buyers largely outnumber the unfortunate buyers, attempts to purchase offshore or in Thailand still ends up badly for too many people.

In my experience, most buyers purchase without taking any of the most basics precautions which led me to conclude that the difference between a fortunate and an unfortunate buyer is sheer luck, not more savvy on one side than the other. The fortunate buyers were simply lucky enough to purchase from one of the honest and reliable developers doing business overseas.

What are the most frequent problems encountered by unfortunate buyers? The stories told by unfortunate buyers are many and varied. For example, one is the story of the buyer who purchases land without first checking if the rights to the land were evidenced by a title deed[5]. After the purchase, this buyer ended-up with nothing more than "squatters' rights".

Another is the story of a buyer who purchases a property without first checking if the seller was indeed the owner and who ends up paying twice the price that would have been paid if the property had been purchased directly from the owner.

Alternatively, there are the stories of those imprudent buyers who purchase land without first checking the applicable zoning regulations and end up being unable to build on the land they purchased, or building a smaller structure than they had intended to. Finally, there are the stories of buyers who purchase high land for the view without knowing that they cannot build on land located over 80 meters above sea level in some parts of Thailand.

All these stories about unfortunate buyers have one point in common. Most traps involving buyers of offshore real estate are "accidents waiting to happen". And, like most accidents, these accidents could have been avoided if the buyers had taken minimal precautions.

The following table summarizes the problems generally encountered by buyers of offshore real estate.

---

[5] There are only three kinds of land worth purchasing in Thailand. Land represented by the *Chanote* (Nor. Sor. 4) are the best buy. Then there is land represented by Nor. Sor. 3 Kor. (Certified Certificate of Use) or Nor. Sor. 3 (Certificate of Use).

TABLE 1 Problems encountered by buyer of offshore real estate	
Problems	**Causes**
The seller fails to transfer the ownership of the property, or to execute or register the lease agreement because:	The seller is not the owner of the property sold, or The property is mortgaged and the seller is unable to clear the mortgage, or The property is not represented by a valid title of property, or The seller is unable to divide the land, or The seller becomes insolvent.
The seller fails to construct or complete the construction of the house or condominium because:	The seller is insolvent or has financial difficulties, or The seller did not receive permission to build, or The construction has ceased because of failure to fulfill zoning or building law requirements.
The seller fails to build or complete the facilities of the project because:	The seller is insolvent or has financial difficulties.
The seller fails to apply or obtain a condominium license because:	The seller is unable to fulfill the legal requirements for obtaining said license.
The seller fails to apply for a land development license when applicable because[6]:	The seller is unable to fulfill the legal requirements for obtaining said license.

Problems may also occur even after the transaction has been completed to the satisfaction of the buyer. There may also be legal issues with the transaction the buyer isn't even aware of, or may be aware of but fails to fully comprehend in terms of the full extent and consequences.

In Thailand, for example, there are restrictions on foreign residential land ownership. Thousands of buyers have circumvented the law by purchasing land using companies that have "*Thai*

---

[6] There are, of course, other problems that may occur, but we will discuss them later.

shareholders who may be deemed nominees" without understanding the full legal implications of such transactions. Other buyers are aware of the implications, but believe the chances of being sanctioned are remote because no action has been undertaken by Thailand's successive governments for nearly 30 years.

Most buyers who have purchased a house and leased land from a developer with the promise of a *"perpetual renewal of the lease"* are unaware of all the legal issues surrounding their *"renewal clause"*. They are unaware that the so-called renewal clause inserted into their lease agreement might not be effective at all; even if the clause is effective, the renewal of the agreement might not be as easy as anticipated. They are unaware that the renewal clause is not automatically transferable together with the lease either by succession or assignment of the lease agreement.

Chapter 3   The First-Time Developers

From experience, we know that most problems occur when buyers purchase property *"off plan[7]"*. Whether or not the transaction has a favorable outcome will depend solely upon one single factor: Did the buyer purchase from a reliable developer or not?

Truth be told, purchasing off plan is no more dangerous when purchasing offshore than in your home country, as long as you are purchasing from a reliable developer who operates in the country where you are purchasing.

Briefly, developers in any country may be separated into two main categories. On the one hand, you have what I call Top Developers. These are mostly public companies listed on the stock exchange, such as in Thailand Raimon Land, Natural Park, Sansiri, Golden Land Property and Land & Houses to name only a few. These companies have substantial capital, access to financing and a track record of success. Purchasing off plan from one of these developers

---

[7] Off plan property is a property that is at the planning stage and is yet to be built or has not yet been fully constructed when it is bought.

is nearly risk–free, because these developers are concerned about their reputations. What's more, when they do make a mistake (no one is perfect), they will endeavor to do their very best in honoring their contractual commitments and delivering the properties purchased to their customers. If they cannot deliver the property to the buyers, then they will reimburse them in full. Moreover, Top Developers are also known to honor their warranty commitments.

On the other hand, you have small- or medium-sized developers. Here again, these are mainly reliable and professional, but the difficulty is there are also many unprofessional ones.

Who are the unprofessional developers? They are mostly investors who may or may not have previously worked in the real estate sector who wake up one day having finally found their true calling. They become land developers over night. In the remainder of the book, I will refer to these people as *"First-Time Developers"*. Not all First-Time Developers are bad, and some of today's start-ups will become the Microsoft's of tomorrow. Bill Gates was not born the chairperson and owner of Microsoft. He started his business from scratch with minimal capital, a company newly registered and with no prior accomplishments. He got to where he is today through dedication and sheer hard work[8]. Therefore, it is possible to be new in a business sector and also be successful.

However, the common denominator of all start-up businesses, including First-Time Developers, is that they are doing business against the odds.

First-Time Developers nearly always launch their projects in spite of the odds against them. Generally speaking, First-Time Developers have no previous record of success in real estate development; or if they have a record, they were employees of a company involved in real estate only in their home countries. First-Time Developers are often foreign investors newly arrived in the country where you are making your purchase. When they are foreigners (as many First-Time Developers unfortunately are), and

---

[8] I guess luck might also have something to do with it.

even if they have experience in this kind of business, they will be unable to refer to their accomplishments when developing their project in their newly adopted country because their experience was gained in a completely different context. When they are foreigners, they are rarely able to speak, much less read, the local language and will have only a superficial understanding of the laws applicable to land development.

The average cycle of project developments by First-Time Developers will take place as follows: In most cases, the First-Time Developer has enough capital to purchase project land[9] and to hire an architect to do some drawings and a master plan. In some cases, they will have enough capital to start the construction of a show house and laying the ground work for the utilities, but rarely more. Their First-Time Developer status will make it hard or impossible for them to access commercial loans for financing their projects. De facto, the First-Time Developer has no other options. Once the original capital has been spent, continued financing for the construction and development of the project will come out of their clients' pockets. First-Time Developers will easily sell the first five to ten units of their projects (10% to 20% of the whole project) to family members and close friends as they commence the construction in earnest. However, the level of sales will soon drop and/or the developer will begin to encounter problems dividing the land, and/or will have used part of the payments made by the customers to build their houses and market the project...

Whatever the cause, the time will come when the First-Time Developer begins to encounter financial difficulties as cash flow is less than anticipated, or the project construction will begin to suffer more and more delays as a result of unwise spending. After a time, those few existing customers will stop making payments and this is when the project fails.

---

[9] In some cases, however, they are First-Time Developers who start a project without even owning the land on which the project is developed. Generally, they'll have paid a deposit and agreed on payments by installment with the landowner.

First-Time Developers are not generally dishonest and they seldom start their projects with the intent of cheating or harming their customers. They firmly believe in what they are doing and, while they do not have the capital to fully finance their projects, they generally invest all of their savings in the projects and will end up broke if they fail. First-Time Developers hold little prospect of success and their projects are likely to fail as the elements of insufficient experience, knowledge and capital combine for the only outcome possible in most purchases from First-Time Developers, and that is failure.

From a buyer's perspective, purchasing from a First-Time Developer means purchasing against the odds. I will, of course, provide you with the tools necessary for helping you separate the wheat from the chaff and distinguish reliable developers from the unreliable ones. However, providing you the tools to recognize good developers is not enough. Experience has taught me that once a buyer has set his mind on a house and on a developer, there is not a lot that can be done to dissuade him from purchasing because, as I explained in the introduction, the decision to purchase an offshore property is usually an irrational and emotional decision.

What makes First-Time Developers so successful, yet dangerous, is that they are most often people with outstanding personalities. You cannot help but like them, especially after they conclude the sale with a *"nice guy"* sales pitch and invite you to dinner at home where you will meet the family. These dinners will often be unpretentious, a barbecue by the pool in an exotic garden and that's it. You're living the dream. You can't imagine anyone else building your dream house and you'll throw all caution to the wind as you refuse to listen to any prudent advice.

The second characteristic that makes First-Time Developers so seductive is that mainstream developers often built generic projects without a soul. While most real estate projects have a theme, they become aseptic at the end of the day and are built to please the greatest number of buyers possible.

Now, foreign buyers who purchase real estate in Thailand want more than a plain mainstream architectural concept and First-Time Developers' projects are often more attractive than big developers' projects, because First-Time Developers, despite all their other failings, will put their hearts into their projects. These projects often look brilliant on paper and have great potential, but for the fact that they are most often developed against all odds.

Chapter 4   Let the Buyer Beware!

The story I am about to tell you is a true. It happened in Thailand, but could have actually happened in any other country that is a favorite destination for offshore real estate buyers. Although the story is true, it's also an extreme example, and what I believe to be a once-in-a-lifetime occurrence (at least in Thailand) as the circumstances were a convergence of events that made this possible only once on such a large scale.

Those I refer to in this book as First-Time Developers generally limit themselves to developing small-scale projects (less than 50 houses). When they fail in their endeavors[10], they generally fail early into their projects. As a result, while they will leave buyers stranded, the overall number of the victims and damages will be limited.

As it always happens, the developers failed in the middle of the construction of the project. The exceptional circumstances were the number of victims and the extent of the damage sustained by the

---

[10] Notice that I do not say if they fail, but when.

victims, because more than 200 buyers had purchased from this First-Time Developer, and according to my estimation those investors have lost more than USD 15 million altogether. The account I give you is the story of the project as I was able to reconstruct it after the fact. The timeline and the chain of events I have described are based on the due diligence of the developer company's corporate documents, financial statements of public record and the information provided by 21 out of 200 customers in the projects (commercial agreements, marketing documents, emails, interviews with some of the buyers and so on). While I do not know the whole story, I believe that the files and information I collected and reviewed were sufficient to establish a pattern that led me to deduce the version of events I present below.

This tale began with the arrival of two foreign businessmen on a beautiful island that had become a magnet to foreign travelers over the years. The island was such an ideal place that they could not help but mingle with the local population and ended up married to two local maidens. As they were not yet old enough to retire, our two businessmen decided to promote themselves as *"Real Estate Developers"* and began purchasing land in a nice location to develop housing projects with confidence they would be able to complete their projects successfully. Unfortunately, their good intentions did not make up for their lack of experience, knowledge and capital.

Their first mistake was that, instead of earning their bones on one small project, they ended up launching not one but six residential projects totaling more than 250 housing units. It's unclear, however, whether the multitude and scale of the projects were their doing or whether they were pushed into commencing more and more projects by the agents and financial brokers involved in this failure.

Launching six projects in parallel is not only a complex task from a legal, administrative and construction point of view, but also a very costly business endeavor. Based on the information I collected, the total funding necessary for developing six projects with 250 houses up to completion, including land purchasing, utility development, common areas and facilities was between THB 600 million and THB 900 million (between USD 16 million and USD 24 million[11])

When purchasing *"off plan"*, the first thing any potential buyer should do is calculate the approximate cost of construction for the project he is purchasing into. The easiest way to do this is to calculate the total selling value of the project and apply that amount to the total obtained for a profit ratio coefficient. For example, the total selling value of the Projects was over THB 1.8 billion or USD 46 million. The selling value of the project is very easy to calculate, as developers always give their customers a price list showing the number and the price of the project units. It suffices, then, to apply a profit margin factor of 30% to 50%[12] to obtain a fair approximation of the development costs of the project. In the case of these Projects, an application of a 50% factor would account for the costs of construction at THB 900 million[13] or USD 24 million. Of course, without access to the factual data, these results will only be an approximation.

Another method for obtaining an approximation of the cost of development for a project is to calculate the cost of construction and the cost of the purchase of the land separately. For condominium projects, the cost of the land is between 10% and 25% of the total selling value of the project, depending upon the location. In determining the cost of construction, it suffices to find the average cost of construction in the destination country. Every country has a professional association or government entity that collects those data. In Thailand, for example, this service is provided by the Valuers' Association of Thailand. In Bangkok, the approximate cost of construction for a condominium building is as shown in the following table:

---

[11] At a rate of USD 1 = THB 38 at the time. (Note that 1 USD is now 34 THB only)

[12] The actual margin of First-Time Developers is far wider because they often finance the projects with buyers' money.

[13] In our case, this approximation was confirmed by an analysis of the development costs recorded in the project company's financial statements in comparison to the project's completion status.

TABLE 2 Buildings Construction Costs in Bangkok			
Type	Specifications	Low Standard Price per sqm	High Standard Price per sqm
Residential building	6 to 15 storey's	THB 9,600	THB 13,700
	16 to 25 storey's	THB 15,500	THB 24,900
	26 to 35 storey's	THB 17,100	THB 27,800
2009 Costs of Construction in Bangkok: Source: Valuers Association of Thailand			

For housing projects, the land and installation of the utilities should cost between 10% and 40% of the total selling value of the project, depending upon the location, the size of the land and the quality of the utilities and facilities.

Then the cost of construction for the buildings will be as follows:

TABLE 3 Houses Construction Costs in Bangkok			
Type	Specifications	Low Standard Price per sqm	High Standard Price per sqm
Detached house	Concrete, 1 floor	THB 10,200	THB 13,200
	Concrete, 2/3 floors	THB 9,300	THB 13,200
Duplex house	Concrete, 1 floor	THB 8,600	THB 11,600
	Concrete, 2/3 floors	THB 7,800	THB 10,200
Townhouse	2/3 floors, 4 m wide	THB 6,800	THB 9,700
Townhouse	2/3 floors, 6 m wide	THB 8,300	THB 11,100
2009 Costs of Construction in Bangkok: Source: Valuers' Association of Thailand			

Once a buyer has estimated the cost of the development project in which he wants to purchase, the next task is to check whether it is likely that the developer has sufficient capital to develop the project.

In the case at hand, the developers used a myriad of limited companies (we identified six of them so far, but there might have been more) to develop their Projects. Out of those six companies, two handled the bulk of all the transactions. We will refer to these two companies as Developer 1 and Developer 2 from this point on.

Developer 1 was incorporated in 2001 (that is to say, only two years before the launch of the projects). It had paid-up capital of only USD 105,000[14]. Its financial statements for the years 2002 and 2003 revealed that Developer 1 did not have any business activities prior to the launch of the Projects in 2003. During the period from November 2001 up to the end of 2002, Developer 1 did not record any sales or rental income. The only recorded income of Developer 1 over the two-year period preceding the project launches was an amount of THB 483 (or USD 12) from interest.

Developer 2 was incorporated in 1997 with initial paid-up capital of USD 26,000. We were unable to examine the balance sheets of the company for the period from 1997 up to 2000, as records were unavailable and the company may have conducted activities at the time. By the time the project was launched, it had increased its paid-up capital to USD 105,000. During the period from January 2000 up to the end of February 2002, the company did not have any business sales activities and did not declare any sales income. Its only sources of income during this period were USD 8,236 from rentals and interest income in 2001 and USD 9,473 from rental income in 2002.

At the end of 2002, Developer 1 owned USD 100,000 in land and office equipment while Developer 2 owned only USD 65,000 in land. At the end of 2003, Developer 1 owned USD 360,000 in land and USD 250,000 in cash[15] in hand (as opposed to cash in a bank account) plus office equipment, while Developer 2 owned only USD 150,000 in land.

Overall, the two companies that were about to launch 6 Projects with development costs of around USD 23 million had between themselves a total of USD 210,000 in paid-up capital and had seldom owned more than USD 165,000 worth of land by the end of 2002, and USD 510,000 by the end of 2003 when the cumulative

---

[14] As a matter of convenience, we will provide all financial data in USD at a conversion rate of USD 1 = THB 38 as it was the rate applicable at the time

[15] I'm always very skeptical when I see lines such as "cash in hand 10 million baht" on a Thai company's financial statement.

worth of the two companies was less than 3% of the Projects' development costs. In our estimation, the minimum amount required to buy the Projects' land (between 60 to 80 rai[16]) was between USD 1 million and USD 3 million. Therefore, we aren't even certain whether the developers entirely owned the land for the Projects at the time of their launching. One of the possibilities is that they indeed owned all of the land for the Projects at the time of their launching, but maintained the land ownership under the names of the original owners or other Thai individuals for land division purposes. The other option is that they had purchased the project land, but had not yet paid the entire purchase price to the original landowners who, for this reason, had not yet transferred all of the land to the developers' companies.

At the end of the day, it doesn't really matter which was the case. What does matter is that, even if the companies had indeed owned all of the land for the Projects prior to their launching, they did not have the financial resources necessary for developing six projects of this scale. A simple look at their financial statements for 2004 and 2005 sufficiently confirms that the developers financed their projects out of the pockets of their customers because the value of the company assets increased in conjunction with the clients' payments. The value of Developer 2's recorded assets jumped from USD 160,000 in 2003 to nearly USD 4 million in 2004 and USD 8 million in 2005. And the financial statements of Developer 2 provided further evidence that the company had had cash flow problems all along, with only USD 10,000 cash available at the end of 2004 (compared to USD 4 million in assets) and USD 30,000 cash available at the end of 2005 (compared to USD 8 million in assets). The continued flow of payments from their customers was the lifeline sustaining the Developers' Projects. Once the payment well had dried up, there was nothing to prevent the Developers' house of cards from falling.

Ludicrously, the proverbial straw that broke the camel's back and led to the collapse of the developers was actually the developers' own agreements with their customers. In order to build

---

[16] 1 rai = 1600 SQM.

customer confidence, the Project Developers did something very unusual in their standard agreements for payment schedules. Although buyers don't often realize it, a developer's schedule of payments speaks volumes as to the reliability of the developer, because it tells you how the project is financed. In Thailand and other countries, developers currently use two kinds of schedules for payments with buyers that purchase "*off plan*".

Top Developers who are either public companies or highly capitalized private companies with a track record of success and access to bank financing will usually use the 30/70 or 40/60 schedule of payment. The client will pay a deposit (often THB 100,000), followed by 10% of the purchase price upon the execution of the agreement, then 20% in 12 to 24 installments during the construction period. The buyer only pays the remaining balance of 60-70% of the property purchase price upon completion and the registration of the transfer of ownership (freehold), or the registration of the lease (leasehold), of the property at the Land Department. Furthermore, in countries where such facilities exist, Top Developers will generally agree that their customers use escrow facilities as an additional protection.

In contrast, most First-Time Developers will use an 80/20 payment schedule, where the client will be requested to pay a deposit (THB 100,000), then 30% at the signature of the agreement, 25% upon the completion of the foundation, 25% upon finishing the roof and windows, then 20% upon completion and transfer of the property.

Developers that only request 30% or 40% of payment during the project construction and 60% or 70% upon completion or transfer property are developers who have the financial resources to develop their projects without customer payments (whether through equity or financing). A developer who uses a payment schedule requesting the buyer to make payments for 80% of the purchase price prior to the completion and delivery of the property and the last 20% upon delivery needs the client's money to pay for the project development.

Not surprisingly, the Projects' schedule of payments was of the 80/20 type. Clients were requested to make their payments in four installments, starting with a refundable deposit payable upon the reservation followed by the first installment representing 25% of the aggregate property purchase price (less the deposit) and of the entire purchase price of the furniture payable upon or within 30 days of the execution of the contract. What was unusual in the developer's schedule of payments was that the second installment representing 25% of the aggregate property purchase price was payable upon the commencement of construction *and the completion of the land transfer or the registration of the lease agreement*. The third installment representing 30% of the aggregate property purchase price was payable upon construction of 70% of the villa (up to the roof) and a final installment representing the remaining 20% of the aggregate purchase price was payable upon delivery of the completed villa.

The Developers introduced in their agreements a clause rarely seen in Thailand that provided for an early transfer of the land to their buyers, and doing so led them to their doom. They failed to understand that the land appropriation is an easy process only as long as one intends to follow the law. Land appropriation, a process also known as land allotment and consists of dividing land into smaller plots for resale as undeveloped land or within the context of a land development project. In Thailand, the Land Appropriation (or Allotment) Act from 2000 regulates land division. The purpose of the Act is to protect buyers purchasing in housing projects and *"...to specify measures to protect the appropriate land buyer"*[17] and determine the quality of the infrastructure of the project. For example, the law will determine the minimum size of the common area and green area as well as the minimum width of the roads within the project and the minimum standards applicable for utilities. The law also provides an obligation for the developer to transfer the ownership of the common areas and facilities to the project juristic person (equivalent to a homeowners' association).

---

[17] Government Gazette, Volume 117, Part 45 A

The scope of the land appropriation act is as follows: *"Land Appropriation" means disposition of land, which is allotted in many small plots, altogether from over 10 plots, notwithstanding allotment from a sole plot or many plots in successive areas with assets or benefit acquired as remuneration. It also means allotment of less than ten small plots with the addition of former plots later on within three years totaling over ten small plots".* The act furthermore specifies, *"Anybody is forbidden to perform land appropriation, unless permission is granted by the board[18].*

Now, one of the problems with the Land Appropriation Act is that it does not account for the needs of developers who would like to sell housing properties to foreign buyers under a lease agreement. A developer who has received a land appropriation license may only sell the allotted land, not lease it[19]. The second difficulty is that the process of obtaining a land appropriation license requires the preparation of many supporting documents for attachment to the application. For example, the developer has to provide plans for the project's electricity system to be approved by the Electricity Authority of Thailand. While professional developers will have no problems providing the requested documentation, First-Time Developers will find the process cumbersome and costly, preferring to avoid it at all costs. What they do not realize is that trying to circumvent the Land Appropriation Act is far more complicated, time-consuming and costly than providing the supporting documents requested by the local authorities. The difficulty is that the only way to divide the land without falling under the scope of the Land Allotment Act is to divide the land nine parcels at a time every three years. At this rate, it would take 83 years to divide the whole project. To circumvent this time constraint, First-Time Developers will try to keep the ownership of the land divided into the hands of several landowners, apparently independent of one

---

[18] Land Appropriation Act, Section 21

[19] In theory, a developer who only wants to lease land, not sell it, could request an application to divide the land for lease into more than nine parcels at a time. However, if the developer later sells part of the land divided for the purpose of the lease, then it would mean that application to divide the land had been falsified.

another. Each supposedly independent landowner will file an application to divide their land in nine parcels before transferring it to several other landowners who will further process the subdivision[20]. In order to avoid alerting the Land Department that the developer is trying to circumvent the land allotment act, the developer will file one application at a time and wait several months between each application.

This process is complex enough to manage when developing thirty-house projects and it doesn't take a lot of imagination to understand the difficulties the Developers may have encountered in dividing their land for the projects into 250 units. Such complexity makes the demanding procedure of applying for a land allotment license look like a walk in the park.

How could a First-Time Developer not see that whatever legal requirements he needs to fulfill in dividing a land by the book are a hundred times easier than trying to circumvent the law? It should be noted that those who have purchased land and houses from developers in Thailand who haven't applied for a land appropriation license do not need to worry about a possible legal backlash. The Land Department policy is only to prosecute the developers and not the buyers who have purchased within such projects.

According to the information provided by the local Land Department, the Developers of these Projects never applied for land appropriation licenses for any of their Projects. Instead, they chose to try circumventing the law to divide their land. As might have been predicted, the Developers encountered problems in the process and were unable to divide their land into 250 parcels as quickly as they had first anticipated. Because of the slow land division and since the payment of the buyers' second installment was subject to the condition that the Developers transferred the titles to the plots of land or registered the lease agreements to their buyers, the latter delayed their payments. The lack of payments started to affect the

---

[20] You don't actually need so many landowners, because one person who owns two parcels of unconnected land may divide each parcel into nine plots.

project construction, and brought the Projects to a standstill. The Developers' failure left 200 buyers stranded with a total cumulative loss we estimate at between USD 15 and 20 million. Only a few of those buyers will be able to recover any part of their losses. Only the less unlucky who have received the ownership of their land parcels will be able to recover part of their losses.

The reason most buyers won't be able to recover their money has nothing to do with the Thai legal system. The buyers have legal rights under Thai laws and could chose to sue or prosecute the Developers with good chances of success. However, another setback when buying from a First-Time Developer is that the buyers will be left behind with a messy legal situation in the case of a failure. Even with the support of justice, the legal situation will be so complicated that the buyers have no chance of ever recovering their losses.

In this particular case, for example, the first difficulty was that the companies with whom most buyers had executed their agreements, namely Developer 1 and Developer 2, did not own all of the land for the projects at the time the developers failed. Part of the project land was and remains the property of Thai individuals with whom the buyers have no direct legal relationships. What is more, the cash-strapped Developers, as they were when the Projects started to fail, began to borrow money and mortgage many of the project land parcels against small commercial or private loans. As they couldn't borrow enough money from commercial banks, they started to make what we call in Thailand *"Khaifak"* ["nest egg"] transactions.

"Khaifak" originated with a Chinese method for borrowing against land. The closest Western institution would be a *"sale with right of redemption"*, but, while there are similarities, the two transactions remain different. The owner of land will borrow money from a lender and transfer the title of the land to his lender in exchange. If the borrower is able to reimburse the loan to his lender within a certain period, then the lender will be legally bound to transfer the ownership of the land back to the borrower. If the borrower is unable to repay the lender, then the lender keeps the ownership of the land and the debt is deemed repaid. For the

duration of the period of repayment, the borrower will generally become the tenant of the lender. Now, when their clients stopped paying, the Developers who were unable to secure commercial loans started to borrow money under *"Khaifak"* arrangements. As they were unable to reimburse their lenders, third parties with whom the buyers had no legal relationships, ended up owning many parcels of the Projects.

Finally, the last setback in doing business with First-Time Developers is that most of them believe in paying as few taxes as possible, maintaining two sets of books and failing to declare part of their income – if they ever declare any income at all. Even those who do not actively try to cheat the Revenue Department will have messy accounts (when they have any) and it isn't uncommon to see them having problems with the tax administration. At least three out of the six development companies involved in these Projects are currently being audited by the Revenue Department. I am not talking of the mandatory annual tax audit for all companies registered in Thailand. No, we are talking of the nasty tax audit, the one that is so bad that the Tax administration feels the need to notify the Department of Business Development[21] that those companies cannot be liquidated for the duration of the tax investigation.

Now, if at the end of its investigation, the Revenue Department concludes that the Developers have failed to declare part of the companies' income, then the Revenue Department will have cause to claim unpaid taxes and fine the companies. Since the companies are insolvent, they won't be able to pay the Revenue Department back taxes and fines (if any) and the tax authority will have no other alternative than to pursue the liquidation of the companies' assets. Whatever assets the companies still have will be sold through public auctions. As the assets are distressed assets, they will be sold at fair market value and, because the Revenue Department is by law a secured debtor, the buyers will only be able to share whatever is left after the Revenue Department and other secured creditors have been paid.

---

[21] The company registrar.

For all these reasons, we believe that most of the Project buyers will never be able to recover any of their losses, even if legal action is successful.

Chapter 5   The Butterfly Effect

We've all heard of the butterfly effect and its theory that a seemingly innocuous change, such as the flap of a butterfly's wings, unleashes tornado-like forces on the future. While the Developers launched their Projects against the odds and failure was likelihood from the start, the fall-out from their actions might not have been so damaging if not for one additional circumstance. As I've already explained, the most common cause of failure with First-Time Developers is insufficient funds and their absolute reliance on their clients' payments to complete their projects. These developers normally fail early on in the development process due to the lack of sufficient capital and the money necessary to properly market their project. They will only rely on a few local[22] real estate agencies to sell their houses and will only make a few sales before they have to stop because of cash flow problems. Therefore, it isn't uncommon for First-Time developers to leave more than a few buyers[23] stranded. Why, then, were the Developers of the six Projects we discussed in the previous chapter able to do so much damage?

---

[22] But for this particular case the big and reputable real estate agencies do not generally handle the sales of projects developed by First-Time Developers.
[23] Even if a few are too many.

The *"butterfly effect"* resulted from the involvement of an international real estate agency franchisee (hereinafter referred as the *"Franchisee"*) at an early stage of the project launches and of an offshore, financial services brokerage company[24]. The international real estate agency was the overseas representative of a worldwide real estate affiliation of independently owned and operated companies (hereinafter referred as the *"Real Estate Affiliation"*), also known as a franchise network[25]. The problem was that the Real Estate Affiliation in question had spent the past 15 years building a worldwide reputation of undeniable trustworthiness and the association of a Real Estate Affiliation brand with any real estate project inevitably reflects well on the project. This is the Real Estate Affiliation claiming on its website to be *"The best real estate firm in any market"*. The very same firm that claims to provide the *"best possible real estate solutions"* or *"expert local real estate advice"* and a *"pioneering tradition of global breadth and local depth continues today and sums up the Real Estate Affiliation's unique approach to the business of commercial real estate"*.

The only truth was that this Franchisee did indeed have *"a very unique approach to the business of commercial real estate"*, but the problem was in the flaws of this approach. The first mistake the Franchisee made was to mislead the public to believe the Real Estate Affiliation was developing this project in co-operation with the project developers.

The Franchisee prepared and jointly disseminated with the First Time Developers an advertisement called the *"Project Fact Sheet"*. In the top left corner of the document was the Developers' logo while the top right contained the Real Estate Affiliation logo and the catch title *"First-Time Developer is now proud to present its latest world-class development in **cooperation with the** Real Estate Affiliation."*

---

[24] It's important to note that the real estate agency and the finance brokerage company were both located and operating overseas and that no Thai brokers or agencies (including international real estate agency brands operating in Thailand) were involved.

[25] The international real estate agency brand involved has since appointed a franchisee in Thailand, but the Thai franchisee was not involved in these events.

Not only did the Franchisee mislead the potential buyers into believing the Real Estate Affiliation was associated with the Developers, but the Franchisee also advertised the Developers as a reliable and experienced developer. The Franchisee further referred to the *"Developers (...) **latest** world-class development"* in the *"Project Fact Sheet"*, "latest" meaning the "most recent". The use of the word "latest" in the Project Fact Sheet also mislead potential buyers into believing the Developers had already successfully completed other projects, which was inconsistent with the balance sheets of the companies that showed no activities for the three years preceding the launching of the Projects.

Finally, the Franchisee did not have any terms marvelous or dazzling enough to qualify the Projects as *"World-Class Development"* or the Developers *"(...), Utopia Island's **premier developer** of luxury villas"*. Claiming the developers were first in rank among the island Developers was also not supported by their financial statements.

As if misleading potential buyers to believe the Projects were developed in cooperation with the Real Estate Affiliation and making unsubstantiated marketing claims wasn't enough to fool potential buyers, the Franchisee further mislead the buyers to believe the Franchisee had performed complete due diligence on the Developers' Projects.

The Franchisee was sending potential buyers a two-page fact sheet called *"Real Estate Affiliation Developer's Due Diligence for International Projects"*, leading potential buyers to believe the developers of the projects had been subjected to and successfully passed a 21-item due diligence conducted by the Franchisee. Briefly, *"Due Diligence"* is an investigation or audit of a potential investment that serves to confirm all material facts in regard to the purchase of an asset. In this particular case, the due diligence form sent by the Franchisee to the potential buyers led them to believe the Franchisee had performed complete due diligence on the Developers and their projects. The fact sheet sent by the Franchisee to the buyers led them to believe the Franchisee had verified the following information:

PRODUCT CONSIDERATIONS
- A.　Two to three independent appraisals of property value (if available)
- B.　Legal description
- C.　Color pictures of the property
- D.　Location map
- E.　Product details

1. Size in acres (total site and proposed sub-division)
2. Description of proposed physical improvements on property
3. Statement indicating conformance with town planning
4. Any known easements, restrictions or reversions on property
5. Any restrictions or reversions attached to acquisition by Seller
6. Specific proposed use of property
7. Justification for third-party investment requirements
8. Specific sources of funds
9. Property details:
   a. Any outstanding mortgages on property
   b. Assessment of property's salability
   c. External consultant details (construction, architecture, town planning, marketing)
   d. Project development plans
   e. Proof of ownership

10. Developer details:
    a. Track record
    b. Company structure (PLC vs. private)
11. Operating or capital costs associated with purchase
12. Any unusual operating costs resulting from property acquisition
13. Anticipated expenses resulting from property acquisition
14. Investor's financial commitment
15. Any potential liabilities/risks associated with proposed acquisition e.g. any unusual potential for accident, loss of relevant or resultant additional costs
16. Disclaimers and restrictions over project control and management
17. Ownership eligibility (nationalities/vehicles e.g. individuals, companies, corporations)
18. Ownership tenure (freehold, leasehold - perpetual/fixed term)
19. Return on Investment (ROI)
    a. Capital growth (yield)
    b. Cash flow from rental returns - guaranteed/forecast
20. Acquisition process:
    a. Deposits
    b. Payment schedule
    c. Financing
    d. Taxes, stamp duties, legal fees, council/government rates
    e. Ongoing fees (e.g. management, sinking fund, utilities)

    f. Local purchase value vs. foreign purchase value
21. Disposal process:
    a. Capital Gains Tax
    b. Other taxes or fees
    c. Restrictions on foreigners

Because of the reputation of the Real Estate Association, the buyers had no reason to doubt the Franchisee's word on this matter and they relied on Franchisee's claims that it had performed due diligence. Did the Franchisee perform due diligence as claimed or not? As already explained, I am not privy to what the Franchisee did or did not do, but I don't think they actually bothered to perform any due diligence. If they had, they would have found that the developer companies did not own all of the land for the Projects; the Developers' companies had no previous track record and had been idle for the three years preceding the launching of the Projects. Finally, they would have realized that the developers did not have the financing necessary to handle their projects and that they were First-Time Developers. You'd think they couldn't do much worse than lying about the due diligence, but they did.

The Franchisee organized exhibitions overseas to sell the Projects. During the first exhibition, one of the Franchisee Directors brokered an agreement between at least one potential buyer[26] and one of the developer new companies[27] that did not even exist at the time the agreement was first executed. That the company was incorporated a few months later is irrelevant and doesn't make such impossible behavior acceptable, but we haven't reached the bottom yet; there's more to come.

Around July 2004, just one year after the Projects were first launched, rumors started to spread around that the Developers were in financial trouble and didn't own the project land, or at least did not own all of the land. Of course, as soon as buyers started to hear those rumors, they reported them to the Franchisee. In September of

---

[26] In this particular case, I'm aware of one potential buyer, but there may be more.
[27] The Developers had incorporated at least six companies I know of to develop their projects, but even when the clients were signing with those other companies, all payments were made to Developer 1 and Developer 2.

2004, the Franchisee sent an email reassuring the buyers that "*The developer purchased the land with cash and he is the owner of it. He's funded the project himself without any loan from the bank so far.*" This affirmation was, of course, false. Not only had the Developers never possessed the funds to finance all of their Projects, but they also had already started to borrow money as early as 2003. In 2003, the Developers were borrowing money from private persons at an interest rate of 30% per year. How desperate can a person be for money to agree to such terms? (The maximum legal interest rate in Thailand is 15%.) As there were no public records of the private loan, the Franchisee might not have known about it. However, the Developers had started to mortgage several parcels of project land with banks as early as April of 2004. For example, in April 2004, they mortgaged two deeds they had already sold to their clients. In July 2004, they mortgaged another deed representing a parcel of land that had also already been sold to a client.

In my opinion, the most significant part of the Franchisee answer was the last sentence. "*Could you please advise us about the source of the rumor you received? The developer would like to know it.*" At this time, the Franchisee was still in bed with the Developers and, when the rumors started to spread, the Franchisee was not so interested in verifying the facts as squelching them. Indeed, the Franchisee was about to organize a second exhibition to sell more of the Developers' properties.

However, despite attempts by the Franchisee to stop them, the rumors continued and more buyers started to express their concerns about the financial situation of the Developers during the second half of 2004, which compelled the Franchisee to take action. Then one of the Franchisee employees sent this email, which is a masterpiece of irresponsibility: "*FYI, I have done a little of my own personal snooping previously on various Thai forum boards on the Projects site and crew: The Projects crowd have a very good reputation on them in terms of service and standards with nary a bad word and when there has been one it has very quickly been revealed as sour grapes usually from another developer down there. I just thought I would pass that little tidbit on.*"

If there were a hall of fame for corporate irresponsibility the *"little tidbit"* email would definitely have its place there. I mean, that says a lot about this *"Real Estate Affiliations' unique approach to the business of commercial real estate"* and their claim to be *"the best real estate firm in any market"*. Finally, when the Developers started to encounter problems and delays, the Franchisee informed the buyers the delay had occurred because of *"the recent overhaul of the land office was caused by some land ownership issues on the main land and Phuket and has nothing to do with the Developers"*. I believe this explanation given to the buyers was incorrect and that the delays were the direct consequences of the Developers' failure to abide by the law by applying for land allotment licenses to divide the land for the Projects. While the Developers are primarily responsible for this debacle, they would never have done so much damage without the help of the Franchisee, and the Franchisee should be, in my opinion, held accountable for their losses. Unfortunately, this does not help, as the Franchisee also seems to be in bad shape.

In the first edition I had said, *"The only good news from the buyers' point of view is that, in this particular case, the Franchisor himself was operating the Franchisees in the zone where our Franchisee was located. Since the Franchisor is one of those publicly listed multinational companies declaring to attach a high value to the concept of corporate responsibility[28] and as they seem to derive such great pride from the listing of one of their Franchisee on a Corporate Responsibility Index, there is still hope they will step in and do right by their buyers."* Unfortunately, when informed of the situation, the franchise owner did not react. Several groups of Buyers have sued the Franchisee. Hopefully they will be able to recover part of their investments.

Since the first edition was published, I have also learnt that the very same Franchisee was also involved in another failed project, a condominium project on another Thai island; here again, the number of victims is impressive.

---

[28] At least that's what they say on paper and in their press statements.

Chapter 6   Separating the Wheat from the Chaff

If there's a lesson in the example I discussed in the two previous chapters, it is that what happened to the buyers in the Developers' Projects could have been avoided. There was enough evidence available showing the developers to have neither the experience nor the funds to complete the projects in the first place. However, similar to the symptoms of a sickness, evidence must be visible to be useful. How can buyers dig up the information they will need to evaluate the strengths and weaknesses of the developers they are about to purchase from?

Heaven helps those who help themselves, which is why I tried to develop an easy-to-score test any potential buyer could use to test a developer's reliability without having to ask for professional assistance. This test is not one of due diligence. On the contrary, it is to due diligence what a do-it-yourself pregnancy test is to an ultrasound. A positive pregnancy test will tell a woman she's pregnant, but if she wants to know if the baby is well-formed, she'll need to have an ultrasound.

The purpose of the developer test is to look for patterns, and the results of the test will indicate whether there might be one or more problems with a developer.

For the purposes of the test, I've isolated five criteria buyers can easily check as relevant in evaluating developer reliability. Note that, for the purposes of the test, you must check the developer's company, not the company owning the project. Indeed, most developers (even Top Developers) set up one company per project. Therefore, the target of the test is the company of the developer, not the company that owns the project land, except for cases where these two are the same.

(1) The first criterion is the type of company. Is the developer a public or private company? Furthermore, if it's a public company, is it quoted on a public stock exchange such as SET[29]?

Why is a public company better than a private company? In most countries, the conditions of the incorporation in a public company are more stringent than the conditions of the incorporation of a private company. Any Tom, Dick or Harry can ask a lawyer to register a private company. The incorporation of a public company, however, requires more effort and is subject to greater scrutiny. I have yet to see a First-Time Developer who has used a public company as its legal vehicle. It's simply too improbable.[30]

Why is a public company quoted on a Public Stock Exchange better than a non-quoted company? Here again, a good deal of time and financial results are normally necessary before a company can apply for listing on any market. Being listed generally means easier access to capital and financing than a non-quoted company and more transparency. All of the financial records and history of the company can be checked online on the Stock Market website (there is an English version in most cases). In Thailand, for example, you can obtain all information about publicly quoted companies online in

---

[29] Stock Exchange of Thailand.
[30] It's possible, of course, to buy a shell company, but even this operation is costly.

English at the SET website, while records of private companies must be copied at the Ministry of Commerce and translated from Thai to English.

There are 25 Developers listed on the Stock Exchange as follows:
Raimon Land, Sansiri, Major Development, Eastern Star Real Estate, Lalin Properties, MK Real Estate Development, KC Property, NC Housing, Sammakorn, Preuksa Real Estate, SC Assets, LPN Development, Land & Houses, Golden Land Property Development, Rasa Property Development, Property Perfect, Supalai, Asian Property Development, Noble Development, Prinsiri, Quality Houses, Metrostar Property, Charn Issar Development, Krisdamhanakorn, Areeya Property

(2) The second criterion is capitalization. How strong is the developer's capitalization?

Why is capital relevant? Paid-up capital is important, as it's the first indicator of the financial situation of a company. If a developer intends to develop a project that costs USD 5 million[31], but has only USD 100,000 in paid-up capital, then a smart buyer should wonder where the money to develop the project is coming from. Of course, a company may have low capital but numerous assets, which is why the capital criterion must not be examined in isolation, but in parallel with the fifth criterion, the payment schedule. If there isn't enough equity to finance a project, then where does the money come from? In Thailand, for example, Thai commercial banks generally refrain from granting loans to First-Time Developers, especially those who develop land and housing projects targeted at foreign customers and managed by foreign directors. This is why most First-Time Developers either finance the projects themselves or out of their clients' payments[32]. Which option do you think they'll choose?

(3) The third criterion is longevity. How long has the developer company been registered?

---

[31] I've already provided an easy method for buyers to calculate the development costs of a project in Chapter 4.
[32] Very few First-Time Developers have the equity to develop their projects.

Why is the time of incorporation relevant? Because longevity is often the result of good management; therefore, the longer a company is in the market, the better it is for a customer. Longevity is an even more relevant criterion if you consider it in parallel with the developer's record of accomplishment. The longer a company has been in existence, the more projects it should have developed. Here again, it is technically possible to buy an existing company. Therefore, the period of incorporation must be viewed in parallel to the fourth criterion, the track record.

(4) The fourth criterion involves experience. How many projects has the developer completed? The more projects a developer has worked on, the more experience this developer has.

(5) Finally the last criterion, how is the developer's payment schedule structured?

Why are the terms of payment relevant? As discussed in Chapter 4, a buyer who purchases "*off plan*" will be offered two kinds of payment schedules, depending upon the developer. The first type is a table of payments providing for the payment in several installments of 30% to 40% of the purchase price during the period of construction (often in installments); and the payment of the balance, which is 60% to 70% of the purchase price, upon the transfer of the title deed for the completed property to the buyer.

Top Developers in Thailand only use the first schedule of payment, that is to say 30% (before transfer) / 70% (upon transfer). They do not need to ask their buyers for additional payments during the construction stage, because their project is fully financed either by equity or through a mixture of commercial loans and equity.

In the second type of schedule, the developer will request the buyer to pay up to 80% to 90% of the purchase price during the period of construction (between 3 to 4 installments). On the transfer date of the completed property the buyer will only have 10% to 20% of the purchase price to pay. This method of payment is more risky for the buyer and is often an indication the developer is financing the construction out of its customer's money. As already explained above, I have never seen any of the Top Developers in Thailand using this second schedule.

Of course, it's always possible to try and fake the results of a test. For example, a First-Time Developer could increase its paid-up capital to THB 100 million and not actually pay the capital[33], or even purchase a shell company registered 10 years ago. This is why the test doesn't weigh each criterion separately, but in relation to one another. If a developer has THB 100 million in paid-up capital, but still uses an 80/20 schedule of payment, or if a developer company has been incorporated for 20 years but has only one active project, then there's a problem.

This scoring system is easy to use, but is it reliable? I have tested it on both known Top Thai Developers and First-Time Developers. Those developers I call *"Top Thai Developers"*, such as Raimon Land, Sansiri, Golden Land and so on, have all passed the test with excellence and scored 75 pts. However, whenever I used the test to score First-Time Developers, they failed. For example, the companies I referred to as Developer 1 and Developer 2 in Chapter 5 would have failed the test. Developer 1 would have barely scored 10 out of 75 points (1c = 5, 2d = 0, 3d = 0, 4d = 0, 5b = 5) and Developer 2 would have scored 20 out of 75 points (1c = 5, 2d = 0, 3b = 10, 4d = 0, 5b = 5).

In addition, for the test to mean something, the company to be tested should be one registered inside the country where the project is located. Any Tom, Dick or Harry could register a company with USD 20 million in capital in the BVI[34], providing he paid the registration fees.

Please see in the following table the Rene Philippe Developer Test.

---

[33] Illegal, but technically possible.
[34] British Virgin Islands

TABLE 4: The Rene Philippe Developer Test

THE RENE PHILIPPE DEVELOPER TEST TEST YOUR DEVELOPER IN 5 QUESTIONS	DVLP1	DVLP2	DVLP3	DVLP4
THE DEVELOPER :				
1.a Is a Public Company quoted on the Stock Exchange. (15p)	15	-	-	-
1.b Is a Public Company not quoted. (10p)		10	-	-
1.c Is a Private Company. (5p)	-	-	5	5
1.d Is an Individual. (0p)				
2.a Has paid-up capital of USD 25 million or more. (15p)	15	-	-	-
2.b Has paid-up capital of USD 5 million or more. (10p)	-	10	-	-
2.c Has paid-up capital of less than USD 1 million. (5p)	-	-	5	
2.d Has paid-up capital of less than USD 200,000. (0p)	-	-	-	0
3.a Has been registered for 10 years or more. (15p)	15	-	-	-
3.b Has been registered for 5 years or more. (10p)	-	10	-	-
3.c Has been registered for 3 years or more. (5p)	-	-	5	-
3.d Has been registered for less than 2 years. (0p)	-	-	-	0
4.a Has completed more than 10 projects. (15p)	15	-	-	-
4.b Has completed more than 3 projects. (10p)	-	10	-	-
4.c Has completed only one project. (5p)	-	-	5	-
4.d Has never completed a project in the country. (0p)	-	-	-	0
5.a Has Conditions of Payment at 30% prior to and 70% upon completion with transfer of the property at the Land Department. (15p)	15	-	-	-
5.b Has Conditions of Payment at 80% prior to and 20% upon completion with transfer of the property at the Land Department. (5p)	-	5	5	5
TOTAL	75	40	25	10
©Rene Philippe & Partners Ltd.		www.renephilippe.com		

A friend recently told me that my developer test was unfair because there are First-Time Developers out there who are starting from scratch with newly registered companies, low capital and no previous experience who could succeed against all odds, if given a chance. My friend concluded his remarks by saying the developer test would accomplish nothing but drive people out of businesses who could have succeeded if given a chance.

My friend is absolutely right. There is an exception to every rule and I've personally witnessed more than a few First-Time

Developers become successful with their projects, despite the deck of cards stacked against them. Therefore, my purpose in making the test available is not to put First-Time Developers out of businesses. I agree that everyone deserves a chance.

My point is that those who are buying from a First-Time Developer should do so with all of the facts in hand and knowing they're about to engage in a risky transaction. I have no problems with people who want to take chances with their money, but I think it's only fair for them to at least know the risks. For those who decide to knowingly do business with a First-Time Developer, I would also say this:

Hiring professional help is always a first step in the right direction, but is often insufficient. In French, we have this saying: *"The most beautiful woman in the world can only give what she has."* It's the same with a lawyer who will only give you as much advice and help as you require. Hiring a lawyer and requesting a review of your agreement with a First-Time Developer or additional agreements with view to better protection is a good course of action. However, the problem is that all you'll obtain from your lawyer's work is a false sense of security. Just like "applying a bandage to a wooden leg" will not help a one-legged man walk better having a good set of agreements might not be enough when doing business with a First-Time Developer. The main reason has already been explained in Chapter 4: When First-Time Developers go down, they fall all the way to the bottom and leave behind such a legal and accounting mess that there's little hope of recovering anything.

Chapter 7   What is Due Diligence?

As previously discussed, due diligence is a broad term used to refer to the inspection and investigation of a property before a buyer makes the final decision of whether or not to engage in a transaction, such as an acquisition, merger, or loan. Due diligence is a useful tool for estimating the status of a developer.

There are several types of due diligence that may be performed for real estate transactions. The three main types of due diligence are legal, financial and physical. The legal due diligence means a review of all the legal documents associated with a transaction. Depending upon the client requirements, a lawyer may, for example, only verify whether the title evidencing rights to the land exists, the name of the current owner and whether or not there is a charge or a lien on the land, such as a mortgage or servitude. Then the scope may be extended and the buyer may be interested in learning of the history of the title deed (to check whether or not it was lawfully issued[35]), the zoning and building regulations applicable to the land and whether there is any problem with access. A buyer may request the lawyer to

---

[35] Please see Part II on this matter.

widen this scope and look at the seller and/or developer's information. Financial due diligence is the analysis of the financial statements of the developer. In other words, legal and financial due diligences are more about checking the documents and laws applicable to the property, while a physical due diligence involves physical inspections and testing of the property. Now, there are several reasons why most buyers do not hire lawyers to perform full-blown diligence on a developer or seller.

The first reason is that buyers often develop a friendly relationship with their First-Time Developer from the very beginning and feel uncomfortable about investigating their *"friend"* who *"invited them for dinner at his home"*.

The second reason is that it's generally sufficient for the lawyer to make an estimation of the fees for the service to dissuade the average buyer from proceeding with any due diligence.

Finally, buyers generally hesitate between a few developers, and performing full due diligence on each of them would be both impractical and far too expensive.

Even though most buyers end up not conducting due diligence on their developers, I will make a checklist of the questions that must be reviewed for each type of due diligence, because simply reading the checklist will help buyers in their reflection. The questions mentioned below are applicable in Thailand. Although the situation may be different in other countries, the following checklists are still helpful in reminding buyers of potential issues.

TABLE 5: LANDOWNER AND DEVELOPER CHECKLIST[36]

ISSUE	ITEMS TO CHECK
Landowner	
	Legal Name
	Legal Structure (individual ownership, partnership, limited company, public limited company)
	Date of Incorporation
	Capital
	Part of the Capital paid up
	Members, Partners, Shareholders and % of interest
	Last three years' Financial Statements including Profit and Loss Statements
	Last three years' Tax Returns
Developer	
	Legal Name
	Legal Structure (individual ownership, partnership, limited company, public company limited)
	Date of Incorporation
	Capital
	Part of the Capital paid up
	Members, Partners, Shareholders and % of interest
	Last three years' Financial Statements including Profit and Loss Statements
	Last three years' Tax Returns
Development Experience	
	Biography and key principals
	How long the developer has been developing real estate
	List of projects developed or in process of development
	Year of completion of each project
	Status of uncompleted projects
Form of Project Financing	
	What percentage of the project is financed through personal equity?
	What percentage of the project is financed through commercial loans or other sources?
©Rene Philippe & Partners Ltd.	www.renephilippe.com

---

[36] This is a sample checklist only and is not deemed exhaustive.

TABLE 6: UNDEVELOPED LAND CHECKLIST (1)[37]

ISSUE	ITEMS
Land Ownership Documents	
	Does a Chanote[38] title deed represent the rights to the land?
	Does a confirmed certificate of use (NS-3[39]K) represent the rights to the land?
	Does a certificate of use (NS-3)[40] represent the rights to the land?
	Title number
	Owner name
	Size of land as per title
	Location of land as per title
	Was a geometrical survey of the land done?
	When was the title first issued and on what documentary basis?
	Are there any mortgages registered against the land?
	Terms , conditions and mortgage agreements (if any)
	Are there any rights of easement or servitude registered against the land?
	Terms, conditions and easement or servitude agreements
	Are there any other charges or liens registered against the land?
	Terms and conditions of any other liens
	What is the Land Government Assessed Value?
	What was the registered sale price at the time of the latest transaction recorded?
©Rene Philippe & Partners Ltd.	www.renephilippe.com

---

[37] This is a sample checklist only and is not deemed exhaustive.
[38] Please see Book II for the classifications of rights to land in Thailand.
[39] Same as 31.
[40] Same as 32.

TABLE 7: UNDEVELOPED LAND CHECKLIST (2)[41]

ISSUE	ITEMS
Zoning and building regulations	Is the land located in a commercial area?
Warning: Changes in zoning regulations and the fact that there is a high rise on adjacent land does not mean you can still build one.	Is the land located in a residential area?
	Is the land located in an industrial area?
	Is the land located in a warehouse area?
	Is the land located in a rural and agricultural area?
	Does the land have a slope of more than 35°?[42]
Warning: Zones are color coded, but the content of the prohibition attached to a color may vary from one province or city to another.	If the land is located in Phuket, Prachuabkirikhan (Hua Hin, Pranburi), Petchburi (Cha-am), Pattaya, Koh Samui or Krabi, does the land have a slope of more than 25°[43]?
	If the land is located in Phuket, Prachuabkirikhan (Hua Hin, Pranburi), Petchburi (Cha-am), Pattaya, Koh Samui or Krabi, is the land located more than 80 meters above sea level? [44]
	Is the land located in a Navy or Army reserve area?[45]
	What is the *"Floor Area Ratio" (FAR)* in the area?[46]
	Are there any key building prohibitions in this area?
©Rene Philippe & Partners Ltd.	www.renephilippe.com

---

[41] This is a sample checklist only and is not deemed exhaustive.

[42] If land has a slope of more than 35°, it is deemed forest land and no title deed or certificate of use may be owned for this land.

[43] In those provinces, no groundwork (excavation and landfills) may be done on any land with a slope greater than 25°

[44] In those provinces, no building may be constructed on land situated at heights of 80 meters or more above the medium sea level.

[45] When a land is located in army or navy reserve areas there may be special regulations applicable to its use. Also issuance of Chanot title is subjected to Army or Navy approval.

[46] The FAR is the maximum floor area of the buildings allowed to be built in relation to the size of a land.

TABLE 8: UNDEVELOPED LAND CHECKLIST (3)[47]

ISSUE	ITEMS
Zoning and Building Regulations and other matters	
	If you purchase in a sea side resort: How far is the land from the seashore?[48]
	Does the land have direct access to a public road?
	Is the land close to the public electricity network?
	Is the land close to the public water network?
	Is there water on the land and is drilling and pumping for water authorized by the local authority?
	Is the land located near an airport or in the direct line of flights taking off or landing?
	Is the land located in a smelly, noisy, or polluted area?
	Was there mining activity in the area in the past?[49]
	Was there an inland shrimp farm on the land in the past?[50]
	Did you walk on the land and is it vacant of any occupation?

©Rene Philippe & Partners Ltd.   www.renephilippe.com

---

[47] This is a sample check list example only and is not deemed exhaustive.

[48] In Thailand, most sea resort cities have building regulations limiting construction size in relation to the distance from the seashore. The land located farthest from the sea is the land you may build upon the highest. Also, you may not build anything within a certain distance from the seashore in some areas.

[49] For 100 years, Phuket's main activity was tin mining and many lands formerly used for mining were saturated with chemicals at the time.

[50] This land will be saturated with sea salt.

TABLE 9: LAND WITH A BUILDING CHECKLIST[51]

ISSUE	ITEMS
Building	
	Have you had the building inspected?
	How old is the building?
	How is the wiring, plumbing, roof, foundation, structure, water, electricity, air conditioning system etc.?
	Is there a street number or a house registration *(Tabian Ban)* for this building[52]?
	Does the owner have the building construction permit file?
	Were structural renovations made after the construction, and was a construction permit applied for?
	Were floors added to the building after initial construction?[53]
	Is the building vacant?
	If the building is habited, what are the occupants' rights?
	Who is the owner of the building?[54]

©Rene Philippe & Partners Ltd.   www.renephilippe.com

---

[51] This is a sample check list only and is not deemed exhaustive

[52] The Tabian Baan is a house registration certificate. If there is a street number and a Tabian Baan for the building the building is indicated to have been lawfully built

[53] It may happen that a building owner built additional floors on a building without legal authorization or preliminary engineering studies.

[54] In Thailand, there are no documents to establish proof of ownership of a building. There are, however, documents to create a presumption of ownership. The Tabian Baan is not proof of ownership of a building.

TABLE 10: PROJECT CHECKLIST[55]
(when purchasing a condominium or a house in a project off plan)

ISSUE	ITEMS
Authorization	Is the project subject to an Environmental Impact Assessment (EIA) and was the EIA completed?
	Is there a building construction permit?
	If the housing project contains more than nine units sold freehold, did the developer apply for a land allotment license?
	If purchasing an apartment unit, will the developer apply for a condominium license; if not, why?
	If you are purchasing in a housing development, check who owns the common area land and the projects roads.
©Rene Philippe & Partners Ltd.	www.renephilippe.com

The issues listed in the previous tables are applicable in Thailand and some cases are limited to land area in Thailand only. Also some of the issues mentioned above will apply to a particular purchase, but not to another, and they do not always need to be reviewed in entirety.

---

[55] This is a sample checklist only and is not deemed exhaustive

Chapter 8   **Access to Land or Real Estate: Are There Any**

Restrictions on Foreign Land or Real Estate

Ownership?

Many countries in the world still have restrictions on foreign land ownership. In some countries, the land is state-owned and the restrictions on owning land will apply to both local citizens and foreigners. In other countries, the prohibitions on owning land will apply to foreigners only. However, most countries still restricting foreign land ownership have no outright bans as such, but a system of restrictions.

There are three main types of restrictions. In some countries, foreigners are allowed to own land, but there are land quantity restrictions (meaning that a foreign citizen may only own a limited amount of land). Then there are restrictions based on the location of the land within the country. In some countries, for example, foreign buyers are allowed to purchase land, but only in limited designated areas, or may freely purchase land with the exceptions of certain designated areas. (In many South American countries, foreigners may not own land within a certain distance from a border.)

Finally, there are restrictions or allowances based on purpose[56]. Some countries will allow foreign land ownership, but prohibit foreigners from owning agricultural land because the participation in this activity is open only to local citizens. In other countries, land ownership for agricultural or residential purposes will be prohibited, but foreign investors will be allowed to purchase and own land freehold for industrial purposes. However, even when foreign ownership is authorized, it will be subject to additional conditions, such as the minimum amount of investment, minimum duration of ownership before resale, and obligation to resell the land if the activity for which it was purchased is discontinued. In some countries, the foreign ownership restrictions will only apply to land, but foreigners will be allowed to own buildings or condominium units either without restrictions or subject to the fulfillment of a set of conditions. In others, foreigners will be prohibited from owning either land or buildings. Therefore, the first step for a buyer of offshore real estate should always be to determine what access this country grants to foreign buyers of real estate.

The first question any prudent buyer should ask is, "Will I be able to own my property freehold?" If the answer is "No", the second question should be "Does this country offer a valid alternative to freehold, such as leasehold rights, for example?"

When looking at a leasehold option, the points to be considered are the duration of the lease period, renewal options, transferability of the lease by succession or assignment and level of protection granted to a lessee pursuant to the country's legal system[57].

Once those questions have been answered, subsequent questions will be, "How are rights to land represented in this country? Is there a titling system? And, if so, how reliable is this

---

[56] Please see Book II for actual restrictions in Thailand.
[57] Please see the next chapter on the leasehold issues.

system?" Another issue of importance will be use and local zoning regulations to determine "How can I use my property?" The critical issues in relation to the purchase of offshore real estate may be summarized as follows:

TABLE 11: CRITICAL ISSUES IN RELATION TO LAND ACCESS	
Issue	Factors determining outcomes
Access: Is land available, and at what price?	State ownership of land Tribal or communal ownership of land Ownership or use restrictions Zoning and planning requirements Property taxes
Security: What are my rights? Are my property rights secure?	Titling system Registration process Collateral rules Transfer of property rights Courts
Use: How can I use and develop land?	Location permits Construction and building permits Environmental impact assessment Utility connections
Consistency of treatment: Are other buyers treated like me?	Governance Transparency Accountability
Source: World Bank[58]	

---

[58] The whole document can be downloaded at
http://rru.worldbank.org/documents/publicpolicyjournal/300muir_shen.pdf

Chapter 9   **Is Circumventing Local Prohibitions on Foreign**

Ownership Such a Good Idea?

It's a well-known fact that wherever there is a law, there is a loophole, and if there are no clear loopholes, then there will be lawyers devising methods to circumvent the law in some way, and there will be people willing to circumvent, or even violate, the law.

One of the first paradoxes of the offshore real estate market is this: Most buyers are retirees or people preparing for retirement, and many of their preferred destinations are countries wanting to attract retirees who are viewed as the perfect foreign resident. However, many of those countries wishing to attract retirees have legislation that limits or prohibits foreign property ownership.

There were 326.6 million retirees in 2006 and that figure should reach 425.6 million by 2015[59]. For any country, capturing even less that 1% of the retiree market is an incredible financial jackpot. One hundred thousand retirees spending USD 1000 per

---

[59] Source: the Healthcare Coalition Institute, a California-based industry research group.

month means an injection of foreign capital equaling USD 100 million per month, or USD 1.2 billion per year. Each retiree will create jobs for maids, cooks, drivers, nurses and caregivers, and hairdressers. From a retiree point of view, the destination countries must have a warm climate (no more heating expenses), good but often cheap healthcare, low cost of living, safety and political stability.

Between countries like Thailand, Indonesia and the Philippines and retirees, it's almost a match made in heaven but for one very small detail. While those countries want to attract retirees and persuade them to spend part of their life savings in purchasing real estate, they all have restrictions on foreign real estate ownership. Even if those countries have laws allowing foreign investors to purchase condominiums freehold, those laws fail to take into account that not many retirees want to spend their retirement closed up in an apartment building, but would prefer a house with a garden and a private swimming pool.

Of course, those countries generally offer an alternative to land ownership that's usually in the form of a leasehold property. When all is said and done, the leasehold is for a short period from 30 to 75 years. Options for renewal are often available, but, as we'll see in the next chapter, the leasehold options offered to foreign buyers in most countries prohibiting foreign land ownership are full of traps and drawbacks. To those countries, I say that you cannot expect to benefit from the retirees' financial bounty and entice them to invest part of their life savings in real estate without giving them a secure alternative to freehold ownership. This alternative must take into account that retirees not only want their property secure for the duration of their life span, but that most of them would like their children or grandchildren to benefit from their purchase, and that there should be no restriction to transfers made by succession.

Unfortunately, these countries failure to offer foreign buyers[60] a valid alternative to freehold ownership won't stop them from purchasing.

Buyers will ask lawyers to check for loopholes in the law or whether there are any options to circumvent the law. Suddenly, hard-working citizens who have never broken the law in their lives without so much as a traffic ticket will not hesitate to break the laws of the country where they dream of spending their retirement.

Now, what are the risks involved? Most schemes offered to potential buyers of real estate in circumvention of the prohibition on land ownership are using nominees on one level or another. What, then, is a nominee? A nominee is defined as "one designated to act for another in his or her place". It is used sometimes to signify an agent or a trustee. It has no connotation, however, other than "acting for another, in representation of another, or as grantee of another"[61]. In other words, a nominee shareholder is an individual or a company who agrees to hold shares on behalf of another person, the true owner of the shares who retains all rights of ownership and control of the shares, even if those rights appear to be exercised by the nominee.

Is the use of nominees always illegal? No, becoming or using a nominee is not always illegal; for example, a well-respected doctor might not want his family, friends or relations to know he invested in a pub or a bar and might exercise discretion by having another person hold his shares in the company operating the pub. The use of nominees is generally legal as long as no one uses a nominee to circumvent the law.

People who are using nominees to purchase land or real estate assets on their behalf will have a choice between using an individual or a corporate nominee. Buyers choosing to use an

---

[60] As much as I love Thailand, leaseholds for durations of 30 years are a poor alternative to freehold, especially due to the difficulties in relation to renewal and succession (see the next chapter).

[61] Henry Campbell Black M.A; Black Laws Dictionary; vol. 2; pg 947.

individual nominee are generally those whose spouses are citizens of the country where the purchase is made. Now what most retirees often overlook is the issue of succession. What would happen if the spouse who owns the property suddenly died? If a foreigner cannot own land in a given country, the chances are also against the foreigner being able to inherit the land. If the couple has children, the issue may be manageable because often (but not always, so please check) the couple's common children will have dual nationality and will be allowed to inherit the deceased spouse's property. However, what if there are no common children, or if the common children do not have the double nationality, or what if they have the double nationality but are minors? In general, the property will be transferred to the next of kin with whom the foreigner may or may not have a good relationship and the death of the spouse who owned the property on behalf of both spouses often results in a legal mess.

Another alternative often proposed is to purchase the asset through a company that would have local citizens as nominee shareholders. The only issue that will matter from an average buyer's point of view is whether the nominees are safe and reliable and whether the buyer is protected against any possible "coup" from his nominees. However, by focusing solely on this issue, the buyer will overlook other problems that really matter. Owning property through an offshore company is a simple affair involving minimal costs and usually no tax liability. The same cannot be said of owning real estate through a local company. Many countries still have no legal vehicle specially tailored for the ownership of real estate. Therefore, potential buyers in most countries will have to use common local private limited companies. In most countries, private limited companies will have to maintain proper bookkeeping, file annual financial statements and yearly income tax returns. Furthermore, the company will be liable to corporate income taxes and any other applicable taxes. Finally, private limited companies are viewed in certain countries as commercial legal entities obligated to generate profits after a certain period. In Thailand, for example, the Revenue Department will expect a company to start declaring profits within a maximum of five years after its incorporation and you cannot expect to perpetually run a company at losses without attracting the attention of the tax administration.

Therefore, owning property through a local company will generate legal, accounting and audit expenses as well as tax liability.

Furthermore, most buyers do not consider the potential civil, administrative or criminal liability they may incur because of their attempt to circumvent laws prohibiting foreign ownership of land or real estate property in the destination country. In many countries, using a nominee to hold land or real estate assets on behalf of a foreigner in order to circumvent the law is an administrative or criminal offence. Sometimes the use of nominee shareholders may also be an additional offence. The range of applicable sanctions is varied depending upon the country where the offence takes place, but it may go from a fine for both the foreigner and the national assisting him to a jail term. In some countries, and in addition to the sanctions applicable, the government may be entitled to seize the property without any compensation or to force the sale of the property within a certain period[62]. Experience has taught me that you cannot trust the fact a government seems complacent toward the situation. Thailand is a good example in this regard as we will see more in details in chapters 40 and 41.

Before all is said and done, a careful buyer should ask himself, *"Is the game worth the risk, or should I go somewhere else?"*

Please see the table next page.

---

[62] Please see later on the situation in Thailand

TABLE 12 CRITICAL ISSUES TO CONSIDER BEFORE THINKING OF CIRCUMVENTING A PROHIBITION ON FOREIGN LANDOWNERSHIP

Item	Factor determining the outcome
Owning land through an agent	Is the use of an agent (individual or juristic person) to own land on behalf of a foreigner punishable? Is it a criminal or administrative infraction punishable by jail and/or a fine? What are the sanctions for the agent? What are the sanctions for the foreign beneficiary?
Owning land through a company using nominees	Is the use of nominee shareholders (individuals or juristic persons) punishable? Is it a criminal or administrative infraction punishable by jail and/or a fine? What are the sanctions for the nominee? What are the sanctions for the foreign beneficiary?
What happens to the property in the event of a violation of the law?	May the government forfeit the property[63] as an additional penalty? May the government force the sale of the property within a limited period of time?

©Rene Philippe & Partners Ltd. www.renephilippe.com

---

[63] In other words, can the government force you to surrender your property without compensation as an additional penalty?

Chapter 10   **What are the Pitfalls Awaiting Buyers**

Purchasing Under Leasehold?

Many countries becoming the favorite destinations of offshore property buyers have legal systems that prohibit foreigners from purchasing land or real property freehold. In those countries, foreign buyers of real estate will have to purchase their property under leasehold. Thailand is mixed in this regard, as we will see later on with a legal framework which enables foreign investors to own land for industrial or business purposes, but which prohibits them (but for one exception) from owning land for residential purposes. The most common alternative to property freehold ownership is, of course, the leasehold. While the leasehold is one of those legal institutions deemed universal, that doesn't mean every issue pertaining to a lease agreement will be resolved in the same manner in every country. Therefore, any buyers of real estate property who purchase under leasehold in a foreign country should check the issues listed in the following table before executing a lease agreement:

TABLE 13: LEASEHOLD CHECKLIST[64]	ITEMS
Restriction	Can any type of land or real estate property be leased?
Form of the Lease	Does a lease need to be made in writing or witnessed?
Agreement	Is an unwritten lease valid and enforceable?
	Does the lease need to be registered?
	Is an unregistered lease valid and enforceable?
	Is the co-operation of the lessor required to register a lease?
Lease Terms	Is it necessary to agree on a rental fee, or may a lease be rent-free?
	What is the maximum duration of a lease?
	Can the lease be renewed?
	If the lessor sells the leased property to a third party, is the new owner of the property bound by the lease agreement?
	If the lessor sells the leased property to a third party, is the new owner of the property automatically bound by the renewal clause?
	Can the lessee freely sublet or assign the lease to a third party, or is the lessor's consent required?
	If the lessee transfers or assigns the lease to a third, party, is the lessor fully bound to the new lessee? Or are there rights and obligations that do not pass to the new lessee without the express written consent of the owner/lessor?
Death	Is the lease terminated in the event of the lessee's death or bankruptcy?
	In the event of the lessee's death, do all of the lessee's rights and obligations pass to the lessee's heirs, or are there exceptions?
	Is the lease terminated in the event of the lessor's death or bankruptcy?
	In the event of the lessor's death, do all of the rights and obligation pass to the lessor's heirs or not?
©Rene Philippe & Partners Ltd.	www.renephilippe.com

In Thailand, there are many reasons why buyers might buy real estate in leasehold and a few of these are reviewed below.

---

[64] This checklist is indicative only of the items requiring examination and is not exhaustive.

The first reason concerns any person[65] who purchases an apartment or house built on land belonging to the Crown Property Bureau. The Crown Property Bureau[66] (CPB) is the institution owning and managing the assets of the monarchy. Among others, the CPB owns 3,493 acres in central Bangkok and 12,500 acres in the rest of the country. To my knowledge, the CPB does not sell land, but only leases it out for a non-renewable term of 30 years maximum. In central Bangkok, the CPB will lease a land plot to a developer for a 30-year period (generally including the construction period). The developer will build a high-rise building and lease the units for the remaining duration available upon the completion of the construction (generally 27 years). The buyers in these projects will not own their units, but lease them for a single term. At the end of the lease term, the building ownership will be transferred to the CPB, which will decide at that time whether or not it wishes to renew the leases of the building tenants. While the terms of purchase are very restrictive, apartments built on CPB land generally sell very well, because all are buildings located at prime locations. The initial lessee will generally get a return on the investment within 10 years and be able to resell the property at a good price without any problems within the first 15 years of the lease. Therefore, purchasing in an apartment building developed on CPB land[67] is generally a good operation despite the restrictive terms, the proof being that, to date, Thais are the first buyers of apartments in buildings developed on CPB land[68], even though they could purchase anywhere else as freehold.

Foreign buyers may also be prompted to purchase a property in leasehold if they have purchased an apartment in a building built by a developer who has failed to obtain a

---

[65] Whether a Thai or foreign citizen.

[66] According to the Thai Ministry of Foreign Affairs, the CPB owning the assets of the Monarchy is an institution *"which essentially belongs to all Thais"* and must be distinguished from the King's personal fortune.

[67] It's all about location.

[68] In fact, Thais don't generally purchase from First-Time Developers. That should tell buyers something.

condominium license[69], or is unwilling or possibly unable to apply for one[70]. For example, developers that launch mixed projects i.e. projects including residential apartments, service apartments and hotels within the same building may choose not to apply for a condominium license because they may not be able to fulfill the requirements pertaining to commercial activities as per Condominium Act 4.

In addition, we have the case of a condominium project where the foreign freehold quota (49%) has been fully sold. A foreign buyer interested in purchasing a unit in such a building may only do so by purchasing in leasehold from a Thai owner. Finally, the last reason foreign buyers would have to purchase under a leasehold is the case of a buyer who wishes to purchase land and house. Because of the restrictions made on foreign residential land ownership, most foreign buyers in Thailand will choose to lease the land on which their house is built.

Before we discuss the pitfalls awaiting buyers of property acquired under a lease, let's sum up the characteristics of a lease agreement in Thailand. For more information on the lease agreement, please read the chapter "What are the Key Features of the Right to Lease under Thai Law?"

In a nutshell, a lease is an agreement pursuant to which the owner of a property (the "lessor" or "landlord") conveys an interest (the right to use) in the land to another party (the "lessee" or "tenant") generally for a limited period of time (years or life) and against a consideration (a rental fee).

Lease agreements must generally be made in writing to be valid (especially for immovable properties). Moreover, in some countries, leases on immovable properties need also be registered in order to be legally binding.

---

[69] Applications for a condominium license may be filed only when the construction of the building is 95% complete.
[70] There are areas where condominium licenses may not be granted.

Where conditions differ from one country to the next, issues such as the type of immovable property that may be leased, the duration of the lease period, the possibility of renewing a lease agreement, the form of the lease agreement, the obligation to register a lease agreement with the authorities and so on must be considered.

The first issue to consider when leasing a property involves the restrictions associated with the type of properties people can lease. In Thailand, for example, a long term lease (more than 3 years) will be binding beyond three years only if registered with the Land Department. The current problem is that long-term rights to lease a piece of land may only be registered on land represented by a title deed (NS-4) ("Chanote"), or by a Certificate of Use[71] (NS-3), or a Confirmed Certificate of Use (NS-3K) but not on other lands.

It's also necessary to check whether the person renting a property to you is the owner of the property or not. If the lessor is not the owner, then a prudent lessee should first verify under what rights the lessor is authorized to lease out the property.

For example, does the person leasing the property to you have a power of attorney from the owner? If he/she has a power of attorney, is this power valid? Also, are there any limitations to the rights of the grantee?

Or is the person leasing the property to you a lessee on his/her own right? In other words does this person rent the property from the landowner? If so, then you are about to enter into a sub-lease relationship. Two criteria must be checked when executing a sub-lease. First of all, is the main lease between the owner of the property and your lessor valid? As explained above, a long-term lease in Thailand is only valid beyond three years if it is registered; if not, the lease won't be enforceable after three years. Secondly, does the lessee have the right to sub-lease? Potential buyers need to verify the main lease agreement and check whether the lease has a clause

---

[71] In Thai, NS-3 = Nor Sor Sam and NS-3K = Nor Sor Sam Gor or Nor Sor Sam Kor depending upon the translation.

either allowing or prohibiting the lessee to sublet. Notably, most standard lease agreement forms used in Thailand prohibit subletting. Furthermore, the lease agreement's silence on the matter doesn't necessarily mean the sub-lease is allowed.

Many buyers of offshore real estate come from common law countries and are accustomed to contracts covering every essential detail. Now, one thing to remember when coming to do business in civil law countries is that agreements in civil law countries are less detailed than in common law countries. This doesn't mean civil country lawyers are less sharp or lazier than their Anglo-Saxon counterparts, but that the law is the ultimate net guaranteeing the parties' rights to a contract in civil law countries. Therefore, civil law lawyers will deal with an issue in an agreement only if the solution provided by the law is unsatisfactory for their client and providing the issue is not one of those mandatory issues unable to be modified by the parties in a contract. In Thailand, for example, the fact that an agreement doesn't discuss the issue of subletting doesn't mean subletting is allowed because Section 544 of the TCCC clearly states, *"Unless otherwise provided by the rental contract, a tenant/lessee cannot sublet or transfer his rights in whole or in part of the rental/leased property to a third person"*. In other words, the fact that a Thai lease agreement doesn't deal with the issue of subletting doesn't mean subletting is authorized because, in the case of Thailand, the law prohibits subletting unless there is a contractual clause expressly allowing the practice.

Clearly, there is a discrepancy in Thailand between the law, which is very formal, and the people, who are not formal at all when it comes to doing business. It's been my observation and firm belief that this observation is also valid in other countries. When doing business among them, for example, Thai people will rarely register long-term lease agreements[72], but they will generally honor the term

---

[72] When I refer to a long-term lease agreement in this book, I am generally referring to a lease agreement for a term of more than three years, which is valid and enforceable only if registered at the Land Department. On the other hand, short-term leases refer to leases of less than three years, which do not need to be registered.

of duration, despite the fact that the lease is not formally valid beyond three years.

Even when made aware of the legal issues pertaining to the absence of registration, Thais will be reticent to register a long-term lease agreement at the Land Department. The reason is that one of the effects of a lease registration is to inform the Revenue Department about the rental of the leased property with the consequence of having to pay taxes on the rental.

Another issue most buyers purchasing under leasehold tend to overlook is the matter of succession. The TCCC is silent on this matter and fails to expressly provide or prohibit the transferability of leasehold rights by succession. For example, under Section 1411 (Title VI), Superficies, the TCCC, *"Unless otherwise provided in the act of its creation, the right of superficies is transferable and transmissible by way of inheritance."* There is no equivalent to this disposition in the title applicable to "Hire of Property".

Furthermore, the Thai Supreme Court has made several rulings on this matter. In relation to the death of the lessee and in the absence of any *"succession clause"* in the lease agreement, the Court considers a lease agreement to be a personal agreement and the person of the lessee as the essence of the lease agreement. In principle, the contract ends and the rights of the lessee are not transferred to the heirs in the event of the lessee's death. On the other hand, the lessor is not the essence of the lease agreement; therefore, in the case of the lessor's death, the lessor's property in the lease agreement will survive for the initial lease term. This was confirmed by a Thai Supreme Court ruling. In the event of the lessor's death, the lease agreement does not end, but only the *"real lease rights"* pass to the lessor's heirs (please see Chapter 11 for further explanation on the differences between lease rights and non-lease rights).

Therefore, a succession clause must be inserted into the agreement stipulating that the lessee's rights and obligations under the lease agreement will be transferred or assigned to the heirs of the lessee in the event of the lessee's death. The effect of this clause will, however, be limited in the sense that only *"real lease rights"* will be transferred to lessee's heirs to the exclusion of *"non-lease rights"*. The renewal clause, for example, is deemed a non-lease right.

Therefore, whenever a long-term agreement is made between individuals, it would be better to have not only the lessor and the lessee as the parties, but to also include the heirs of both lessor and lessee as parties to the agreement.

Note that this will be possible only if the heirs of the lessor and lessee have reached the age of legal maturity at the time a lease of more than 30 years is executed (please see the chapter, "Can the Thai Spouse or Thai Child of a Foreigner Own Land Freehold?" for more information on this issue). This way, even if one party dies, the lease continues between the surviving parties. Finally, the heirs of both parties will be bound by the renewal clause because they were parties to the agreement containing that clause.

Of course, the succession issue arises only if the lease agreement is executed between lessor and lessees who are individuals. If both lessor and lessee are companies, the issue of succession is irrelevant.

To avoid all succession and assignment problems, there are developers who offer buyers an alternative option whereby the developer incorporates an offshore company. The offshore company will be the lessee who leases the land on which the buyers' houses are located. Each buyer will receive a share in the company. Depending upon the type of project, the share will represent *"ownership"*[73] of: (1) the house and land on which the house is built, as well as a share of the common area, or (2) *"ownership"* of the plot of land on which the house is built and a share of the common area[74],

---

[73] I used "" and italics with the word "ownership" to point out that, despite statements in the articles associated with offshore companies, the share is not a valid title establishing rights to land ownership.

[74] In cases where the buyer is the direct owner of the house (Foreigners are allowed to own buildings in Thailand.)

or (3) in the case where an apartment building is built on the land, *"ownership"* of an apartment unit and a share of the common area land and facilities.

The Ministry of Interior has recently caught up with the developers who were offering this type of structure. Pursuant to a circular dated 21 July 2008, the Ministry of Interior has requested Thai Land Departments to examine the registration leases by foreign juristic persons as pertaining to the purposes of the foreign companies in doing so. The Land Department shall refuse the registration of leases for any foreign company leasing land or receiving a long-term right to land for the purpose of leasing land or the purpose of holding land on behalf of foreigners or in breach of the Foreign Business Act of 1999.

While the text of this directive clearly targets offshore companies leasing a whole lot of project land, we are not yet sure how it will be enforced by Land Department officers and whether offshore companies may still be used to lease a single plot of land and houses as in the past[75].

Another important issue is assignment. The lease agreement needs to contain a clause prohibiting the landowner to sell, transfer, or give the land to a third party during the term of the lease agreement or any period of renewal without the agreement of the Lessor. The fact that you have been granted a registered lease agreement by the landowner does not mean the landowner cannot sell the land. It only means that the new buyer will be bound by the lease for the initial term if the landowner sells the land. The buyer will not, however, be bound by the renewal clause because, as stated above and as we will discuss in greater detail in the next chapter, the renewal clause is a non-lease right.

Another current issue to consider when renting a building or an apartment is that, pursuant to Section 567 *"If the whole of the property is lost, the contract shall be terminated"*. If you do not want

---

[75] According to the Land Department officers, this regulation will not be enforced for the time being due to the difficult economic situation at present.

this to happen, please be careful to have a clause to this effect inserted into the agreement.

As far as buyers are concerned, however, the two most crucial elements are the duration of the initial lease and the possibility of renewal, which are issues we will be discussing in the next chapter.

Chapter 11   The Pitfalls of the Renewal Clause

The main drawback to purchasing a property under a lease agreement is the time limitation. Depending upon the country where the lease is executed the duration of a long-term lease may be for a period from 1 up to 999 years. In Asia all of the 13 countries surveyed (please see the comparison table next page) allow foreigners to lease immovable properties. While the right of foreign buyers to lease is granted everywhere there are huge variations as to the extent of the rights granted to them and the conditions attached to the right to lease. In Asia the average lease duration is approximately 50 years.

Cambodia, Malaysia and Singapore offer the longest lease periods with 99 years each. The shortest lease period is to be found in Myanmar where immovable property may only be leased for 1 year when leasing from the private sector (up to 30 when leasing from the government with the MIC approval). Thailand scores number 10 out of 13 in term of residential lease duration (based on a single lease period approach).

TABLE 14: COMPARING LEASEHOLD DURATION IN ASIA

Rank[76]	Country	Lease Duration	Remarks
1.	Cambodia	99 years	
1.	Singapore	99 years	
3.[77]	Malaysia	99 years	Land Lease of more than 10 year require Foreign Investment committee approval
4.	China	70 years	
5.	Vietnam	50 to 70 years	
6.	Hong Kong	50 years	
6.	Korea	50 years	
6.	Philippines	50 years	Renewable for 25 years
6.	Taiwan	50 years	Renewable for 30 years
10.	*Thailand*	*30 years (residential)* *50 years (commercial)*	*Renewable for 30 years (residential) or 50 years (commercial)*
11.	Laos	20 to 30 years	
11.	Indonesia	Right to use land 20 years Right to built on land 30 years	In both cases an extension of 20 years is possible
13.	Myanmar	1 year when leasing from private sector Up to 30 years when leasing from government with approval of MIC	

©Rene Philippe & Partners Ltd   www.renephilippe.com

---

[76] Note that for the purpose of the classification below countries that compare equal receive the same ranking number, and then a gap is left in the ranking numbers.

[77] Malaysia is ranked 3 because while it offers a 99 years lease option to foreigners who wants to lease immovable property a lease of more than 10 years must received the authorities approval

But for Indonesia, Myanmar and Laos, Thailand is currently at the bottom of the list in terms of residential lease agreement period with a duration that cannot currently exceed 30 years[78] for a residential lease. A proposal has been forwarded by the Property Committee of the Joint International Chamber of Commerce to the Thai government for an extension of the registration period up to 60 years. If this proposal is accepted it would be a considerable progress even if I would personally prefer an extension to 99 years as I believe that only a lease period of 99 years may permit to solve the problem of foreign investors that have purchased land through companies having Thai nominees

Once the buyer has checked the maximum lease period allowed by law, the second issue requiring verification is whether or not the laws of the country provide an option to renew the lease at the end of the initial period. The renewal issue is critical in countries providing short term lease periods (under 50 years).

In Thailand, the law stipulates an option to renew the lease period for another term under Section 540 of the TCCC: *"The aforesaid period may be renewed, but must not exceed thirty years from the time of renewal"*.

Although the legal allowance for an option to renew is a good thing, it's not enough. It's also necessary to ask a local lawyer whether there are legal issues to potentially reduce the effectiveness of the renewal clause.

In Thailand, for example, many First-Time Developers claim that one of the benefits of their renewal clause in the provision is an option for the buyer to renew the lease in perpetuity, thus granting to potential buyers a quasi-right of ownership.

No claim could be more false because the renewal of a lease in perpetuity is simply not possible in Thailand. Worse, there are so many restrictions attached to the renewal clause in Thailand that it

---

[78] The duration of a lease for commercial purposes, however, is 50 years.

would be nothing short of a miracle if half of the buyers who purchased under a lease agreement were actually able to renew their lease agreements at the expiration of the initial term.

Briefly, the renewal clause is a *promise* that, 30 years from now, the owner of the land will renew the lease agreement.

Now, this promise will not always be binding. To be binding and valid, this promise requires the following content: (1) an agreement to renew the lease; (2) the duration of the renewal period *and* (3) the amount of the rent during the renewal period. If one of these elements is missing, the promise shall not be binding. To agree, for example, that the rental fee for the period of renewal shall be not more than 15% of the rental for the initial period is insufficient, because the rent cannot be determined, thus making it impossible to say the parties have agreed on the rental fee for the period of renewal.

I have some concerns regarding the validity of a renewal clause reading, *"no additional rent shall be due for the renewal period".* Indeed, one element of a lease agreement is the payment of rent. A rent-free renewal period would not qualify as a lease agreement. Any renewal clause failing to stipulate the rent should not be enforceable.

It would be preferable to draft the renewal clause as follows: *"The total aggregate rent is [xxxxxx Thai baht only] (hereinafter referred to as the "Total Land Rental Fee") and is broken down as follows: (a) the rental for the period of the lease shall be a sum of [xxxxxx Thai baht only] (hereinafter referred to as the "Lease Fee"); (b) the rental fee for the renewal period shall be a sum of [xxxxxx Thai Baht only] (hereinafter referred to as the "Rental Renewal Fee"); (c) the rental for the additional period (if any) shall be a sum of [xxxxxx Thai baht only] (hereinafter referred to as the "Additional Rental Fee"). The Lessee further agrees to prepay the Rental Renewal Fee due for the renewal period and the Additional Rental Fee due for the additional lease period together with the Lease Fee due for the Lease period, and the Lessor agrees to issue receipts accordingly".* I believe such a clause would be preferable, because it shows: (1) the parties have already agreed upon the rental fee for the renewal period; and (2) the lessee has prepaid the rental fee for the renewal period. In other words, not only has the lessor agreed to a rent, but the lessor has also already received payment of that price[79].

A clause of renewal providing for perpetual renewal of a lease agreement would not withstand the scrutiny of Thai courts. Similarly, to my knowledge, the Thai Supreme Court has not yet had the opportunity to decide upon the validity of a renewal clause providing for a first and second renewal of a lease agreement.

Most lawyers agree that the fact that Section 540 stipulates, *"The aforesaid period may be renewed, but must not exceed thirty years from the time of renewal,"* excludes the possibility of a second renewal clause. This is the reason why so many leases often contain two separate clauses, the first providing for the renewal of the agreement and the second clause containing a promise to execute a new lease at the end of the renewal period. To my knowledge, however, the validity or invalidity of this practice has not yet been corroborated by any Supreme Court judgment.

To date, the fact is that promises made by developers about lease agreements including two additional 30-year renewals and thus giving the buyer a 90-year lease overall, are not yet supported by any law or case law.

Drafting a side agreement stipulating the parties' intention to execute a 90-year leasehold won't fly either, because the TCCC stipulates, *"If it is made for a longer period, said period shall be reduced to 30 years"*.

Even more critical is the problem of the assignment or transfer of the right of a third party to renew. Over the years, the Thai Supreme Court has rendered a series of judgments, mostly in relation to Section 569 of the TCCC, which regulates the assignment

---

[79] Note that while we believe a pre-payment for the renewal period may provide a stronger case against the Lessor if the renewal issue ends up in Court, there are no guarantees for this type of case.

of a lease agreement and the transfer of lease rights from the transferor to the transferee, wherein the Thai Supreme Court has established the following principles:

The Thai Supreme Court has ruled that *"real lease rights"* and *"non-real leased rights"* must be treated differently in cases of transfer or assignment of a lease agreement and that only real lease rights are transferred in cases of assignment of the lease.

Suppose, for example, that Mr. A has leased land to Mr. B and the agreement between Mr. A and B contains a renewal clause upon the expiration of the initial lease and a clause allowing Mr. B to assign the lease, so Mr. B assigns the lease to Mr. C. Now, is Mr. A. legally bound to renew the lease of Mr. C following the transfer of the lease at the end of the initial agreement?

Unfortunately, according to the Thai Supreme Court, Mr. A is not legally bound to renew Mr. C's lease at the end of the initial term, because the renewal clause is not a real lease right and may not be transferred. The only way around this obstacle is to either have a written agreement drafted between Mr. A and Mr. C on the matter of renewal, or to register a new lease between Mr. A and Mr. C.

This issue is not specific to Thailand, because the decision of the Thai Supreme Court actually rests upon a legal principle called "privity of contract" that is also known in other jurisdictions. The privity principle limits the obligations between parties who have executed an agreement party to the exclusion of third parties who were not initially part to this contract.

In other words, a promise to do something is generally only binding between the parties who have executed the promise. In the same way, as explained above, if the owner of the land sells the land to a third party during the term of the lease agreement, only the real lease rights and obligations will be transferred to the buyer of the land (to the exclusion of the non-lease rights). Therefore, the buyer of the land will be bound to execute the lease agreement for the initial period, but not for the clause of renewal contained in this agreement. It should be necessary for the buyer of the land to sign a renewal agreement with the lessee for him to be bound by the clause.

Another difficulty most buyers fail to fathom when it comes to leaseholds is that the clause of renewal is not automatic. If the parties do nothing, the lease agreement will simply end after 30 years without the need for any notice. The extension of the lease is an active process requiring the cooperation of both parties to the lease agreement. Firstly, they must execute a new lease agreement for the period of renewal; secondly, they must register the new lease at the Land Department. In other words, a renewal clause is only a promise to renew, not an actual lease agreement.

Also ineffectual is the option offered by some developers to their buyers consisting of immediately signing three 30-year lease agreements back-to-back. This cannot work because the lease already executed for the next period is insufficient. Indeed, a long-term lease is enforceable beyond three years only if registered with the Land Department, which means the lessee will still require the cooperation of the lessor in registering the second and third leases 30 and 60 years from the expiration of the original.

Furthermore, chances are that a new lease would still have to be executed at the time of the renewal anyway, because the person who was the authorized director of the landowner company (if the landowner is a company) might not be around 30 years or 60 years from now. Finally, having the lessor sign all of the forms required for the registration of the second and third leases today is pointless. What are the chances the Land Department will still be using the same forms 30 or 60 years from now?

Of course, one solution would be to register both the first and second leases in advance. While our understanding is still that the Land Department would normally not agree to register two or three back-to-back lease agreements, we have heard of two cases where the parties to a lease agreement were able to register with the Land Department for the initial period along with the lease for the renewal period. In the first case, both consecutive leases would have been executed and registered between the same lessor and lessee. From what we heard, the parties only let a few days lapse within the two leases in order to get the officers to agree to the registration. For example one lease would have expired on 30 August 2030 and the second lease would have begun on 3 September 2030. In the second case, the parties executed a first lease agreement between the lessor and one offshore company and a second lease following the end of the first one which would have been between the lessor and a second offshore company. Of course, the two offshore companies belong to the same owner.

My first remark is that the second offshore company will cost the happy lessee at least USD 1,000 per year in maintenance fees for the next 30 years, which amounts to USD 30,000 over the duration of the first lease agreement.

My second remark is this: One of Thailand's problems is that it will always be possible at some point to find a Land Department officer who will agree to a solution proposed by the parties i.e. to pre-register two subsequent leases of 30 years on a title deed as in the previous case. However, the fact that those successive leases have been successfully registered in two cases does not mean this will become the norm in Thailand[80]. On the contrary, if this practice becomes more widespread (assuming those leases have really been registered), the risk is that someone higher in the government will hear of it, find fault with the process and request the cancelation of the second leases due to a suspicion that the parties had the intention of circumventing the law, for example. Finally and as already explained above, the fact that an agreement is registered does not make it immune from termination.

Lastly, some cases have been reported were Land Department officers have refused to register lease agreements including a renewal clause in favor of foreign lessees. Here again, it depends upon who you are talking with at the Land Department or which province you are in at the time. You may hear, *"Under lease law, the rights of foreigners or Thais are the same and there is no*

---

[80] It may however become the norm in a near future

reason not to register a lease agreement including a clause of renewal simply because the lessee is a foreigner" or you may also hear officers telling you, *"We will not consent to registering a lease including a renewal clause when the lessee is a foreigner, because the parties' intention is to circumvent the law".*

If you find yourself in this situation, i.e. if the Land Department requests that the renewal clause be removed prior to the registration of the lease, then request that your landlord execute an amendment to the lease agreement postdated from after the date of the registration of said lease agreement pursuant to which the landlord and the lessee agree to a clause of renewal. Note that this amendment is also a promise not to renew the actual lease.

I read an article the other day where a lawyer advised foreign buyers to execute a lease for life instead of for a 30-year period, the premise being that lifetime leases may be more than 30 years and this could be one way to avoid the whole renewal problem at the end of the first 30-year period.

Yes, this is a tempting option at first look, but the problems are as follows: Firstly, lifetime may be more than 30 years, but it can also be for a shorter period; there are no guarantees. Secondly, if a contract is for the life of one party only, there is no way to transfer the rights resulting from it by inheritance. Once life ends, so does the agreement.

Now, the solution proposed by this lawyer is to have not only the parties to the agreement, but also their heirs sign the agreement. In this way, the contract is not terminated if one lessee dies but continues for the duration of the life of the other parties. As nice as that sounds, Section 540 of the TCCC, which we have already mentioned, clearly states: *"The duration of a rental term for immovable property cannot exceed thirty years. If it is made for a longer period, such period shall be reduced to thirty years".* So, at the end of the day a lease for life will also be valid and registered for a period of 30 years maximum and will have to be renewed at the end of the 30-year initial period in the same way a 30-year lease would.

Overall, the renewal of lease issue is one of the legal headaches Thailand is famous for and the fact remains that there are so many questions attached to this issue that I just don't understand how developers can seriously *"guarantee"* to their clients *"90 years"* with a 30+30+30 leasehold.

To sum it up, when a developer offers to sell you a 30+30+30 leasehold, what he is actually offering you is not 30+30+30 (it looks so simple) but:

- ➢ 30 +
- ➢ The promise to lease to you for another 30 years, assuming, however, that, (1) the clause is actually binding (it may not be binding if, for example, there is no agreement on the rental fee for the renewal period); and (2) there has been no succession or assignment of the contract during the first 30 years, or if there has been a succession or assignment wherein the new landlord or new lessee has agreed that a renewal clause be written, the landlord does not terminate the lease for causes in between, and/or where the landlord is willing to sign a new lease agreement for the renewal period and to execute the formality or renewal and so on.....
- ➢ The promise to lease to you for another 30 years, assuming that..............

It's not as simple as it first seemed, is it? Renewal clauses are like religions: you need a lot of faith (no disrespect intended)...

For my part, all I can do is warn buyers of the issues and offer a few solutions to improve the odds without being able to guarantee that the renewal will indeed happen:

- If the lease agreement is between an individual lessor and an individual lessee, the agreements should be executed between the lessor and the lessor's heirs and the lessee and the lessee's heirs, so the death of one party doesn't affect the agreement. However, our recommendation is to lease only from a company, as companies don't die. They can, however, become bankrupt or abandoned by their owners, which is why the lessee should be granted a say (a right of participation) in the affairs of the landowner company within acceptable limits as set forth by Thai law (minority participation only to the share capital and the board of directors).

- If this option is still available, incorporate an offshore company of which you become a shareholder and director, and have this offshore company execute the lease agreement on your behalf. In other words, the offshore company becomes the owner of the house and the lessee of the land. If you subsequently sell your property, all you need to do is transfer your shareholdership and directorship to your buyer. The use of an offshore company will not improve your chance to obtain the renewal per se, but will reduce some of the risks potentially affecting the validity of the renewal clause during the initial 30-year period (such as succession or assignment of the lease). In addition, this scheme will permit the parties to save on government fees and taxes in Thailand in case of resale as the owner of the property will remain the same. Note, however, that the drawback is that there might be other tax issues[81], especially if the company is renting out the property and when you have to pay the company annual maintenance fees.

- The agreement should contain a clause stipulating that the landowner may not sell or transfer the land to a third party for the duration of the lease agreement without the written consent of the lessee[82].

- This clause should further stipulate that the lessee may reasonably withhold his consent to the transfer of the land if the buyer of the land refuses to execute a written promise to renew the lease for the lessee. The agreement should further

---

[81] Years of experience taught me that there is never a perfect solution to propose. Any scheme will always have a drawback

[82] If it does not, the landowner may evade the renewal clause simply by transferring the land to a third party.

contain a clause compelling the lessor to execute a promise of renewal of the lease with any third party to whom the lessee would transfer his lease in the future.

- The clause of renewal <u>must not</u> be *"rent-free"*, because the payment of a rent is one of the three elements of a lease agreement (the other two are the agreement to lease a property and the duration of the lease). The renewal clause must, therefore, stipulate a rental fee for the next 30-year period. The rent must be determinable; otherwise, the clause won't be valid. The amount of the rent for the second period should be at least equivalent to the government-assessed value of the land at the time of payment and it should be pre-paid by the lessee. Furthermore, the lessor should issue a receipt attesting reception of the prepayment of the lease for the renewal period.

- Finally, the renewal clause should not be perpetual or provide for two successive renewals, because I don't believe such a clause would withstand the scrutiny of a Thai court for reasons explained above. A promise to execute a new lease at the end of the renewal period is preferable, even if we have no guarantee this promise to execute a new lease will withstand the Thai court's scrutiny.

- If you find yourself in a situation where the land officer refuses to register a lease agreement including a clause of renewal, our recommendation is to register the lease agreement without any clause of renewal and to make a separate *"Amendment to the Lease Agreement"* for the purpose of regulating the matter of the renewal. This amendment will have the same content as discussed above. This amendment should be dated after the date of the registration of the initial lease agreement.

The following pages contain two tables. The first table summarizes the relevant criteria for comparing leasehold options between countries; the second table summarizes the renewal issues.

TABLE 15: THE RENE PHILIPPE LEASEHOLD TEST CRITICAL ISSUES WHEN COMPARING COUNTRIES & RESIDENTIAL LEASEHOLD LAWS	SCORING	THAILAND	COUNTRY 2
DURATION OF THE LEASE			
1a. The maximum duration of a lease is 99 years or more.	15	-	-
1b. The maximum duration of a lease is 65 years or more.	10	-	-
1c. The maximum duration of a lease is 50 years or more.	5	-	-
1d. The maximum duration of a lease is less than 50 years.	0	0	-
RENEWAL OPTIONS			
2a. The lease is renewable at the end of the term.	15	15	-
2b. The lease is not renewable at the end of the term.	0	-	-
TRANSFERABILITY OF THE RENEWAL CLAUSE			
3a. The renewal clause is transferable together with the lease rights.	15	-	-
3b. The renewal clause is not transferable together with the lease rights.	0	0	-
TERMINATION OF THE LEASE UPON THE DEATH OF THE LESSEE			
4a. The lease is not terminated by the death of the Lessee.	15	-	-
4b. The lease is terminated by law by the death of the Lessee, but the lease agreement contract may provide for transferability by inheritance.	10	10	-
4c. The lease is terminated by law by the death of the Lessee and the termination is mandatory and may not be modified by contract.	0	-	-
TERMINATION OF THE LEASE UPON THE DEATH OF THE LESSOR			
5a. The lease is not terminated by the death of the Lessor and all rights and obligations included in the lease agreement are transferred and binding upon the Lessor's heirs.	15	-	-
5b. The lease is not terminated by the death of the Lessor, but only the lease rights are transferred and binding upon to the Lessor's heirs to the exclusion of non-lease rights.[83]	10	10	-
5b. The lease is terminated by the death of the Lessor .	0	-	-
MAXIMUM SCORING	75	35	
TOTAL			

©Rene Philippe & Partners Ltd.   www.renephilippe.com

---

[83] In Thailand, for example, the right of renewal is a non-lease right not transferable with the lease agreement. A new renewal clause must be executed between the lessor and the new lessee, or the new lessor and the lessee.

TABLE 16: LEASEHOLD RENEWAL ISSUES

PERIOD	Nature of Agreement	Remarks
Initial Term of 30 years for Registered Lease The lease rights appear at the back of the title deed. The renewal promise does not appear on the title deed.	**Lease Agreement** The lease agreement must be registered with the Land Department to be valid more than three years. The registration of a lease agreement is only a condition for the validity of the lease beyond three years. Contrary to common belief, the fact that the lease is registered does not give stronger rights to the lessee and a registered lease agreement may still be terminated by the landowner if the Lessee violates the terms of the lease agreement.	1. If the agreement does not contain a clause to prohibit it, the landowner has the right to sell or transfer the leased land to another party providing that the third party agrees to execute the lease for the term. 2. Note that the new buyer is not bound by the renewal clause executed between the former landowner and the lessee (even if the clause is mentioned in the agreement registered at the Land Department), because renewal is deemed a "non-lease" and a personal right by the Thai Supreme Court that binds only the signatories 3. By law, a lease agreement is terminated upon the death of the lessee if no clause stipulates the contrary in the agreement. 4. In the case of the Lessor's death, the lease is maintained up to the end of the term but the lessor's heirs are not bound by the renewal clause. 5. In cases of the assignment of the lease, only the "lease rights" are assigned to the exclusion of non-essential rights, such as the renewal clause.

First 30-year Renewal

Note that there have been cases where officers of the Land Department have refused to register lease agreements including a clause of renewal on the presumption that the foreign lessee and the Lessor were trying to circumvent Thai laws prohibiting foreigners from owning land.

Promise to Renew

Is binding only if it includes an agreement on

(1) Object of the Lease
(2) Duration
(3) Rent for the period of renewal

If the lessor terminates the lease before the initial first term for whatever cause, the renewal clause will automatically be affected.

Reminder: The promise to renew is for *"non-lease"* rights i.e. rights deemed non-essential to the lease agreement by the Thai Supreme Court with the consequences explained above.

The promise is not a lease agreement and a new lease will have to be registered 30 years from the execution of the original lease.

In other words, the renewal is not automatic and requires the active participation of the Lessor.

I have heard that some Land Department Offices have accepted the registration of a first lease agreement and then a second 30-year lease agreement. To the best of my knowledge, this practice is to date an exception and not yet common practice. Furthermore, if it were to become a common practice, there are chances within the current context that a higher member of the Land Department would find fault with the process. If title deeds can be cancelled 10 years after they have been issued, I don't see why the same thing could not happen and the second lease being later cancelled by a higher authority on the premise that this second lease was granted to circumvent current restrictions.

Second 30-year Renewal Now, TCCC Section 540 stipulates, *"The aforementioned period (30 years) may be renewed, but must not exceed thirty years from the time of renewal."*	Most lawyers agree that this paragraph means there may be only one renewal period. Therefore, in this context, it is difficult to seriously offer a third term.	
Additional New Period of 30 years	Some Developers will try to avoid the second renewal problem by including in their agreement a promise to conclude an additional contract at the end of the period of the first renewal instead of a promise for a second renewal.	It is anyone best guesses what such clause is worth?

©Rene Philippe & Partners Ltd   www.renephilippe.com

Chapter 12   Fractional Ownership vs. Timeshare

In theory and from a legal point of view, a genuine fractional ownership is the joint ownership of a real estate asset. There are several ways to accomplish this. For example, two or more people can get together and jointly purchase the asset or one person who already owns the asset and one or more people may purchase shares in the asset, or one person who already owns shares in the asset may sell those shares. Then the operation may be structured with direct or indirect rights of ownership for the asset. For example, the co-owners may directly own the property and their names may be entered as co-owners of the asset in the local Land Registrar. The co-owners may decide to form a company or a partnership and the company or partnership would then own the asset, and each shareholder of the company or member of the partnership would own a share of the company or partnership owning the asset.

Whether you are purchasing a property as a single owner or a co-owner, the situation is the same in terms of critical issues and necessary precautions. The difference lies in the fact that the buyer will have to consider the following additional issues: liability issues i.e. who is responsible for what and whether the buyer's potential liability will be limited or excluded for the actions of other co-owners; exit issues i.e. how to exit and at what cost; whether partners have the right of first refusal in the event of resale; and management issues i.e. how the property will be managed, who decides what, how disputes will be resolved or how to protect against abuse from the majority of the other co-owners.

The buyers in a timeshare relationship don't own the property. The owner is generally a service provider who sells the buyers a right to use the property on a weekly basis. In other words, a timeshare buyer doesn't actually own the property or even a share of the property, but only purchases a license to use the property for a limited period.

Timeshare issues are mostly contractual, so the questions buyers need to ask are: How binding is the agreement? How will my rights be classified in case of bankruptcy of the property owner? Are my rights fully transferable by succession or assignment? And the list goes on...

Timeshare is generally cheaper than fractional ownership, because the buyers only receive a right to use the property, not to own it. In addition, time ownership is generally sold by the week and buyers may acquire only 1/52 or 2/52 rights to use, while fractional ownership will generally be divided by the month or trimester.

In both cases, buyers need to check whether the country of destination has a specific law regulating fractional ownership or timeshare. In the absence of such laws, a lawyer can be asked to review whether the common legal dispositions of this country actually cover all of the issues relevant to fractional ownership or timeshare.

My personal recommendation is that timeshare is more interesting than fractional ownership in terms of common sense. It is a cheaper investment and buyers are often able to exchange right of use from one property to right of use in another or to exchange the period of use in one property against the use of another. The tenants of fractional ownership will point out that this method grants stronger rights on the property, and that buyers actually own a piece of it. However, just look at all the potential problems at the level of a co-owners housing association when all of the neighbors own their own property. Are you really eager to repeat this experience at the level of one property only? Owning a property is a costly investment and, because it is costly, a property should always be purchased in single ownership. Joint ownership should be reserved for within the family circle only.

This is the only chapter in this book where I have no valuable insight to give you on this matter yet, because fractional ownership and/or timeshare have only recently been re-introduced in Thailand and I haven't had the opportunity to review an actual transaction yet.

Chapter 13   Rental Guarantee: Gimmick or Reality?

Nowadays, most offshore real estate is sold with the promise of a rental or minimum return guarantee. Can we really believe developers' promises of a return guarantee? My first remark is that Top Developers don't generally offer a rental or minimum return guarantee because they don't need to[84]. In other words, in my experience, developers who actually offer a rental guarantee are mostly First-Time Developers who see rental guarantees as a marketing tool. In other words, they offer a *"return guarantee"* without having any clue about how to actually implement one.

Promises are cheap, but an actual return guarantee is not a cheap endeavor and the face value of the guarantee will depend entirely upon who the guarantor is. For example, a rental guarantee backed by a five-star hotel group will not have the same value as a return guarantee offered by a First-Time Developer. My point is, how can you trust a First-Time Developer who often doesn't even have the money and experience to finance and develop his project to guarantee you a return on your investment? Indeed, managing a

---

[84] They don't in Thailand.

rental guarantee requires a high level of professionalism. In order to provide a return guarantee, First-Time Developers will often pre-calculate the cost of the guarantee over a 2- or 3-year period, and then add the cost to the price of the property. Therefore, the buyer not only finances the construction of the project, but also foots the bill for the cost of the so-called return guarantee. Moreover, there are no guarantees the First-Time Developer won't have spent all the money he/she overcharged for return guarantee purposes by the time the guarantee becomes effective. Therefore, the first thing to understand is that the value of the guarantee given depends exclusively upon the worthiness of the guarantor.

Another difficulty is the actual content of the guarantee. The promises of return will vary from one developer to the other. Generally, developers offer between 8% and 15% of the yearly return. Some offer a net return, while others offer a gross return or a profit sharing return. Essentially, the developer will offer the buyer the opportunity to have his/her property managed by the developer on his/her behalf. In exchange, the developer will either pay a fixed return or take a service fee, generally 40% to 50% of the rental income, while the balance is paid back to the owner of the property. While the fixed return guarantees are easy to grasp, the profit sharing-based guarantees are more complex. Be sure the developer's share of the profits is calculated upon the basis of the net profit, not the gross profit. It's also necessary to determine whether the definition of net profits is complete and make sure there are no hidden costs left out of the picture that would have to be paid for out of your share of the profits. For one thing, First-Time Developers often don't have a clue about the tax issues related to the guarantee. For example, in the projects I discussed in Chapter 5, it took a smart buyer and 18 months for the developers to realize the rental return they were selling to their buyers would be subject to a 15% withholding tax.

The content of the guarantee is not the only matter of concern. Another issue is whether the developer can actually deliver, because providing a rental guarantee is not as easy as it looks. Buyers will generally come during peak season and the developer will take it as a given that rental guarantee tenants will just turn up.

The first difficulty is that, wherever there is a high season, there is also a low season. Furthermore, in some locations, the duration of the high season doesn't exceed three to five months per year.

Moreover, renting out a pool of properties on a daily or weekly basis is a professional business and may only be possible if the property is managed in the same way as a hotel. There will be extensive work upstream (negotiating agreements with travel agencies...) and downstream (services, cleaning, and services maintenance). If you're really looking for an investment product, you should purchase a house in a well-known hotel group compound. At the very least, you'll know professionals will manage your property. In other words, the worthiness of the guarantee will also depend upon the professional experience of the guarantor.

Prima facie, a developer whose main business is to build houses doesn't seem to be the ideal candidate for providing a rental guarantee. Whenever a developer offers to execute a management agreement with a service management company, please check whether the management company actually exists and has an actual track record, or whether it's no more than a start-up company with low capital and no previous track record.

Finally, the last issue to consider is whether or not the guarantee is actually legally valid. Every legal system has specific requirements regarding the form in which guarantees can be given. Is a guarantee in the form of a letter sufficient? Or, does this guarantee need to be made in the form of an agreement executed between the guarantor and the beneficiary?

For example, the Developers of the six failed projects we discussed in Chapter 5 were offering their buyers a 12% annual guarantee of return on their investment over an 8-year period. Now the guarantee itself was in the form of an 8-year leaseback agreement. In other words, upon completion of the construction of their property, the buyers would lease their properties back to the Developers for a period of eight years. Curiously, we can't help but wonder why this guarantee for the return agreement was actually a long-term lease agreement when the agreement did not contain any clauses requiring it to be registered with the local authority. In Thailand, a long-term lease agreement is not enforceable beyond three years unless it's registered. In other words, in the absence of any registration, the guarantee of return given to these project buyers was only valid for three years and not eight years as promised by the Developers.

Generally speaking, if you want to purchase a property offshore, then you should do so for the right reasons. Select your property based upon the reliability and experience of the developer as well as the property's location and design, but don't buy only in consideration of the promise of an eventual return, especially if the guarantee provider doesn't have a proven background in the hospitality business.

If you purchase from a First-Time Developer, refuse the return guarantee and request a price reduction. You can still change your mind later and decide to join the pool of properties managed under a return agreement.

Please see on the next page our rental guarantee checklist.

TABLE 17: RENTAL GUARANTEE CHECKLIST[85]	ITEMS
Form	Is the validity of the guarantee subject to fulfill the minimum legal form requirements?
Face Value of the Guarantee	Is the guarantee of return backed by any security such as bank guarantees, etc.?
	Is the company providing the guarantee of return a start-up company?
	Does the company providing the guarantee of return have any proven track record in this sector or in hotel management services?
	If the developer provides the guarantee of return, does he have a proven track record in hotel management services?
	Are equivalent properties sold in the project vicinity without rental guarantee cheaper than the developer's property?
Content of the Guarantee	If the rental guarantee is a fixed amount payable every year, is this net amount subject to any charges, taxes or withholding taxes?
	If the rental guarantee amount is based on profit sharing, is the developer's fee calculated on the gross or on the net profit? And, is the buyer's share subject to any taxes? Are there any hidden costs?
©Rene Philippe & Partners Ltd.	www.renephilippe.com

---

[85] This checklist is not deemed exhaustive and is indicative only of the items possibly needing to be checked.

Chapter 14   "My" Agent

Most buyers purchasing offshore real estate will be purchasing through the services of an agent. The first difficulty is that most preferred destination countries chosen by buyers of offshore properties have no regulations (if there are, they aren't enforced) that obligate professional real estate agents to formally notify the buyer that they're acting as the seller's agent. While this information may pop up in the conversation, the effect on the buyer is not the same as signing a form to this effect.

How many times have I met with customers who came to see me with a cute girl they proudly introduced as *"my"* agent?

It's always evident that the client sincerely believes the agent's trying to get him the best deal possible, when all she really wants is to close the deal as soon as possible so she can receive her commission. While the buyer's interest is in purchasing the property with the best quality per price ratio, the agent's interest is in selling to the most expensive property or the one promising the best commission. In other words, a seller agent will have no real incentive to negotiate a sweet deal on your behalf because the sweet deal would reduce the commission.

Except for cases where you paid an agent to find a property on your behalf, always remember that, in most cases, the agent will be a seller agent, meaning she is not working for you.

As with all service professions in Thailand, you will have a choice between the local and international agents as nearly all international real estate brokerage or agency franchises have made it to Thailand. As we've seen in Chapter 6, the fact that an agent represents an international brand isn't always a guarantee of reliability.

What are the main benefits a buyer might gain when using an agent? Firstly, buyers will definitively save time, because agents generally have a listing of properties for sale and help buyers through it. Beyond this, quality depends upon the dedication of the agent.

The commission rate an agent receives in the case of a successful sale will, of course, vary depending upon the country where the property is purchased. In Thailand, the commission rate is generally 3%, but First-Time Developers will often offer from 5% to 10% in commissions to motivate agents into putting their projects forward.

Less recommendable are agents who agree to a fixed price with a landowner and try to resell the property at a higher price (up to double the actual price of the property).

Agents specializing in the sale of offshore real estate and organizing offshore real estate exhibitions in your home country generally receive commissions between 10% and 15% of the selling price. Notably, the highest rate of commission is not pure profit as those agents invest a lot in exhibits and marketing.

One thing buyers don't always realize is the agent's right to a commission as soon as the buyer has paid the deposit. Buyers who change their minds and don't go through with the transaction after having paid deposits will, in most cases, lose the entire deposit. What is often a complete loss for the buyer is no loss for the agent, because most agents will still collect a commission on the forfeited deposit (usually 30% of the forfeited deposit).

If you've lost your deposit after a change of mind, there's no need to profusely apologize to your agent, because the chances are in favor of the agent still making money out of the transaction. Furthermore, in most cases where buyers change their minds, it's because they were pressured by the agent to close the deal too quickly and didn't have proper time to decide whether they really wanted to purchase the property or not.

What should you never tell an agent?

Never tell your agent real estate seems cheaper in Thailand than at home. Those kinds of small remarks will kill any chances of a bargain. Should you give a maximum price to the agent? It depends upon the situation. Yes, doing so will save you from wasting time looking at properties that are too expensive, but it will also motivate the agent to search for property at the top of the price range while overlooking the bottom of your price range.

Agents generally like to close deals quickly, so they might sometimes say you don't really need to hire a lawyer. Although this is generally true when dealing with a Top Developer in Thailand, it's less true when dealing with a First-Time Developer.

Please see our Agent Checklist on the next page.

TABLE 18: CRITICAL ISSUES WHEN HIRING THE SERVICES OF AN AGENT

Item	Always keep in mind:
The agent is acting for the seller.	The seller agent has his/her own best interests at heart, then the best interests of the seller, then yours until you've paid your deposit. The seller is paying a commission to the Agent. The agent commission is a percentage of the purchase price. Never tell an agent that real estate in this country is cheaper than home, because the agent will only show you the more expensive properties. Do not show your interest in a property to an agent too openly; once the agent knows you're hooked he/she has no further incentive to negotiate a discount, because doing so would reduce the commission. Be aware that giving an agent a price bracket may mean the agent decides to offer you only properties in the top of the bracket, because these offer a better commission. Be aware that if two properties are of similar quality, the agent may decide only to present you the more expensive one of the two. Be aware that, once you've paid a deposit, the agent generally receives a commission whether you close the deal or not. When agents tell you they've done due diligence on the property, ask to see the report and don't trust your agent only on his/her word. Never just trust an agent's word that there are no problems with the agreement or the property, because the agent is not a lawyer. If you decide not to hire a lawyer, let it be your own decision and never let the agent dictate your course of action.
The agent is cute	Take a cold shower and remember she's not YOUR agent!

     www.renephilippe.com

Chapter 15   How to Improve the Odds When Buying Off Plan

from a First-Time Developer

If you decide to go ahead with the purchase of a property off plan, there are a few measures you may want to take in order to improve the odds in your favor. Those measures are indispensable if you are purchasing from a First-Time Developer, but matter less if you purchase from a Top Developer.

The first measure is the use of escrow. Escrow is a formal procedure when an independent third party called the escrow agent is used to secure the completion of a transaction between two parties. Simply put, an escrow transaction requires the involvement of an impartial escrow agent who will act as an intermediary between the buyer and a seller, to collect documents and/or funds for delivery to the appropriate parties upon completion of the terms and conditions of the escrow instructions or contract. Why does the use of an escrow agent make real estate related transactions safer?

Firstly, as soon as an escrow agreement has been executed between the seller and the buyer of immovable property, the escrow agent will usually have the duty of notifying the local land registrar. The land registrar will record the property as being subject to an escrow arrangement and no transaction will be allowed on the property for the duration of the escrow agreement unless allowed in writing by the escrow agent. As a result, the buyer will be protected against any attempt by the seller to mortgage or transfer the property without the buyer's knowledge during the construction period.

The second benefit of the escrow agreement is that the buyer's payments are deposited into the escrow account until such time as the property is ready for transfer. Your money will be remitted to the developer or the seller only upon the transfer of the completed property. As a result, the buyer is protected against the insolvency or failure of the developer.

The main difficulty with the implementation of this measure is that not all countries have escrow legislations. Thailand, for example, only implemented an Escrow Act in 2008. Furthermore, most countries with escrow acts do not make the practice mandatory[86].

Therefore, the decision about whether or not to engage an escrow agent is left to the parties involved. Of course, a First-Time Developer who needs his clients' funds to develop his project will never agree to an escrow arrangement. Therefore, whenever escrow is not mandatory, only reliable developers who have pre-financed their projects will be able to agree to the arrangement. The fact that a developer refuses the use of an escrow agent is another indication that this developer's project is not financed out of equity or commercial loans.

Another measure for improving the odds, especially when purchasing in a housing project developed by a First-Time Developer, is to require the developer to transfer the ownership of the buyer's land plot or register the lease agreement on the buyer's land plot to the latest upon the buyer's payment of the first or second

---

[86] Escrow is not mandatory in Thailand

installment[87]. If the developer fails, the buyer will still have the rights to the land. While this measure is plain common sense, it's actually not easy to convince a developer to agree, because the developer will be wary of what might happen if the buyer fails to pay. If you purchase a condominium, the transfer of the ownership of the unit during the construction period is usually impossible. In Thailand, for example, the developer can only apply for the condominium license after having completed 90% of the construction and individual titles representing the units are only issued by the Land Department after the condominium license has been obtained.

Get regular updates on the construction before each payment. Make sure the developer gives you photographs of the site and doesn't just tell you what stage the building is at. Furthermore, ask for pictures of the whole site, including the common areas and facilities. Keep yourself informed and don't make any payments before those payments are actually due. Be careful that the payment terms make a clear relation between the stages of construction that must be reached before a payment is due to the developer. Please remember that the laying of the foundation and the erection of a house structure are only a small part of the construction costs. So, never accept an installment schedule that would have you pay 50% or more of the construction cost by the time the house structure is built. If you purchase in an apartment building or a condominium, you should not pay more than one installment before the construction of the building actually starts.

If you purchase into a small housing project, hire a professional surveyor to survey the house at each milestone[88] because small-time developers are known to cut corners and the quality of the whole house may be affected. This precaution is worth the expense. Request the developer to provide you a copy of the application for the construction permit for your house before you make the payment of the second installment. Finally, verifying the

---

[87] When problems arise with a First-Time Developer, they generally start after the payment of the second installment.
[88] For five visits over the construction period, the cost should be between THB 50,000 and THB 100,000.

agreement provides a clause for damages in case of late delivery, or authorizes earlier termination by the buyer in case of delays. Also, check what kinds of guarantees the developers give you on the finished structure and the quality of the property. All these precautions might improve your situation. However, if you're purchasing from a First-Time Developer, remember that only the first recommendation (use of an escrow agent) will fully protect you from the risk of the developer's insolvency.

TABLE 19: CRITICAL ISSUES TO IMPROVE THE ODDS

Action	Effect	Remarks
Using the service of an escrow agent.	Your payments are passed into the hands of a third party and transferred to the developer only upon transfer of the ownership of the completed property to you.	Not available in all countries. If not mandatory, there are few chances a first-time developer will agree to it.
Requesting an early transfer of the right to ownership or the right to lease on the land.	If the First-Time Developer fails and becomes insolvent, you have secured a right to the lands to show for your money.	Reselling land in a failed project at a good price may not be easy. The developer might not agree to it.
Negotiate clear terms of payments that clearly state every milestone.	The developer may only call for your payment providing he has reached the required milestone.	Progress payment does not protect you against the developer's insolvency.
Negotiate terms of payment that give you fair value against payments.	Installments will be paid only against real construction.	Paying 25% of the price upon completion of the foundation or 25% of the price upon completion of the structure of the house is not fair value.
Hire a surveyor and/or request regular photographic updates.	To prevent the developer from cutting corners when building your house. To assure each payment matches an actual milestone.	Request not only pictures of your property, but also of the project to be sure of the overall construction progress.
©Rene Philippe & Partners Ltd		www.renephilippe.com

Chapter 16   Handover and Warranty

The initiation of the handover process will be the same whether you are purchasing from a Top Developer or a First-Time Developer. When the date of completion approaches, the developer will send you a notice letter (usually 30 days in advance) informing you the property will be soon ready for transfer.

In general, the developer will also schedule a date for a joint visit at the property prior to the transfer. If you are overseas and unable to come immediately, the developer will usually accommodate you to a certain extent and reschedule the meeting for a more convenient date.

This process starts to differ after the joint visit. Top Developers don't make a practice of forcing their buyers into the transfer of defective property (at least they don't in Thailand). On the contrary, they will first repair the defects and schedule another visit or send pictures to the buyer attesting to the completion of repairs and only after all defects have been repaired will they request that the buyer accept the transfer of the property.

However, First-Time Developers often do not consider the repair of defects as precluding the transfer of the property to the buyer and the payment of the last installment. In fact, they will often promise to correct the defects after the transfer and try to get their buyers to accept the transfer of the property and pay the last installment before taking any action in the way of repairs.

Before you agree to purchase from a First-Time Developer, verify your agreement. A fair clause for the buyer should stipulate the following minimum requirements: "*The work inside and outside of the villa is complete, except for minor omissions and minor defects. Minor omissions or minor defects are those which do not prevent the land plot and villa from being reasonably used for the intended purpose whereby the rectification of minor omissions or minor defects will not prejudice the convenient use of the Land and Villa. For example, a scratched window or chipped wall edge is acceptable, but missing or dysfunctional parts or equipment are unacceptable. Any rectification work causing the builder to remove tiles, wood floors or work that creates excessive amounts of dust and noise are deemed to prejudice the convenient use of the villa. Finally, all equipment listed in the Specifications List attached herein has been properly tested and found to be in working order.*"

In other words, the agreement should not allow the developer to force the transfer of a property on the buyer as long as there are defects and/or omissions affecting the property in such a way that it cannot be reasonably used for the intended purposes, or cannot be rectified without prejudicing the convenient use of the property. Be careful to review the Specification List in detail to assure that everything the developer has promised is listed as a specification and that the specifications actually conform to your needs.

What kind of warrantee should buyers request? Warrantee terms vary from one country to the other and there are no general rules. A warrantee should be no less than five years on of all the property's structural elements (pilings, foundations, supports, beams, floors, roof and bearing walls) and two years on non-structural elements.

If you purchase from a Top Developer, you won't need to worry about the execution of the warrantee. As previously discussed, well-known Top Developers with land development as their core business have too much to lose in terms of reputation by not honoring their warrantee commitment.

The same cannot be said of First-Time Developers who are often new to the business. Furthermore, First-Time Developers generally use small contractors they don't pay well, and the construction agreements First-Time Developers have with their contractors[89] often overlook the matter of the defect warrantee. The safest way to ensure that a First-Time Developer executes his warrantee commitment is to negotiate a clause of "retention". This clause will allow the buyer to retain a proportion of the contract value (usually 5% to 10%) of the property purchase price for a determined period (usually one to two years) after the transfer of the property has taken place in order to ensure that the First-Time Developer fulfills his warrantee obligation. If he fails to do so, the clause should authorize the buyer to hire third-party contractors and pay them out of the retention money after a specified notice period. In this way, buyers can at least be sure the warrantee will be executed and it's always better to be safe than sorry.

TABLE 20: ISSUES TO ADDRESS IN RELATION TO THE HANDOVER

Actions	Effects	Remarks
Negotiation of precise conditions for the handover	Prevents the developer from forcing the transfer of the property before all apparent defects have been repaired.	You may never be sure if and when First-Time Developers will repair the defects once you've transferred the property and fully paid them.
Warrantee	Request at least five years for the structure and two years for non-structural work.	
Retention	Retain from 5% to 10% of the purchase price.	This guarantees the good execution of the warrantee.
©Rene Philippe & Partners Ltd.		www.renephilippe.com

---

[89] I have seen more than one case where the First-Time Developer did not have an actual agreement with his contractors.

Chapter 17   Membership and Management of a Co-Owners'

Association

One of the most recent evolutions in the real estate sector is the phenomenon of more and more buyers purchasing properties located within private communities versus individual stand-alone properties. A community living environment (whether a building or a housing project) is a form of living environment including a private area (houses and land plots or apartments) to be sold or leased out to the residents in addition to various common areas.

In a housing project, the common area is characterized by a closed perimeter of walls and fences, controlled entrances for pedestrians, bicycles and automobiles, small residential streets and various amenities, depending upon the size of the project. Typical amenities offered can include pools, tennis courts, community centers or club houses, playground areas, exercise areas with exercise machines, steam rooms, saunas and golf courses or marinas in resort areas. If the project is a building, the common areas will consist of the building entrance, the walkways, the parking facilities and various amenities. In principle, people buying into a community living environment (whether a housing project or a condominium) will purchase two things. They'll purchase a private unit for residential purposes as well as a fractional share of the common area and facilities normally held in an undivided ownership interest by the co-owners association or the juristic person.

Buyers purchasing in a community environment overseas will concentrate on the terms and conditions applicable to the purchase of their residences, but they rarely pay attention to the matter of ownership and the management of the common areas of the community they'll be living in. In my opinion, this is a critical mistake, because those matters are of utmost importance for several reasons. Unfortunately, some countries haven't implemented the legal framework for the issues of the construction, ownership and management of common areas while others have only rudimentary legal frameworks covering those areas.

In countries where these issues are regulated, verify whether the law provides minimum standards for the construction of the common areas. Legal standards may set a minimum ratio between the size of the residential area and the size of the common area, or a minimum number of parking slots in relation to the number of units. Laws may also set minimum compliance requirements, such as width of the internal roads, electricity system or water drainage system and size of the green area. There may also be total prohibitions or limitations in relation to the exercise of commercial activities within the community property. Another issue is the matter of the legal ownership of the common areas. Can the developer retain the ownership of the common areas and facilities? Or, is the transfer of the common area to the co-owners association mandatory?

Then there's the problem of the management of the co-owner association itself.

Gated communities or condominiums are "privately managed" mini-cities and co-owner associations are like privately managed governments. Within the territory of the community, the association will not only provide services to the co-owners but will also regulate activities, levy assessments, and impose fines. It shall also operate within the limits of the housing project tasks, such as the security, maintenance of the project's internal roads, regulation of and restrictions on traffic and so on. However, unlike a municipal government, co-owner association governance is subject to corporate law and some specific legislation governing homeowners' associations, but not to the administrative constraints public governments are obligated to abide by.

In contrast to a local government authority, a homeowners' association can only enforce its regulations through private legal action under civil law. Boards appoint corporate officers, and may create subcommittees such as architectural control committees, pool committees and neighborhood watch committees. Association boards are comprised of volunteers from the community who are elected by owners at the annual meeting to represent the association and make decisions for all homeowners.

An important point from a buyer's point of view is to check whether the local legal framework contains measures to protect the interests of minority buyers against abuse from the majority or against abuse from the board. We've all heard of co-owner associations run like "mini dictatorships" by directors who abuse their power to satisfy their self-interest or because they dislike their neighbors. After having spent a whole lifetime working, who would like to spend their retirement taking the abuse of a "dictator" type co-owner association? Careful buyers, therefore, must also consider this matter.

If you're purchasing in a country where foreign ownership is prohibited or limited, you might have to purchase your property through leasehold. Now, one issue to consider is that voting in a homeowner association or condominium juristic person is generally based on property ownership and only property owners are eligible to vote in elections to the exclusion of the lessees. Therefore, buyers considering long-term leases need to check into the possibility of obtaining irrevocable proxy from the property owner allowing buyers to exercise voting rights in the owner's stead.

Another matter of concern is sinking or reserve funds and management fees. Is there a legal obligation to constitute a reserve fund? If not, did the developer organize one anyway? The reserve fund will be a special account to which every co-owner contributed at the time of the property transfer. The money paid by the co-owners must be held in reserve for important special repair needs (not the day-to-day repairs paid for by the management fees).

Management fees are shares of common expenses and usually calculated per-unit or based on square meters. These expenses generally arise from common property, which varies dramatically depending upon the type of association. Some associations are quite literally towns complete with private roads, services, utilities, amenities, community buildings, and pools. Other associations may have no common property, but may charge for services or other conveniences. In order to facilitate the sale of their projects, or simply because they're ignorant of the management costs of a community, First-Time Developers tend to underestimate the cost of management of their projects; hence the cost of the yearly management fees.

We've seen several projects developed in Thailand by First-Time Developers where the co-owners were forced to double the amount of the management fees within the first year in order to cover day-to-day expenses. Note that many expenses are not compressible. The minimum incompressible expenses include the salaries of the housing association manager, the repairmen (minimum of one to three if 24-hour maintenance is required), a gardener and security guards (minimum of two for 24-hour security). In addition, the homeowners' association will have to pay for expenses, such as garden and pool product expenses, common area electricity and water, accounting expenses and other miscellaneous expenses.

In Thailand, the cost of managing a Grade A building with 150 apartments will be roughly equivalent to the cost of managing a 12-house high-end gated community. The 12 units' housing project costs are about 75% of the 150 units' building management costs. In the first case, however, the costs will be shared among 150 owners, while only 12 owners will be sharing the burden in the second case.

Note that when you purchase in a community, the long-term value of your property will be directly linked to the quality of the common area management. Cutting corners in common area expenses to save money for the short run is the decision a co-owners' association may take.

Another essential issue associated with management fees is whether the local law or the contract (if the local law is silent on the issue) imposes a liability on the developer to pay for the maintenance fees of the unsold units. If there is no legal or contractual obligation on the developer to pay for the cost of the maintenance of unsold units, then the impact will be felt in the budget of the co-owner association and the quality of the maintenance of the common area from the beginning.

Motivating the owners to participate in community living and the meetings of co-owner associations is already challenging in projects where all co-owners have their principal residence. Now, can you imagine how complicated it will be to manage a co-owner association in a second residence project where most of the owners aren't living at the site most of the year? While a selected board of directors has the power to handle the day-to-day management within the limits of the bylaws, the power to change the bylaws or make important decisions (such as increasing the management fees) all fall under the jurisdiction of the co-owners' general meeting. The problem in a second residence project is reaching an actual quorum when organizing general meetings as a lot of the co-owners do not bother to come.

Finally, if you ever agree to accept a directorship in a co-owner association, it's understood that the position isn't only honorary and that there is a lot of work involved, especially during the warrantee period. A good board will periodically check the quality of construction in the common areas and see if any defects appear. If defects are discovered, the board will be responsible for the handling of the warrantee claims, managing and supervising the employees, handling co-owners' complaints, enforcing the payment of management fees and so on. Therefore, if you purchase a property offshore, don't overlook the matter of the co-owner association because it will affect not only the quality of your life within the community, but also the long-term value of your property.

Also don't believe the other co-owners will all be pleased by your hard work. There will always be unhappy co-owners who will have nothing better to do than criticize the decision of the board. Please see the table below which shows the critical issues to consider when purchasing into a community project.

TABLE 21: CRITICAL ISSUES TO CONSIDER WHEN BUYING INTO A COMMUNITY PROJECT	
Item	Issue to check
Common Area Ownership	Does the law or the contract provide for the transfer of the common area ownership to the co-owner association?
Common Area Compliance	Are there minimum compliance standards for the construction of the common area and did the developer fulfill them?
Reserve or Sinking Fund	Will a reserve or sinking fund be established and are all co-owners required to contribute?
Management Fees	What are the management fees? Do the management fees seem reasonable? Or does the developer grossly underestimate them? (Check neighboring projects) Is the Developer responsible (by law or contract) for the payment of the management fees of unsold units?
Protection of Minority Rights	Are there legal dispositions or bylaws that protect the minority from being abused by the majority?
Quorum & Proxies	What is the quorum necessary to hold a general meeting of the co-owners and is it possible for a member to be represented by proxy?
©Rene Philippe & Partners Ltd.	www.renephilippe.com

PART 2 PRACTICAL ISSUES TO CONSIDER WHEN BUYING

PROPERTY IN A FOREIGN COUNTRY

Chapter 18   **What are the Main Factors Affecting Offshore**

Real Estate Prices?

Another matter you will have to consider when purchasing property in another country is that property prices don't undergo the same changes in every country. In other words you cannot simply assume that, because the property value has increased by 5% per year in your home country for the past 10 years, the same will be true in your destination country.

Indeed, while the main factors with potential impact on the prices of property are generally the same in every country, the fact is that the evolution of those factors will depend upon very local circumstances in a particular area or country. Note that, while we discuss each factor separately, all of these factors are actually interrelated.

The first factor is land scarcity. In most countries, for example, downtown land has become very scarce and is generally reserved for the development of office towers or commercial buildings. Whenever a developer launches a residential building in the center of a city, the selling prices of the project units will generally be higher than average, not only because the project is more costly to develop, but also simply because such projects are so rare that developers may list units at a higher price than they would if the project were located on the outskirts of the city. Location is also an important factor. A condominium unit close to a prestigious school and the sky train or subway will have more value in the long run and will always be easier to resell. The same is also true with prime beach land which has become very scarce in Thailand.

The second factor potentially affecting the price of real estate is the balance between supply and demand. As long as supply and demand are balanced, or as long as there are more buyers than properties for sale, the property prices will rise. But a perpetual rise in price is not a given. There will always be bumps along the way.

There are several other factors with a potential impact on supply and demand e.g. population changes, wages and employment levels, construction costs and labor availability. The last factor is the government's fiscal policy, because the demand will vary with the difficulty or ease of obtaining credit.

While most of the factors to consider are local, the fact is that the prices of property in any particular country may also be affected by events elsewhere in the world. In this regard, the two best examples are the 1997 and the 2008/2009 financial crises. One interesting aspect of the latest world financial crisis is that the prices of real estate in Thailand did not plummet as they were expected to because as Thailand was into the middle of a political crisis that has lasted three years to date, local developers had already started to reduce supply before the onset of the current economic crisis. The fact that Thailand was already in "crisis mode" when the financial crisis started helped to diminish its effects in the real estate sector.

Of course, I know a few clients who ended up purchasing properties in Thailand at dramatically discounted prices, but these discounts were not the result of a general drop in prices. Rather, they were the consequences of the individual sellers' personal situations. Nor did real estate prices in Thailand drop because.

Chapter 19   What and Where Should You Buy in Thailand?

Is it always difficult for a new buyer who has just arrived in a country without knowledge of the market to make an informed decision on what and where to buy? I have been living in Thailand for 12 years, and I believe I have a good understanding of the market. Despite my experience, however, nary a day goes by when I don't learn something new.

In this chapter, I will discuss the situation in Bangkok for the most part, because it's the market I know best.

Should you trust your agent to recommend the best product available? You may, of course, but you could also try to find out about the situation for yourself, because agents are more interested in the commissions they may receive on a property than in knowing whether this property is the right investment for you.

Where can you find accurate information? The first source of information is the Real Estate Information Center http://www.reic.or.th which has a site in both Thai and English. You will find a lot of information on this site regarding the situation of the real estate market in Thailand. Unfortunately, much of the data on this site remains solely in the Thai language, but some useful information has been translated. This website, however, deals mainly with general information on the market situation in Thailand. What should you read if you want to buy a condominium in Bangkok? Another free source of information is the Raimon Land Condominium Focus publication, which you can download for free from the Raimon Land website at:

http://www.raimonland.com/en/condo/Condo_Focus_Aug_2009.pdf

Unfortunately, the Raimon Land publication concentrates on Bangkok's inner city center and Pattaya, which are the two core markets were Raimon Land is active. If, however, you want to purchase in one of those two areas this document is a "must read" before making your purchase, especially because this publication is updated every three months and provides accurate and unbiased information.

For example, two interesting surveys were recently published in the newspapers in August 2009. The first survey from Aquarius Estate Co., Ltd was a study of the recent evolution of average prices per square meter for new condominium units in Bangkok. According to Aquarius study the above mentioned prices have risen by 28% from 2007 to 2008, climbing from THB 57,600 per square meter to THB 74,000 at the end of 2008. However, average prices dropped to THB 70,000 in the first eight months of 2009. Regardless, average prices have risen tremendously since 2007. That's not bad when you consider Thailand has suffered from an ongoing political crisis since the second half of 2006 and from the aftershock of the global economical crisis[90].

Foreign buyers generally purchase in Bangkok's inner city center where prices for new units may be anything from THB 90,000 per square meter and prices can exceed THB 250,000 per square meter.

---

[90] Please note that those are the average prices for the whole Bangkok area (including Bangkok outskirts with all condominium types confounded)

Speaking of prices, the Global Property Guide published a survey on 28 August ranking 112 cities from the most expensive to the least expensive place to purchase a condominium. The study compares the purchase prices of secondhand high-end 120 SQM condominium units in 112 countries.

Of 112 cities, Bangkok is listed as number 82 with an average price of USD 2,238 per square meter which makes Bangkok look fairly affordable. The second part of the survey lists the cities offering the highest gross rental yield. Here again, Bangkok fares well at 21 out of 98 with a rental yield estimated at 7.97%.

Now, while I'm always happy to see Bangkok faring well in real estate surveys, I think the Global Property Guide survey results for Bangkok are a bit too optimistic.

In Bangkok, a USD 2,238 (THB 76,092) per square meter condominium unit would for 120 SQM translate to a THB 9,131,040 price tag. While I know condominium units are indeed available at this price per square meter, they will not usually be located in the center of inner Bangkok. When they are, they will generally be in buildings already aged 10 years or more.

If you are looking to purchase on the resale market's high-end units in Bangkok's inner city center in buildings aged less than 5 years, the average selling price will be somewhere between THB 90,000 (USD 2,647) and THB 120,000 (3529 USD) per SQM for a 120 SQM condominium unit based on transactions for secondhand units I've overseen during the past 12 months. This evaluation is further confirmed by Raimon Land's latest Condominium Focus mention of an average price of THB 95,000 per square meter for secondhand units in Bangkok's inner city center where most high-end units are located.

No. 82 is the correct rating for Bangkok if you average the prices for the whole city. However, if you look only at Bangkok's inner city center where most of the high-end units are located, Bangkok pricing ranking would more accurately be placed between No. 71 (Budapest or Phnom Phen) and No. 50 (Krakow or Zurich) which, by the way, is still a good rank.

While I confirm the possibility of purchasing a secondhand apartment at THB 76,092 (even cheaper) per SQM in Bangkok, based on my experience, current prices for high-end secondhand units are closer to THB 90,000 to THB 120,000 per square meter, especially if you want to purchase in a condominium building located in the city center and completed within the past five years.

To sum up, while surveys are extremely useful in terms of showing market trends, it is not possible to reduce a city like Bangkok to a single market. Mega-cities like Bangkok are in this regard "countries" in their own right, with each area or each district being its own market with its own average prices. As both surveys indicated, it is possible to purchase new or secondhand condominium units in Bangkok at 75,000 THB per square meter or even lower, but those units will generally be located far from the city center or may possibly be city center secondhand units in buildings aged 10 years or older.

Chapter 20   **Are they any tricks when selecting a property in**

Thailand?

Are they any "insider tricks" I could pass on to help you purchase a condominium unit in Bangkok? Yes, of course there are but at the end of the day, however, it's just pure common sense.

Firstly, whether you purchase as a user or an investor, the most important thing is always location, location, and location. The most highly regarded condominiums units right now are those located adjacent to or near the mass transit system and this is a trend that will continue in the long run.

According to the study from Aquarius, the best condominium sales this year were in the Lad Prao and mid Sukhumvit area between Soi 71 in Prakanong and Soi Onut (Soi 77) with sales rates of 79% and 78% respectively, in comparison to an overall rate for Bangkok of 64% (46,137 units sold out of 71,581 units offered).

Why were those two areas favored by buyers? The answer is that both areas have BTS and MRT stations nearby but are also located far enough from the inner center for new condominiums to be sold at prices lower than the going rates in Bangkok's inner city. In other words, those two areas offer a valid alternative to buyers who are working in Bangkok city center but cannot afford a condominium there. In this way, they can buy in areas where prices are lower but offer commuting solutions via the mass transit system. I believe these areas will continue to be a good buy for the next two or three years.

What are the other tricks you should know about when selecting your condominium unit?

Another trick is to look at the map of Thai high schools (private schools, most of which are Catholic schools) and buy a condominium in an area near both a Thai high school and the transit system. You'll then have a winner no matter what happens. You cannot lose money on such a unit, because there will always be parents of students wanting to buy your unit for convenience when their children are in high school because most reputable high schools are in Bangkok's inner city center and families who do not live in the city center have a choice between waking up before dawn to take their kids to school or moving closer by. Focus on high schools, not universities, because, most universities have moved or are about to move their campus to Bangkok outskirts. For example, a condominium purchased three years ago in such an area (between the sky train and a high school) at THB 75,000 per square meter is now worth now THB 125,000 per square meter according to a Thai bank evaluation (note that the evaluation was made a few months ago, while we were still in the midst of the current economic crisis). Although the downside of living near a school will be horrible traffic in the mornings and afternoons, you can't have it all.

Another good buy would be a condominium unit located riverside, especially now that the sky train has finally crossed the river. Purchase a river view unit near the sky train and you'll have another winner. What I mean is a condominium unit with a price that can only appreciate in the long run.

Now it's time for the big questions. Should you wait or should you buy now? And why do condominium prices continue to rise over time? I think the reason is simple: developers and banks have learnt from the 1997 crisis and developers have regulated themselves by freezing projects while the banks have done the same by reducing their loan offers to developers. For example, a few years ago, banks were still lending to developers who had pre-sold 30% of their projects. Now developers need to pre-sale 40% to 50% of their projects to have a chance at obtaining bank financing.

This is not only the case with condominiums. The same can be said of the Bangkok house market, which is particularly healthy because most SET listed developers have delayed launching new projects due to the political and economic situation and have pushed the sales of their inventory instead. As a result, the number of listed properties affirms that Bangkok's new home stocks have significantly diminished during the second quarter of this year. Also, the demand for new houses has been growing steadily during the first five months of this year. According to the REIC (Real Estate Information Center), 28,800 house units were transferred during the five first months of 2009, 9,650 of which were transferred in May. Overall, this is 5% more than last year, which is good news. Even better news is that two recently launched projects were fully sold in a matter of days.

Is there any good condominium deal to be made? Those who are waiting for prices to drop in Bangkok so they can purchase a condominium unit are making a costly mistake. Yes, you may still have an opportunity to find a private buyer in financial trouble that has to sell at any cost on the resale market, but this kind of opportunity is rare and you just have to be in the right place at the right time to do so.

Why should you buy a condominium in Bangkok now? Simply because developers and banks have been too reasonable; there were fewer projects launched in 2007 than in 2006 and 2008 saw fewer projects launched than in 2007. The same happened during the first half of 2009. Overall, developers have cut over three years from their offer (by nearly half) and concentrated on selling their stock. As the global economy seems to be back on track then I believe we'll have a two-year window period (starting 2010) when the supply will be lower than the demand, because the demand for condominium units will increase more quickly than the offer and it takes around three to four years from blank page to project completion.

What about buying a house in Bangkok now? Unfortunately for my readers who are foreign buyers, the bad news is the Bangkok home market is not for you. The reason is that the housing market in Bangkok is dominated by the 25 listed developers and those developers only launch projects developed under land allotment licenses. When a project is developed under a land allotment license, the developer may only sell the land and house units to the buyers. Developers may not lease the properties developed under a land allotment license. Furthermore, the projects are designed with the needs of Thai customers in mind and foreign customers may not like them. Therefore if a foreign buyer wants to purchase a house in Bangkok he will have only two solutions. Investing 40,000,000 THB in Thailand and purchase one rai of land freehold (please see Chapter 39 for more information on this option) or set up a company with Thai nominees to purchase the land on its behalf, which is not the best thing you can do at this time.

If you don't want to purchase in Bangkok then I recommend you to buy a condominium in Bangkok, Hua Hin, Phuket or Pattaya, but only within projects launched by top Thai Developers such as Raimon Land, Sansiri, Preuska, Land & House[91] and other developers listed on the stock exchange of Thailand as the financial situations of those developers are healthier than the financial situations of smaller developers.

What about buying a house in one of Thailand's seaside resorts? It is very difficult to make an accurate prognosis of the

---

[91] Please see Chapter 6 for the 25 listed developers' names

housing market in a province, especially with respects to properties with potential to attract foreign buyers. It suffices to say that the new house market targeting foreign customers in Thai seaside resorts is mostly in the hands of First-Time Developers who have suffered tremendously for the past two years. So, it is not unusual to see projects launched in 2005 or 2006 still "on sale" with sales of only one-third of the total amount of the units to date. Also, if you purchase a house in leasehold, you'll be faced with all the issues pertaining to the renewal clause I discussed in a previous chapter. Will this market pick up again? One thing is certain: the extension of the lease period from 30 to 99 years would help stranded First-Time Developers sell again.

For the time being, my recommendation is to purchase a condominium instead of a house as ownership issues are less complex at present, especially if your retirement is 10 or 15 years away. If you select the right type of condominium, you can rent it for the next 10 years, then sell it with a margin and use the money to purchase your dream home, because leasehold periods will hopefully in 10 years' time have been increased from 30 to 99 years.

Note that if you want to purchase a seaside condominium unit, you'll have to purchase off plan and preferably upon the launching of the project, as those types of units are very popular with foreign buyers and that there is a 49% foreign quota limiting the number of foreigners buying into a given project. As you will have to purchase off plan, we recommend that you purchase from SET listed developers.

Chapter 21 What is the Rental Yield in Bangkok?

In the second part of the surveys I discussed in chapters 19, the Global Property Guide ranked 98 cities from the highest gross rental yield to the lowest.

Here again Bangkok does fairly well with a ranking of 21 out of 98 and an average 7.97% gross rental yield. Unfortunately, I think that the survey is too optimistic in its estimation of rental yields that may be achieved in Bangkok

A rental yield of 7.97% would mean:

- a rental of THB 727,743 per year or THB 60,645 per month on a 120 SQM apartment at THB 9,131,040 (THB 76,092 per SQM).

- a rental of THB 860,760 per year or THB 71,730 per month on a 120 SQM apartment at THB 10,800,000 (THB 90,000 per SQM).

- a rental of THB 1,147,680 or THB 95,640 per month on a 120 SQM apartment at THB 14,400,000 (THB 120,000 per SQM).

In my experience, a reasonable maximum yield for a 120 SQM secondhand unit would be between THB 50,000 and 75,000 THB per month. In other words, the rental yield would be from 6.5% in the case of a unit purchased at THB 9,131,040 and rented out at THB 50,000 per month to 6% in the case of a unit purchased at THB 14,400,000 and rented out at THB 72,000 per month. And for really expensive units priced at THB 20,000,000 or more, one should not expect a rental yield of more than 5% to 5.5%.

Note that I'm talking here of ordinary condominium as opposed to serviced apartments with higher rental yields. In terms of rental yield, therefore, my opinion is that Bangkok should rank between 33 (like Toronto) and 48 (like Zurich) out of 98, which is still a fairly good ranking. Bangkok, however, may do better than Toronto or Zurich in that management service fees (common property charges) and taxes are certainly lower here than they are in Toronto or Zurich.

Also, while I believe the gross rental yield in Bangkok to be lower than indicated in the surveys mentioned above, the fact remains that Bangkok is still a good place to buy, because you may realize a substantial long-term capital gain in addition to the rental yield if you choose the right property.

Chapter 22   The Foreign Exchange Risk Factor

In the next few chapters, I will discuss a few financial issues. While they are not exactly within the scope of my experience, I believe these issues should be addressed in this book, because they are important for potential buyers.

Once you've located the offshore property of your dreams and are about to make an important purchase in a foreign currency, you'll begin to wonder about the risks and whether or not there are any solutions to protect yourself. The main issue to address when purchasing offshore property is the currency volatility risk as shown in the examples below.

Note that the case I've made here is only to illustrate the currency volatility risk. My meaning is that I'm taking only fluctuations in the currency exchange rate into account in my examples. There are, in fact, many other factors to be taken into account regarding whether the buyers in my examples made a gain or loss over the period from January 2002 to January 2009 and what their gain or loss actually amounted to. Among the other factors I haven't taken into consideration are inflation and changes in the housing value index during the same period in the US and France, etc. This is because the purpose of this example is not to give an accurate result of the actual gains or losses realized by my subjects, but simply to illustrate the following to my readers:

(1) They must consider fluctuations in foreign currencies against their own currency when purchasing a property offshore.

(2) This issue must be taken into account, not only when purchasing property in an exotic country, but as soon as you purchase a property with values expressed in a currency other than your own. This is valid whether you purchase in the US, Europe or more exotic destinations, such as Ecuador, Belize, Cambodia or Thailand.

Example 1: Purchasing Property Ready for Immediate Transfer

Our first buyer is Albert Dupont, a French citizen who purchased property in the US in January of 2002. The purchase price of the property was USD 1,000,000 (or EURO 989,410 at that time).

Our second buyer is John Smith, a US citizen who purchased property in France in January of 2002. The purchase price of the property was EURO 989,410 or USD 1,000,000 at that time.

For the sake of this discussion, we'll assume that Albert Dupont and John Smith have purchased properties with equivalent features.

While both John Smith and Albert Dupont paid the same price for their properties in 2002, if you take only the variation between the Euro and US dollar over the past seven years into consideration, John Smith and Albert Dupont are no longer in the same situation. Indeed, in January of 2002, one US dollar was worth EURO 0.98941. In January of 2009, however, one US dollar is only equal to EURO 0.7411.

If Albert Dupont were to resell his US property in January of 2009 at the same purchase price he paid in 2002 i.e. USD 1,000,000

(EURO 989,410), he would receive only EURO 741,100 at today's exchange rate. In other words, if he were selling his house at the same price he purchased it in 2002, Albert Dupont would receive EURO 248,310 or USD 335,055 less than he paid seven years ago, amounting to a loss of 33.5%.

On the contrary, if John Smith were to resell his French property today at the same price he purchased it i.e. EURO 989,410 (USD 1,000,000 in January of 2002), John Smith would receive USD 1,335,000 for a gain of 33.5% in comparison to the original purchase price.

Example 2: Off-Plan Purchase of Property Ready to Transfer in 24 Months

If you're purchasing property off plan with the price expressed in another currency, never forget to take into consideration that the price of the property you're buying may fluctuate during the two or three years before the project is ready to be transferred. To illustrate my point, I'll once again compare the situations of Albert Dupont and John Smith.

Just imagine what would happen if John Smith and Albert Dupont made reservations in January of 2002 to purchase properties off plan for delivery in January of 2004 instead of purchasing property ready to be transferred in January of 2002.

Both John Smith and Albert Dupont have made deposits representing 30% of the property purchase price in January of 2002, with the remaining balance of 70% of the total purchase price due at the time of the transfer in January of 2004.

Our first buyer, Albert Dupont, purchased a property off plan costing USD 1,000,000 (or EURO 989,410 in January of 2002). He made a deposit of USD 300,000 (or EURO 296,823) in January of 2002. In January of 2004, Albert Dupont needed to transfer the balance due on the purchase price i.e. USD 700,000 (or EURO 558,692) to the developer.

Overall, Albert Dupont spent a total amount of EURO 855,515 to purchase his property in the US instead of paying EURO 989,410 if he had made his payment in full in January of 2002. Therefore, Albert Dupont, paid USD 169,217 (or EURO 133,895) less for his property than he would've paid had he paid the full price in January of 2002.

Our second buyer, John Smith, purchased a property in France off plan in January of 2002 at a price of USD 1,000,000 or EURO 989,410. He made a deposit of EURO 296,823 (or USD 300,000) at the time of the reservation. In January of 2004, John Smith needed to transfer the balance due on the property purchase price i.e. USD 875,305, or EURO 692,587, to the developer.

Overall, John Smith spent a total amount of USD 1,175,305 to purchase his property instead of USD 1,000,000 as initially anticipated based on the exchange rates of January, 2002.

Note that if John Smith and Albert Dupont were to resell the property they purchased off plan in January of 2002 and transferred in January 2004 at the initial purchase price, their situation would be essentially the same as in the first example. John Smith would still make a marginal profit and Albert Dupont a loss. However, Alain Dupont's loss would be less here than in the first example. In the same way, John Smith's gain would be also less than in the first example.

As explained above these, two examples are not completely accurate in terms of the gain or losses realized by John Smith and/or Albert Dupont (if only because I assume the properties were sold at the same price as their initial purchase)[92]. I continue to find them fascinating, not only because they demonstrate the potential risks of the currency conversion gain/loss, but also because they show how the passage of time can affect a potential currency gain or loss. In

---

[92] Under normal circumstances, the value of both properties would have appreciated during the course of the seven years and none of the owners would be selling them at their original purchase price.

other words, today's loss may be tomorrow's gain and then a loss again the day after.

Being no financial wizard, I have no particular insight into how buyers can protect themselves against the volatility of exchange rates when purchasing real estate offshore. I'm not even sure a perfect method to do so actually exists without taking a bet on the future value of the foreign currency[93].

Although I don't have a solution, I still believe this issue is worth mentioning, if only to raise awareness among potential buyers of offshore real estate that the issue exists. As a rule, brokers or developers selling offshore real estate will generally emphasize the potential capital or rental gains to be made, but remain silent on the exchange risks.

Since this book was first published, one of my clients was victim of fluctuations in the foreign exchange rate. He purchased a condominium off plan from a medium-sized developer in 2005. The condominium was, according to the contract, to be delivered at the end of 2007. Unfortunately, the developer was late and the unit was only transferred in March of 2009. While the purchase price of the condominium unit did not vary in THB, the British pound had lost value against the Thai baht over the past two years (from 62 THB to 55 THB for 1 British pound). Of course, the contract provided for a damage clause but, all matters considered, we recommended our client to settle with the developer. While the developer made a gesture, it did not cover the entire exchange loss.

To conclude on this subject, another factor to consider when purchasing real estate property in another currency is the time and place for exchanging your money. For example, any given currency exchange rate may differ, depending upon where you make your transaction. In some countries, the amount of foreign currency

---

[93] If any of my readers have valuable insights on this subject, please do not hesitate to send me your comments.

you'll receive for your Euro or US dollar may not differ whether you ask your bank to purchase the foreign currency on the international market or whether you transfer your US dollars or Euros directly to the destination country and convert to the foreign currency locally. There are no absolute rules regarding which solution is most advantageous for you. In some cases, it's more advantageous to convert the foreign currency on the international market. In other cases, it's more advantageous to convert on the local market.

Offshore buyers need to be careful, however, because there are still many countries only authorizing foreign buyers to purchase real estate on the condition that the foreign buyer transfers foreign currency into the country. (e.g. if you're purchasing a condominium in Thailand). If you're purchasing in a country with this requirement, you'll have to instruct your bank to transfer foreign currency to the destination country even if it's more costly for you to do so.

Chapter 23   Foreign Exchange Control

Of course, a careful buyer will also need to check what local foreign exchange control regulations are applicable in the destination country.

Indeed, you want to be sure that (1) there are no regulations requiring you to transfer foreign currency, (2) there are no regulations that would make your transfer onerous (e.g. a withholding tax that would apply to inbound transfers[94]), and (3) your transferred money will be exchanged at a fair rate and not at a pre-fixed rate determined by the government of the country in which you are investing. Finally, you want to be sure you'll be allowed to transfer your money out of the destination country once you have sold your property.

---

[94] For example, at the end of 2006, the Bank of Thailand imposed a 30% retention requirement on categories of inbound capital payments made in foreign currency. While numerous transactions were specifically exempted, this measure dramatically affected foreign investment. Fortunately, this measure has since then been discontinued.

In Thailand, the Exchange Control Act of 1942 and Ministerial Regulation No. 13 of 1954 set forth the exchange control policies. The Bank of Thailand is in charge of administering foreign exchange.

Firstly, there is no restriction on the amount of Thai baht brought into the country. Secondly, and contrary to popular belief, you may transfer foreign currency into Thailand or bring it in cash without any limit.

This being said, and while foreign currency may be freely imported, a reporting requirement applying to any person purchasing, selling, depositing, transferring or withdrawing foreign currencies in an amount of USD 20,000 or more must be mentioned. The same requirement applies to anyone bringing foreign currency in cash into the country.

If you are bringing cash into Thailand to pay an installment on a condominium purchase, do not forget to declare it to the customs officer, even if the amount is below USD 20,000. Indeed, at the time when the developer or the seller transfers the condominium unit, you will have to verify your payment of the total amount of the condominium purchase price in foreign currency. Therefore, you will need a receipt from the Customs officer for any amount of cash you brought for this purpose.

Thai banks will require you to complete a form called the Foreign Exchange Transaction Form ("FETF") for any transactions above the amount of USD 20,000.

The table on the next page is not the actual FETF. It only describes the information you will be requested to provide whenever you have to sign the form. Note that FETF forms for most banks are in both English and Thai.

TABLE 22: THE FOREIGN EXCHANGE TRANSACTION FORM
(For transactions valued at USD 20,000 or above or equivalent to the market rate)
Name of Authorized Financial Institution Branch

1 Customer Information	Identification Number, Name, Nationality, Address, Country, Telephone Business Type
2 Beneficiary or Sender Information	Name, Nationality, Address, Country Relationship with Customer: Affiliate or Shareholder/Others
3. Foreign Exchange Transaction	Type: Purchase, Sale, Deposit, Withdrawal, Neither Sale Nor Deposit, Receipt, Payment Account Number Name of Account Owner Payment Method: Note, Draft, T/T, T/R, M/T, SWIFT, Other Currency: Amount, Exchange Rate
4. Specified Purpose:	Please Specify the Name of the Exporter or Importer (For Trade Purposes, Please Specify the Name of the Exporter/Importer If the Beneficiary/Sender Is Not An Exporter or Importer). Competent Officer's Letter of Approval (if any), Number, Date of Issue.
5. Foreign Currency Loan	Type: Direct Loan, Issue Debt Securities (Type/Maturity, Term/Year(s)/Month(s)/Day(s)), On Demand, Not Specified Repayment: Full Repayment Date, Number of Installments, Installment Period in Month(s), First Installment Date. Interest Rate: No Interest, SIBOR + ...% Per Year, Fixed ....%, LIBOR + ...% Per Year Other (Please Specify). Loan Repayment or Debt Securities Redemption, Loan Principal Repayment. Amount, First Withdrawal Date, Repayment, Early Repayment at Maturity. Type, Loan Proceeds Brought In, Loan Proceeds not Brought In, Maturity: One Year/Not More Than One Year/Over One Year Debt Securities Redemption Type: Proceeds Brought In, Proceeds Not Brought In, Redemption Full Partly, Issue Date, Amount, Interest Repayment Amount

6. Certified by Customer	I hereby attest to the truth and accuracy of the above statement. Customer Signature Date
7. Certified by Authorized Financial Institution	We hereby certify that the above transactions have been verified in terms of truth and accuracy and in compliance with the Exchange Control Law. Signature and Stamp of Authorized Financial Institution Date
©Rene Philippe & Partners Ltd.	**www.renephilippe.com**

As always in Thailand (and everywhere else), read the fine print before signing a form and do not give false information, because doing so is the surest way to get you into a lot of trouble. The fine print on the FETF is as follows: *"Any person who contravenes or fails to comply with the Ministerial Regulations, Notifications, or Directions issued under the Exchange Control Act of 1942 shall be subject to a maximum fine of twenty thousand baht or a maximum imprisonment of three years, or both."*

When transferring foreign currency into your Thai bank account, be aware that any amount above USD 20,000 will be put on hold until such a time when the account beneficiary has remitted the completed FETF to the bank. Most banks request the form be remitted as an original. Therefore, if you intend to transfer money on your personal account while abroad, anticipate and complete the form in advance and leave it with your lawyer. It is only after the remittance of the original form that the money will be credited into your account.

Even if the amount to be transferred is below USD 20,000, make certain the bank has filed a contact number for a person who may be contacted when you are abroad. Indeed, most banks will contact the recipient by phone upon any foreign exchange transaction to ask the purpose of the transaction and inform you of the exchange rate.

Never accept the first exchange rate offered to you, because Thai banks will only offer you their best exchange rate if you ask for it.

Finally, even if the transaction is below the limit of 20,000 USD, and even if you are not requested to execute a FETF, always ask the bank to issue a foreign exchange credit advice receipt, because you will need these supporting documents if you ever want to repatriate your capital overseas one day.

The next issue is whether a foreigner may hold foreign currency or maintain a foreign currency account in Thailand. Yes, you can but note that, pursuant to Bank of Thailand regulations, *"any person in Thailand (foreign or Thai) receiving foreign currencies from abroad is required to sell such foreign currencies to an authorized financial institution or deposit them into a foreign currency account with an authorized financial institution within 360 days of the receipt thereof."*

The only exceptions to the above rule are (i) foreigners temporarily staying in Thailand for no more than three months; (ii) foreign embassies and/or (iii) international organizations, including their staff with diplomatic privileges and immunities.

May you legally purchase foreign currency with Thai banks? Here again, the answer is positive but foreign currency purchases are limited to general allowance in relation to an underlying international trade or investment. In other words you may only purchase foreign currency in Thailand in relation to a specific need e.g. purchasing foreign currency to pay an invoice abroad or buying cash foreign currency before a trip overseas. Document requirements will depend upon the specifics of the transaction, so please check with your bank about what documents you will need prior to the transaction.

Is there any limit as to the amount of Thai currency one person may export from Thailand? Any person travelling to Thailand's bordering countries, including Vietnam, is allowed to take out up to THB 500,000 without authorization. If you are traveling to a non-neighboring country, you will have the right to take up to THB 50,000 with you without authorization.

Is there a maximum amount of Thai currency a foreigner may hold? Yes, there is, and foreign investors may not have more than THB 300,000,000 in aggregate in all of their bank accounts in Thailand. To date, this is one of the few regulations that has never bothered me, although I sincerely hope to be bothered by it one day!

Chapter 24   Opening a Thai Bank Account

Can a foreign citizen open a bank account in Thailand? The answer is, of course, "Yes," or, more accurately, "Yes, but…"

As a matter of fact, the issue of opening a bank account by a foreign non-resident is one of the most confusing issues because there are huge discrepancies between theory and practice. If you are living and working in Thailand, and even coming here as a tourist, you will in theory be entitled to open and maintain a Thai baht or foreign currency account as explained above.

The complications begin with the number and the type of documents you will be requested to provide in order to open your bank account, which will not only depend on your status but also on the individual policies of each bank. The worst part of it is that, while each bank is supposed to have a clear policy that policy is not applied uniformly in each branch or even within the same branch, and depends upon which employees you're dealing with. In general, there will be fewer requirements to fulfill and fewer documents to provide if you are working or living in Thailand on a long-term basis and more if you are only a tourist. For example, below are the document requirements of Bangkok Bank. My personal preferences as a bank user are Kasikorn Bank Public Limited Company for Thai banks and HSBC for foreign banks in Thailand.

TABLE 23: DOCUMENTS & CONDITIONS TO OPEN A BANK ACCOUNT

APPLICANT STATUS	DOCUMENTS	ADDITIONAL DOCUMENTS
You are working in Thailand	Passport **and** work permit.	No other requirements.
You are living in Thailand permanently	Passport, **or** Certificate of residence, **or** alien certificate and house registration.	No other requirements.
You are living in Thailand temporarily or you are a tourist	Passport **and** the following required documents:	A letter of recommendation from a person acceptable to Bangkok Bank (Bangkok Bank staff or customer of Bangkok Bank; a university teacher, a company director or senior executive). A letter of recommendation must be prepared on the Bangkok Bank's letter of recommendation form. You must attach the recommending person's certified true copy of identification document e.g. ID card or government official ID card to the letter; **or** A letter of recommendation from a reputable organization located in Thailand, such as an embassy or an international organization; **or** A letter of recommendation from your bank abroad, acceptable to Bangkok Bank, sent to Bangkok Bank via SWIFT; **or** Your driver's license containing your photo.

©Rene Philippe & Partners Ltd.   www.renephilippe.com

Remarks: The above are the document requirements of Bangkok Bank. Other banks may have other requirements.

Is there a catch? Yes, there certainly is. As is often the case in Thailand, theory is one thing and practice is another. While bank document requirements do not seem excessively complicated, even if you are a tourist, many foreigners have seen their requests for the opening of a bank account refused by one bank or another despite having provided all the documents required by that bank.

In other words, yes, you can open a bank account, but it is like the *"Quest for the Holy Grail"* and you might have to go through several trials (several banks or bank branches) before you fulfill your quest. If you need help, just contact my office and we will help you with this matter. Minimum deposit requirements are very low and you will only need to deposit THB 500 to open a Thai baht saving account. To open a foreign currency account, the minimum deposit will be between USD 5,000 to USD 10,000 and you will generally be requested to perform the first deposit by wire transfer.

Upon opening a Thai baht savings account in Thailand, you will immediately receive an ATM[95]/ bank debit card allowing you to deposit and withdraw funds at the ATM. Debit cards are easier to obtain than credit cards especially if you are a foreigner. Bank practices based on the Bank of Thailand policies are only to issue credit cards to foreign applicants holding "Non-Immigrant Visas" and work permits with a history and proof of income. Banks and/or card issuers will generally request that a foreign applicant have a one-year work permit and with a history of working with the same employer in Thailand from three to six months before approving his/her credit card application.

To sum it up, there will be no major difficulties in opening a bank account and obtaining an ATM and/or debit card. Finally, all Thai banks have internet banking services available in English.

---

[95] Of course you will have to request it (we heard that some Thai banks do not give ATM cards in the case of joint accounts)

Chapter 25   Should You Make Your Offshore Property

Purchase in Cash or Through Financing?

How should you purchase your offshore property? Should you pay for it in cash or apply for financing? If you apply for a loan to finance your purchase, should you borrow in your home country; or from a bank in the country where your property is located? Should you mortgage or take out a second mortgage on existing property in your home country to finance your offshore purchase? These are the issues we'll try to address in this chapter.

This might come as a surprise to some of my readers but, while I'm a firm believer in offshore real estate, I definitely believe the purchase of offshore property should be a cash purchase. If you finance your offshore property through a loan, the loan should be done with a bank willing to accept the offshore property as security whenever this option is available. Unfortunately, this option is not yet available to foreigners in Thailand.

I don't believe buyers of offshore real estate should take out a first or second mortgage on their main residence to finance the purchase of offshore real estate assets. In my opinion, first or second mortgages on a primary residence should always be a last resort for very specific events, such as education, hospitalization and so on.

Now, before my readers misinterpret the content of my above remarks, let me restate, *"I'm a believer."* What's more, I've seen many satisfied customers make gains as a result of investments in offshore real estate. However, as I mentioned in the book's introduction, there are still some unfortunate buyers among the many fortunate ones. And even if I hope there will be fewer offshore real estate fiascos as a result of this book, the fact remains that the purchase of offshore real estate involves potential risks with no easily procured means of protection. In other words, when you purchase a real estate asset in another country and currency, there are numerous factors with potential impact on the value of your investment over which you have no control e.g. currency fluctuations or political risks. Therefore, I would recommend that buyers of offshore real estate exercise caution and not mortgage their main residences to purchase their dream houses offshore (especially if they purchase from a First-Time Developer).

At the risk of sounding elitist, I believe the purchase of offshore property should be reserved for those who can afford to pay in cash or that buyers should be permitted to finance offshore property purchases by mortgaging the offshore property rather than a primary residence in the buyer's own country.

Chapter 26   Is it Possible to Finance the Purchase of Your

Property Through a Loan with a Thai Bank?

The question of whether or not foreign non-residents may borrow in Thai baht from Thai banks is another issue that generates a great deal of confusion.

Note that the concepts of "non-resident" and "resident" in this chapter are defined by immigration law. In a nutshell, you are a resident if you have the Thai resident blue book[96]. If you don't have it, you don't qualify as a resident but as a non-resident, even if, like me, you've been around for a few years and have a legitimate work permit with a one-year visa.

According to the Bank of Thailand, Thai Banks may not lend Thai baht to foreign non-residents but for a few exceptions as shown in the table on the next page.

---

[96] The Resident Blue Book I'm referring to is the book delivered by Thai Immigration to foreigner with Resident status. Not to be confused with the Tabien Baan or house registry book which is also blue for Thai people and Yellow for foreign non-resident.

TABLE 24: LOAN REQUIREMENTS FOR FOREIGNERS	
TYPE OF LOAN TO NON-RESIDENT	CONDITIONS
Issuance of credit card	➢ Non-Immigrant Visa and work permit, history and proof of income (three to six months).
Personal consumption loan *(purchase of a car or consumer goods in leasing or by installments)*	➢ Valid work permit of more than one year; the amount must not exceed THB five million, and ➢ The loan must be fully collateralized.
Loan to non-resident residing in a neighboring country	➢ Prior approval from BOT must be sought on a case per case basis.
©Rene Philippe & Partners Ltd.	**www.renephilippe.com**

While a foreign non-resident may theoretically borrow up to THB 5,000,000, this applies to only to the purchase of consumer goods such as cars, bikes, furniture, computers and so on.

To date, I've never heard of a foreign non-resident investor borrowing THB 5,000,000 from a Thai Bank to purchase real estate assets. Anyway, I don't see how a foreign investor could borrow from a Thai Bank to purchase land for residential purposes as foreigners are prohibited from owning land in the first place. In the same manner, a foreign buyer purchasing a house and land under a leasehold could not borrow, because, unlike a 50-year commercial lease, the 30-year leasehold may not be collateralized.

As for condominiums, the condition for a non-resident to purchase freehold is to bring foreign currency for the amount of the purchase price. Therefore, a non-resident who wants to be allowed to own a condominium freehold will first need to bring foreign currency into Thailand and close the door to any possibility of borrowing in Thailand by doing so. To date, only residents who've been granted a Resident Book may borrow from a Thai Bank in Thai baht to finance the purchase of a condominium.

Chapter 27   Visa Issues and Living on Your Dream Property

Another issue that needs to be taken into account when purchasing a property offshore is immigration. It's all very well to purchase a property overseas, but it's even better if you can easily get a visa to live there long-term.

In Thailand, property owners may have a choice between two kinds of visas: the Investor Visa or the Retiree Visa. Of course, there are numerous other types of visas (working or business visas for example), but most property owners will not come to Thailand to work but to enjoy their retirements. In this chapter, we will review the conditions applicable to each of these two types of visas. We will start first with the Non-Immigrant Investment Visa.

The concept of the Investment Visa is not new in Thailand. For example, following the crisis of 1997, an investment visa with a minimum investment amount of no less than THB 3,000,000 was created as an incentive to help Thai developers sell their stock of condominium units leftover from the crisis to foreign investors. This visa was discontinued in October of 2006.

Discontinued only means that new applications for this particular Investment Visa were not accepted after 1 October 2006, but foreign investors who had invested not less than THB 3,000,000, entered Thailand, received Immigration Department permission to stay before 1 October 2006 and have since renewed their visas each year without any interruption are still benefiting from this promotion.

Now, as a result of the current Thai political crisis and the 2008 global economic crisis, Thailand has reintroduced the concept of the investment visa. The only difference from the former investment visa is that the minimum investment requirement has been increased from THB 3,000,000 to THB 10,000,000.

Is this new investment visa a good thing? The new investment visa is very welcome, because it allows the filling of a gap in Thai visa offers. Indeed, for the past three years, we did not have a real visa alternative to offer wealthy foreign citizens below 50 years of age who wanted to live in Thailand on a long-term basis without working. The gap is now filled and this change is good news for everyone.

Of course, the minimum investment ceiling has been raised considerably from THB 3,000,000 to THB 10,000,000, but with new condominium units ranging in price from THB 80,000, to THB 350,000 per square meter, most investors purchasing condominiums or leasing houses in Thailand will fulfill the minimum investment criteria.

Furthermore, if the condominium you purchase costs less than THB 10,000,000 then you will still have the option of combining two types of investments in order to reach the ceiling e.g. a condominium purchased at the price of THB 7,000,000 and the purchase of state bonds for THB 3,000,000.

The conditions for obtaining a new Investment Visa are quite straightforward. The foreign investor who wishes to obtain a one year visa investment must have the following:

(1) A non-immigrant visa ; *and*

(2) Evidence of transferring funds into Thailand amounting to no less than THB 10 million; *and*

(i) Agency or government-issued evidence of investment into the purchase or rental of a condominium unit for a period of no less than three years at a purchase or rental price of no less than THB 10 million; *or*

(ii) Evidence of investment in the form of a fixed deposit of no less than THB 10 million with a bank registered in Thailand with Thai nationals holding more than 50 percent of its shares; *or*

(iii) Evidence of investment in the purchase of government or state enterprise bonds valued at no less than THB 10 million; *or*

(iv) Evidence of making an investment as set out in criteria (i), (ii), or (iii) above with a total value of no less than THB 10 million.

The only catch is that this promotion only applies to foreign investors who invested after the 25 November 2008 and onward. Unfortunately, those who have purchased condominium units between 1 October 2006 and 25 November 2008 do not qualify.

You will need to provide the following documents:

➢ Passport or travel documents with validity of no less than six months at the time of the visa application at the Thai Embassy and no less than 18 months when applying for your one year extension.
➢ Completed visa application form.
➢ Recent passport-sized photograph (4 x 6 cm) of the applicant taken within the past 6 months.
➢ Documents to support your investment of THB 10,000,000 in Thailand, such as Foreign Exchange Transfer Forms, Bank Credit Advice, Sales and Purchase Agreement, Title Deed and so on....

If you fulfill all of the conditions mentioned above and if you are able to provide all of the documents required, you will be able to receive a one-year extension period each year for as long as you maintain your investment in Thailand.

If you've purchased a property of less than THB 10,000,000 in value but are older than 50 years, then the option for you will be to obtain a Non-Immigrant Visa "O-A" (Long Stay) Visa.

The Non-Immigrant Visa "O-A" (Long Stay) is a visa for people aged 50 years and up who wish to stay in Thailand for a period not exceeding one year without the intention of working. Be warned that employment of any kind while holding a Non-Immigrant O Retiree Visa is strictly prohibited. A stamp affixed near the visa on the passport of the beneficiary generally confirms this stipulation.

The process normally requires two steps and you may chose between two options to accomplish the first step as follows:

The First Option will be to apply for a 90-day Non-Immigrant "O" Visa at the Thai Embassy or consulate of the country of your nationality or the country of your residence at the time of the application.

The Second Option is applicable only if you are a national from a country where citizens benefit from a visa exemption privilege; if this is the case then you may simply choose to come into Thailand without a visa and file an application with the Immigration Office for a change of visa upon your arrival.

However, you may do this only if you have all the documents required to obtain a retiree visa with you and providing that you do so within nine days after your arrival in Thailand. Once your change in type of visa has been approved by the Immigration Department you can then apply for a one-year visa. We recommend that you use the first option because, while it obliges you to make a trip to the Thai embassy of your country of residence before coming into Thailand, the process for the extension to a one year visa will be smoother.

Once you've entered Thailand, you'll have to apply for the one-year extension of your visa at the Immigration Office assigned for your location. If you come with a Non-Immigrant "O" Visa issued by a Thai Embassy, you will have to wait in Thailand for 60 days before to file your application at the Immigration Office. Furthermore, if you're eligible for visa exemption status, you'll first have to change the type of your visa within nine days after your arrival before applying for the one-year extension.

To be eligible for this type of visa you will need to meet the following criteria:

(1) Age of 50 years or more.

(2) No prohibitions from entering the Kingdom as provided by the Immigration Act of 1979.

(3) No criminal record in Thailand or the country of the applicant's nationality or residence.

(4) Nationality of or residence in the country where applicant's application is submitted.

(5) No prohibitive diseases e.g. leprosy, tuberculosis, drug addiction, elephantiasis, third phase of syphilis as indicated in Ministerial Regulation No. 14 of 1992.

You will have to provide the following documents:
- ➤ Passport with validity of no less than 18 months.
- ➤ Three copies of the completed visa application form.
- ➤ Three passport-sized photos (4 x 6 cm) of the applicant taken within the six months preceding the application.
- ➤ A copy of a bank statement showing a deposit of an amount equal to and no less than THB 800,000, or an original income certificate with a monthly income of no less than THB 65,000, or a deposit account plus a monthly income totaling

no less than THB 800,000. If you are submitting a bank statement, the original letter of guarantee from the bank is required.

When you are applying for a 90-day Non-Immigrant "O" Visa at the Thai Embassy without a Thai Bank account, you may instead provide a statement from your bank in your country of origin to verify you have more than 800,000 THB (or its equivalent in foreign currency) in savings.

When you file your request for extension of stay at the Immigration Office, you'll have to provide documented evidence that you've transferred money to Thailand and showing a total of no less than THB 800,000 (less if you combine it with a pension; in this case, savings + pension must reach more than THB 800,000 per year).

The money must have been deposited in Thailand at least 60 days before you go to the Immigration Office if you're applying for your Non-Immigrant "O" Visa and 90 days if you're applying for a renewal. The required amount must have been left untouched during the validation period of 60 or 90 days. Therefore, transfers must be more than the requested amount to cover your living expenses during this period.

When you file your application for the one-year Retiree Visa extension at the Immigration Office in Thailand based on your monthly income, you'll have to provide a certificate from your embassy in Bangkok to confirm that you have a pension or a monthly income of THB 65,000 more per month. You have to apply for this certificate prior to going to the Immigration Office. Please check with your embassy in Thailand about how to proceed to do so.

(6) A letter of verification issued from the country of your nationality or residence stating that the applicant has no criminal record. Verification will be valid for no more than three months and should be notarized by a notary public or the applicant's diplomatic or consular mission.

While this final document is on the required document list mentioned on website of the Ministry of Foreign affairs, retirees are not yet required to actually provide the document when applying for a their one year visa at immigration but this may change in the future. Note that we recently heard that a few Thai Embassies overseas were starting to request criminal records from retirees applying for their Visa O retiree.

(7) A medical certificate issued from the country where the application is submitted and showing no prohibitive diseases as indicated in Ministerial Regulation No.14 (1992). This certificate will be valid for no more than three months and should be notarized by a notary public or the applicant's diplomatic or consular mission.

Here again, while the medical certificate is also on the list of required documents on the website for the Ministry of Foreign affairs, it is not yet necessary to provide this document at the embassy when applying for a visa. You will, however, be required to pass a medical visit with a Thai doctor and obtain a medical certificate before applying for your one year extension at the Immigration Office.

As long as you fulfill all of the conditions and provide all of the documents required, the Immigration Department will grant you a one-year extension and permission to stay in Thailand for one year. Before concluding this chapter, however, I would like to add a few remarks common to both type of visas mentioned above.

Firstly, you must understand that the documents and requirements listed above are the minimal applicable requirements and the fact that you have provided all of the documents requested does not always guarantee a favorable outcome.

Secondly, the one-year extension period is always calculated from the date of first entry, not from the date of approval. For example you entered Thailand on the 1st January 2010. Your one year visa (retiree or investor) was approved on the 15 March 2010. You will be allowed to stay in Thailand until the 31 December 2010 only as the one year period is calculated from the 1st January 2009.

Thirdly, note that you are required to apply at the Immigration Office for a re-entry permits (single or multiple) before departure if you wish to travel out of Thailand during your one-year visa extension period to leave and re-enter the country without losing your visa.

If you benefit of a one year visa extension period but leave Thai territory without a re-entry permit, your one-year extension will become void. Therefore, our recommendation is to apply for a re-entry permit immediately upon the approval of your one year visa. Apply immediately for a multi re-entry permit, even if it's more costly, because I've seen more than one client purchasing a single re-entry permit and forgetting about losing their visas after an unexpected second trip out of Thailand.

Finally, once you've obtained your one-year visa and had your re-entry permit processed, there is one last matter to remember, the reporting requirement.

At the end of any uninterrupted 90-day period of stay, you will have to report to the Immigration Officer of your residence area and report again every subsequent uninterrupted 90-day period of presence in Thailand. The 90-day period is calculated from your last actual entry. If, for example, you travel frequently in and out, you need to recalculate the 90-day period from the last time you entered Thailand.

There are many other visa options available, but the above two are the ones applying to most foreign buyers of property in Thailand

Chapter 28   Overseas Ownership of Immovable Property in the Event of Death

Most people who purchase offshore real estate are in their 40s or older at the time of the purchase. They already own real assets in their home country and, as a result, most buyers of offshore real estate already have a will and don't feel the need to make a new will in relation to their offshore assets. The truth is that you don't always need a will when purchasing assets offshore, but you may need one in certain cases. Therefore, the next issue is how to determine when a person who owns overseas assets needs a will.

In the matter of succession, the most important thing is to determine the laws applicable to the devolution of the succession, because these laws will determine:

- The capacity of a person to affect the devolution.
- The form of the will.
- The capacity of the heirs to inherit.
- The rights of the heirs.

- The minimum portion of the estate to be distributed among the legal heirs[97] of first rank (if any).
- The portion of the estate that may be freely disposed of by the testator[98].

There are as many rules for succession as there are countries, so the ability to determine in advance what rules will be applicable to the devolution of assets located outside your home country is of utmost importance.

It is a generally accepted principle of international private law that the transfer or devolution of immovable property takes place in accordance with the law of the country where the property is located *("situs"* law). On the other hand, the transfer or devolution of movable property passes in accordance with the law of the deceased person's domicile at the time of death.

Therefore, the laws applying to the devolution of a real estate asset owned overseas will depend entirely upon the method of ownership. If the testator personally owns the immovable property, then the object of the succession is the immovable property itself. If the testator does not directly own the property, but has purchased it through a company for which he owns the shares, then the object of the succession is not the immovable property, but the shares of the company owning the property.

Note that, for the time being, there are no succession taxes in Thailand per se. In case of a succession that results in the transfer of an immovable property, the heir will have to pay the usual transfer taxes and fees at the Land Department.

Please see the table on the next page to help you decide whether or not you need a will in Thailand.

---

[97] Many countries have a mandatory reserve, i.e. the minimum mandatory share of an estate that must be transmitted to primary heirs, such as spouses and children.

[98] Testator is a person who made a will or a person who dies having made a will

TABLE 25: CRITERIA TO DETERMINE IF YOU NEED A WILL IN THAILAND		
Object of the succession	Law applicable to the devolution of the succession	Do you need a second will in the country were the asset is located?
Immovable Assets Condominium House Land	The law of the situation of the immovable property.	Yes. If an individual directly owns an immovable asset in a foreign country, a second will is the safest thing to do.
Movable Assets Shares of a company owning immovable property.	The law of the deceased person's domicile at the time of death.	No. You do not need a second will if you only own shares in a company that owns offshore real estate.
©Rene Philippe & Partners Ltd.		www.renephilippe.com

If you ever move overseas, please do not forget to name a contact person in your new country of residence and give instructions to this person about what to do in the event of your sudden demise. It isn't uncommon for people who move overseas to lose contact with their families in their home country and families are often unaware of the death of their relatives.

I once heard the story of a Swiss citizen who owned a condominium in Bangkok and died in Thailand. At the time of his death, he was living with a Thai girlfriend. He was not married to her. Upon his death, however, she filed a claim based on her status of *"common law wife"*. By the time the Swiss citizen's family finally learnt of his demise, the Court had already ruled in favor of the girlfriend. She was awarded the ownership of the condominium unit and, by the time the family acted, the condominium had long been sold. Therefore, if you have loose ties with your family, you need to have a contact person located in your country of residence who can inform your family in the case of death.

BOOK II

THE CASE OF THAILAND

PART 1

LAND TENURE SYSTEM, ZONING, BUILDING CONTROLS AND

OTHER REGULATIONS PERTAINING TO LAND

DEVELOPMENT

Chapter 29   Why is Knowledge of Land Tenure and Land Use

Law So Important?

Why discuss the Thailand land tenure system and the difference between public and private land or the matter of expropriation, in a book intended for buyers of private properties? After all, who needs to know the theory of combustion to buy and drive a car?

There are three reasons why a person interested in purchasing offshore real estate should have a basic understanding of the land tenure system in the destination country.

Firstly, and like in many other countries that have become preferred destinations for offshore property buyers, the titling system in Thailand is still in progress. Over the last 60 years, the Thai titling system has been overhauled several times, and there have been several reforms granting land to farmers. In any country, a developing titling system in conjunction with land grant reforms for farmers is always accompanied by fraud and the issuance of unlawful land titles. Thailand has been no exception, and there are still in circulation many land title deeds or certificates of use that were issued unlawfully. In the past, the Thai government has revoked those unlawfully issued documents, and will continue to do so. Just looking at a title deed document, won't tell you whether or not it's been legally issued, but having an understanding of the local land tenure system might help you determine whether they may be problems with the land you are considering to purchase and what type of questions you should ask before purchasing or leasing land.

Over the past 50 years, Thailand has joined many other countries in becoming aware of the necessity to protect its land resources through the creation of national parks and forest reserves. Most countries initiating those reforms within the last 50 years have had to deal with a common impediment: part of the land designated as national parks or reserves were not wild at the time of the designation, but already inhabited by farmers. In addition, those countries often have contradictory policies. On the one hand, they were motivating their farmers to extend cultivation areas while on the other hand, they were declaring potential cultivation zones protected areas, which resulted in encroachment.

In Thailand, the territories of some of foreign travelers' favorite destinations such as Koh Tao (the diving paradise of Thailand) and Koh Samet are composed mostly of public lands, national parks and reserves. Most houses or businesses located on those islands are actually located on public land, some legally and others illegally. Even when a person is given the right to occupy public land lawfully, this grant is generally limited to a specific purpose (farming, for example) and is in general not transferable, or only transferable in a limited manner (by succession, for example). A recent high profile scandal serves to illustrate this. General Surayud Chulanont a former Thai Prime Minister and member of the Privy Council ended up owning a plot of land in Khao Yai Thiang Mountain that should never have been his in the first place. Indeed, this plot of land was part of land granted to the poor (landless farmers) under a Cabinet resolution dated of April 29, 1975 and was not transferable. If Thai Attorney General's recommendation is followed General Surayud will have to give back the land to the Royal Forest Department, which will then give it to landless farmers.

Those of you who come to Thailand one day will inevitably meet a person offering you the deal of your life: beachfront property for peanuts. The land is so incredibly cheap because the seller is not actually offering you the purchase of the land, but the right to occupy a parcel of public land. Often, the seller[99] won't bother explaining to you that the rights of occupancy he's about to sell to you were granted for farming only. Neither will he tell you that those rights are not transferable, or that you might not be able to build legally on this land. Nor will he tell you that a part of the rights offered to you might actually be encroaching upon a protected area and cutting trees in a protected area is a prosecutable offence. Believe me, more than a few buyers have agreed to such deals.

Finally, many buyers of offshore properties are purchasing in countries they view as less developed than their countries of origin. In some cases, the destination country is less developed, but this perception is mistaken in other cases. Thailand, for example, is now a developing country. One of the most common misconceptions of foreign investors is to believe that less developed countries are like lawless states in the *"Wild West"* where anything goes. This misperception is often aggravated by the cavalier attitude that locals have for the laws in their country.

While Thailand has a very complex and formal legal framework, Thais are the most informal people I've had the opportunity to meet and they won't always follow the letter of the law when doing business. If Thais want to build on land they occupy without formal title or authorization, they'll build it whether the construction is legal or not and without construction permits if they have to. Other Thais will purchase the *"right"* to occupy this land (which may or may not be transferable) and the house that is illegally built on the land without blinking an eye. Neither the original occupant and builder nor the buyer will lose one minute of

---

[99] Most of the time, the sellers are not fully aware of those limitations, or if they are aware of them, they fail to understand their legal implications. While Thai laws are very formal, Thai people are not, and whenever they engage in this kind of transaction, they often fail to comprehend all of the legal issues.

sleep thinking about any of the legal issues involved. It sounds like the Wild West, but it's not. The fact that a country's citizens are prone to disregarding applicable laws in relation to specific matters doesn't mean that laws don't exist to be enforced at some point in the future.

All those potential issues are why a careful buyer should have a minimum understanding of the laws regulating land tenure and land use in the country chosen for the purchase.

Chapter 30   Public vs. Private Land Systems

King Chulalongkorn (Rama V, reigned 1868-1910) first introduced the concept of individual land ownership in Thailand in 1872. Before this date, the King, who owned all lands, would make grants to nobles, officials and other free subjects. The recipient of a land grant could transmit the grant to his heirs, mortgage it or even sell it. Farmers at that time were entitled to make an informal land claim after three years of continuous cultivation. Formal title deeds first appeared in 1901, which was also the year when the Department of Land (DOL) was established. From then on, there have been several reforms of the land registration and tenure system leading up to the enactment of the Land Code Act B.E. 2497 (1954)[100] and its subsequent amendments.

The Land Department is the agency in charge of implementing the land registration system in Thailand under the responsibility of the Ministry of Interior.

---

[100] The Thai calendar started 543 years earlier than the Christian calendar.

There are Land Department offices in every province and district of Thailand. Under the Land Code, the Land Department's primary responsibilities are to issue land ownership or land utilization titles to the people and deliver services of registration of rights and juristic acts upon land and other immovable property. Furthermore, the Land Department is also in charge of making cadastral surveys and maps and issuing certificates for the royal title upon the public land and crown property land and of controlling private cadastral surveys, land allotments and condominium licenses.

Finally, the Land Department is responsible for providing the Department of Treasury with the data needed to assess the value of immovable property in Thailand.

Typically, land and condominiums have three values in Thailand. The first value is the *"assessed value"*. The assessed value is the value of a property as determined by the Treasury Department based upon the data provided by the Land Department. The assessed value is the *"official"* value of land in Thailand. The second value is called the *"registered value"*. The registered value is the registered sale value of a property i.e. the price the parties to an immovable transaction are declaring as the actual selling price of the property. Finally, there is the *"market value"* i.e. the value of a property on the open market. In principle, a property may not be transferred at a price below the assessed value except when the seller can provide an explanation. Assessed value is used to calculate the government fees to be paid upon any transaction at the Land Department. Registered sales value is used to calculate taxes, such as the Special Business Tax or Withholding Tax, which are to be paid upon the transaction.

Similar to most developed countries, the Thai legal system classifies land into two categories i.e: public and private land. The Land Code Act is the core legislation applicable to land matters, but not the only one, and there is much legislation pertaining to land use e.g. the Town Planning Act; the Building Control Act; the Factory Act; the Land Development Act; the Forest Act; the National Park Act; the Industrial Estate Authority Act; the Land Allotment (or Appropriation) Act; the National Forest Reserve Act; the Commercial

Forestry Act; the Wildlife Preservation and Protection Act; the Highway Act; the Environmental Quality Promotion Act; the Land Consolidation Act; and the Land Readjustment Act[101].

The first purpose of the Land Code Act of 1954 was to establish the administration responsible for administrating the Land Code as well as describing its powers and duties. The Land Code Act also contains provisions to define terms, such as land, land rights, land trade and public land. Furthermore, the Land Code Act regulates the allocation of public land and the land acquisition process, the classification of the different types of documents evidencing rights to land and the procedures applicable to their issuance. It also regulates cadastral surveys and the operation of the title register. Finally, it outlines the principles applicable to defining controls over the land holding rights of foreigners, aliens and certain limited companies, partnerships or associations operated by foreigners. Ministerial and departmental regulations issued in application of the Land Code Act provide more details or impose more controls.

The Land Code Act states that *"any land which is not vested in any person shall be deemed the property of the state"*[102], but the actual definition of the public domain is to be found in Section 1304 of the Thai Civil and Commercial Code. *"The public domain of State includes every kind of State property which is in use for the public interest or reserved for the common benefit such as: (1) wasteland and land surrendered, abandoned or otherwise reverted to the State according to the land law; (2) property for the common use of the people e.g., foreshores, water-ways, highways, lakes; (3) property for the particular use of the State e.g., a fortress or other military buildings, public offices, warships, arms and ammunition."* Note that public land may also be assigned to purposes other than those indicated above (to the use of religious establishments, for example).

Public property is inalienable: *"Any property which forms part of the public domain of State is inalienable, except by virtue of a*

---

[101] This list is not exhaustive.
[102] Land Code Act Section 2.

special law or a Royal Decree[103]". Because public land is inalienable, private individuals may never claim public land by way of acquisitive prescription or hostile possession, whatsoever the duration of their occupation: *"No prescription can be set up against the State with regard to any property which forms part of its public domain[104]."* Finally, *"land property of the State may never be seized[105] whether such property forms part of its public domain or not."*

---

[103] Section 1305 of the Thai Civil and Commercial Code.
[104] Section 1306 of the Thai Civil and Commercial Code.
[105] Section 1307 of the Thai Civil and Commercial Code.

Chapter 31   Private Property Rights

If any land not vested in private ownership is public land then, by consequence, private land is any land for which private persons or companies have legally claimed ownership. The rights to private property are guaranteed under the Kingdom's new Constitution of 2007 that states: *"The property right of a person is protected[106]"*, while the content and exercise of property rights are regulated by Book Four of the Thai Civil and Commercial Code.

In Thailand, as in many countries, the protection of property rights is not absolute, but may be limited by due legal process: *"The extent and the restriction of such rights shall be in accordance with the provisions of the law.[107]"* In other words, a person may only exercise private property rights within the boundaries of the law and there are in Thailand, as the list provided earlier shows, many laws to restrict or direct the utilization of a land plot.

---

[106] Section 41 of the Kingdom's 2007 Constitution.
[107] Section 41 of the Kingdom's 2007 Constitution.

The type of use further classifies private land. There are four main types of private land: agricultural land, commercial and service area land, industrial land and residential land[108]. Of course, each category of land is regulated by a specific set of legislation.

Under some circumstances, privately owned land may return to the public domain e.g. if an owner has abandoned land, the State has purchased it back, or the land documents evidencing private rights to the land were issued unlawfully.

Section 6 of the Land Code Act exemplifies the first case when private land may return to the public domain. In accordance with Section 6 of the Land Code Act, landowners may lose land rights to the State if they fail to use the land for a certain period. The duration of this depends upon the type of land documents, but will be 10 consecutive years if a title deed evidences the rights to the land, and 5 consecutive years if a certificate of use evidences them. An owner who abandons land does not automatically lose the rights to the land, but according to due legal process. In order for the land to revert to the State, the Director of the Land Department will have to file a petition with the court. This petition will state that the landowner has left his land uncultivated and in waste for the legal period and request the cancellation of the land documents and the immediate return of the rights to the land to the State without compensation.

The second case when private land may revert to the public domain is through compulsory purchase or expropriation. Section 42 of the Constitution of the Kingdom of Thailand defines the framework within which the State may exercise its right of expropriation. Section 42 of the constitution provides the following:

"The expropriation of immovable property shall not be made, except by virtue of the law specifically enacted for the purpose of public utilities, necessary national defense, exploitation of national resources, town and country planning, promotion and preservation of the quality of the environment, agricultural or industrial development,

---

[108] Forest land is part of the public domain, which is why we don't mention it here.

land reform, conservation of ancient monuments and historic sites, or other public interests, and fair compensation shall be paid in due course to the owner thereof as well as to all persons having the rights thereto, who suffer loss by such expropriation, as provided by law.

The amount of compensation under paragraph one shall be fairly assessed with due regard to the normal market price, mode of acquisition, condition and location of the immovable property, loss of the person whose property or right thereto is expropriated, and benefits the State and the person whose property or right thereto is expropriated may receive from the use of the expropriated property.

The expropriation of immovable property law shall specify the purpose of the expropriation and clearly determine the period for fulfilling that purpose. If the immovable property is not used to fulfill such purpose within such period of time, it shall be returned to the original owner or his heir."

The main law regulating the expropriation process is the Immovable Property Act of 1987. This act enumerates the valid causes of expropriation, the method of calculation of the compensation to be paid to the landowner and the steps of the expropriation procedure.

There are many other laws authorizing government agencies to engage in the purchase of private properties (e.g. the Airport Authority Act, the Public Irrigation System Act.). Some of those other laws include specific procedures for the expropriation, while others do not. If a specific law does not contain procedures, then the Immovable Property Act will be applicable.

As Thailand is still developing its infrastructure, cases of expropriation by the state are still common. Therefore, before purchasing land or registering a long-term lease on land or accepting land as security for a loan, one should verify whether or not there are plans for developing infrastructure projects in the area concerned. In general, such plans are developed a few years before the actual commencement of the project and the expropriation process. The fact that no such plan exists at the time of the purchase of a land is no guarantee that such issues may not arise later on[109]. However, buyers must retain the belief that, if expropriation ever becomes an issue for them, they will be treated fairly and with due legal process.

The most problematic case is when land for which private ownership documents have been issued reverts to the public domain because of the revocation of the land documents. The revocation of unlawfully issued land documents may occur at any time (sometimes years after the issuance of the titles and after the land has been transferred several times). Of course, the land will in such cases return to the State without any compensation. The examples mentioned below illustrate that the revocation of land title deeds is far more than just an academic problem. On 24 July 2008, the Bangkok Post reported[110] the Land Department had revoked title deeds issued to land plots in the Phuket and Phang Nga provinces. Among the titles revoked in Phuket were NS-3K land occupation papers issued to 29 land plots in Phuket's Tambon[111] Rassada, Muaeng District. In Phang Nga Koh Yao District, the Department revoked NS-3K papers issued to 21 plots, and NS-3K land deeds issued to 598 out of 628 plots being investigated in the Kapong District. In Surat Thani Province (Koh Samui), the Department has recently revoked two deeds issued in relation to a property development project and may eventually revoke titles to four other plots in the same project.

---

[109] Note that one of our clients was victim to an expropriation last year and that, as far as we were able to judge, the procedures and the indemnity this client received were fair.

[110] For the full article, please see http://www.bangkokpost.com/ 240708_News /24Jul2008_news10.php

[111] Local government units are called "Tambon" (Sub-District), "Amphoe" (District) and "Jangwat" (Province). Municipalities are "Thesaban" and are divided into three levels: *Thesaban Nakhon* (populations of at least 50,000 and a population density of 3,000 per square kilometer); *Thesaban Mueang* (provincial capitals, or populations of at least 10,000, a population density of 3000 per km^2 and sufficient income to cover the functions of a town); and *Thesaban "Tambon"*, are the lowest municipality level (gross income of at least 5 million baht, a population of 5000, a population density of 1,500 per km^2, and the consensus of the population of the area). Finally, there are *"Mubaans"* (Villages), the lowest administrative subdivision of Thailand.

The land documents in Koh Samui were revoked because they were issued on forest land (encroachment), while those in the Phuket area were cancelled because they were based on incorrect claims.

An article published last year in the Property Report stated that, while Koh Samui has a total area of only 150,000 rai[112], the cumulative size of the title deeds issued on the island is said to be about 200,000 rai[113]. If those figures are correct, and if the authorities act on them, then we are talking of the possible revocation of 25% of the land title deeds or certificates of use ever issued on the island of Samui.

The two main causes of issuances of unlawful land documents are encroachment or the falsification of land claim documents on whose basis the land documents were first issued.

Encroachment[114] is *"the act of entering gradually or silently upon the rights or possessions of another; unlawful intrusion"*. Encroachment of public lands in Thailand is mostly done on forest land.

An official survey in 1992 revealed that, while forests have officially become state properties since the creation of the Royal Forestry Department in 1896, there were more than 1.3 million households living on forest lands at that time. Most of these households were farmers who had cleared forested areas to expand their farmland. One of the paradoxes is that those farmers were in some way encouraged to encroach upon forest land. Thailand development policies are stated by five-year National Social and Economic Development Plans, which outline government policies regarding natural resources. Until 1991, however, six successive NESPD plans made agricultural development for export a priority and the government itself encouraged farmers to expand their

---

[112] 1 rai = 1600 sqm
[113] Source: The Property Report, March 2008 http://www.property-report.com/
[114] Webster's Revised Unabridged Dictionary.

farmland, thus resulting in encroachment of forest land. While encroachment on forestland was initially the fault of farmers, businessmen were not far behind in trying to acquire valuable land holdings through this process.

The Land Department recently announced it was about to expand the fight against encroachment and was comparing current pictures of protected areas with pictures taken in the 1970s for this purpose. Indeed, the Land Department has a comprehensive database of aerial pictures taken by the Thai Air Force in the 1970s, because it was using aerial pictures at the time to map the land in order to accelerate the organization of the land registration system. The Land Department is now taking new pictures of the protected areas using satellite-recorded pictures and GPS-based methods of survey to compare them with the pictures taken by the Air Force. While the Land Department decision is commendable, the fact remains that the implementation of the fight against encroachment will certainly generate more than a few disputes and social problems. It's one thing to cancel the deed of a businessman who illegally acquired public land and another thing to cancel the rights of a farmer who may have worked a land plot for generations.

The second cause of unlawful issuance of land documents lies with the Thai government's launching of several land reform plans to reduce the pressure on land resources resulting from the increase in the population. In order to accelerate the implementations of those reforms, the Land Code Act was amended for a time to allow the issuance of land titles, even when there were no documents, occupancy or land claim certificates and, in some cases, without a field survey. Furthermore, upgrading an occupancy claim to a certificate of use or land title documents is not an exact science. For example, the Sor. Kor. 1 document, which serves to establish an occupancy or possession claim, does not give the precise location of the occupied land. Therefore, it's not impossible for an unscrupulous businessman to use a Sor. Kor. 1 document issued for one piece of land to make a claim over another piece of land at a nearby location[115]. Over the years, many certificates of land use or titles have been issued based on incorrect claims.

Finally, another problem may also arise in the future. mentioned above, there are many laws to regulate land use in Thailand. Many laws also mean many agencies. At some point, Thailand has up to 21 different agencies involved in land use management, some of which had prerogatives overlapping. Several of these agencies have also had the power to issue occupancy certificates or other kinds of rights or claims to land, and it's not implausible that one or more agencies had at some point in time issued documents acknowledging claims on land boundaries overlapping one another.

---

[115] Such Sor.Kor.1 are referred too as *"Flying"* Sor.Kor.1

Chapter 32   Zoning, Building and Construction Regulations

Land development is one of the most regulated activities in Thailand and there are now many laws to control land use and building construction, such as Town and City Planning Acts and the Building Control Act. Thailand's zoning system is quite elaborate and recorded in maps called *"country planning law maps"*. All cities have one including Bangkok.

Land zoning determines land use restrictions applicable in each area. Briefly, there are five main zoning categories[116] and each is classified by designated use: (1) commercial, (2) residential, (3) industrial, (4) warehouse and (5) rural and agricultural areas.

Determining the zone may not be enough because a zone may be further divided into sub-zones. In Bangkok, for example, the residential zones include three sub-zones, each of which has a different set of limitations. Each zoning category is attributed a color on the city planning map. For example, commercial zones are designated in red, rural and agricultural zones are designated in dark

---

[116] National parks, forests and other special zones are not included.

green, industrial in purple, and warehouse zones (also called light industry) are in light purple. You may not, however, rely solely upon the color code to determine whether or not a zone has been sub-divided. For example, the Bangkok commercial zone is represented only by red irrespectively of the sub-zoning, while each sub-zone of the Bangkok residential zone has its own color code. For example, high density residential areas are brown, medium are orange and low are yellow. It's also important not to confuse the terms and the colors. In Phuket, for example, the green zone within the city allows construction, while the green zone outside the city does not.

Bangkok City Planning Map

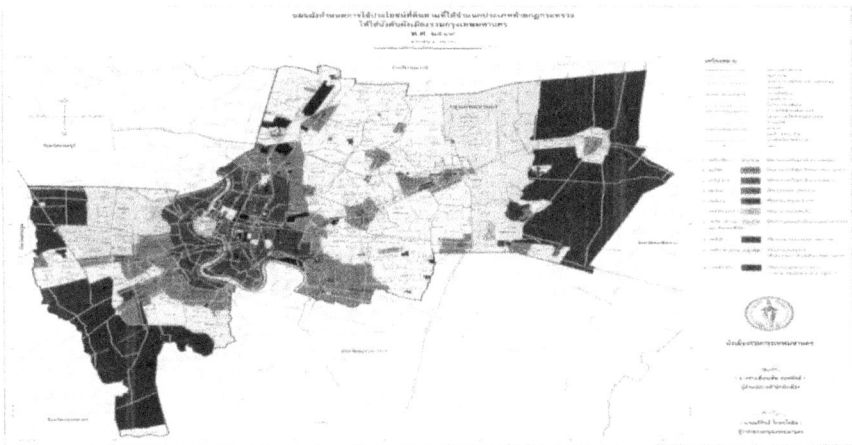

In addition to classifying land by categories of use, the law also provides the Floor Area Ratio (FAR) and the key prohibitions applicable to land use in each category or each sub-zone.

The *"Floor Area Ratio" (FAR)* also called *"Floor Space Index" (FSI)* is some countries is the ratio determining the maximum floor area of the buildings to be constructed in a determined area in relation to the area of land. The prohibitions are additional restrictions applicable in certain zones or sub-zones. For example most of Bangkok's Central Business District is classified as red (commercial) or brown (high density residential), and is the area of

Bangkok with the highest FAR (up to 10.1). A ratio of 10.1 authorizes the construction of a building equivalent to 10 times the area of the land.

However, this doesn't mean each land plot located in the CBD may benefit from the highest FAR ratio applicable in this area. Indeed, in addition to the FAR, the law also provides a list of key prohibitions for each zone. One of the limitations introduced in Bangkok in 2006 was a limitation in the size and height of buildings in relation to the width of the frontage road.

The width of the roads leading to a plot of land in Bangkok is often an important factor in determining the maximum authorized height of construction for a specific land plot. The construction of a building more than 15 meters high on a land plot not located on a road wider than 10 meters or a building of more than 23 meters' height on a land plot not located on a road wider than 20 meters is generally forbidden. Similarly, a building of more than 10,000 sqm may only be constructed on a land plot located on a road wider than 30 meters. When the land plot is not located on one of Bangkok's main roads, such as Sukhumvit or Sathorn, it isn't enough for the road directly in front of the land plot to be 10, 20 or 30 meters wide. In order for the criteria of road width to be fulfilled, the side street must be wider than 10, 20 or 30 meters from the point where the side street branches off from the main road up to the point where the land is located

To summarize, checking the zoning of the area where a land plot is located is the first step. In some cases, this will be enough, but we often find that zones are further subdivided into sub-zones with specific limitations or prohibitions. One of the most common mistakes made by land buyers is the assumption that land plots will be allowed the use same as their neighboring plots where high-rise buildings have been built. Although two plots of land may be adjacent to each other, they may be subject to a different set of regulations and prohibitions, because they are not located in the same zoning area.

In addition, zoning regulations are not set in stone, but will change with time. In Bangkok, for example, land plots that would have qualified for the construction of a high-rise building before the introduction of new zoning regulations in 2006 no longer qualify for such constructions, so developers hurried to apply for high-rise construction permits before the enactment of the new building regulation. The effects of Bangkok's new zoning regulations were quickly felt and, while the number of building construction permits issued in 2007 was 15% higher than in 2006, the total construction area permitted decreased by 25%.

Changes have also occurred in several resort cities. In Phuket, Pattaya and Hua Hin, for example, it was possible to construct high-rise buildings next to the seashore up until a few years ago. Now, most resort cities in Thailand have zoning regulations forbidding or limiting the construction of high-rise buildings near the seashore.

In Phuket, (Phuket City Planning Map, Pathong-Karon) the construction of buildings next to the seashore is limited as follows: The red zone starts from 0 to 50 meters from the seashore measured at high tide. No building or construction may be built within the first 20 meters from the coastline, and building heights above ground level are limited to a maximum of 6 meters for residential purposes and 5 meters for industrial purposes. Building area coverage is limited to a maximum of 25% for residential buildings, or 60% for industrial buildings. The second zone is called the "yellow zone" and starts 0 to 150 meters from the boundary of the red zone. In the yellow zone, building heights above ground level are limited to a maximum of 12 meters for residential or industrial purposes. Building area coverage is limited to a maximum of 70% for residential buildings, or 90% for industrial buildings.

Building construction regulations must not only be taken into account when purchasing a building, but also when renovating a building. It would be impossible to envisage all scenarios here. As a rule, however, if you own or lease a building, you won't need to apply for a construction permit just to redo the interior. As soon as you start to modify the structure of a building, it will be necessary to apply for a construction permit prior commencing the work. When in doubt, it's better to be cautious and check with the administration to see whether a construction permit is required. Never add a floor to a building or close an existing rooftop without first applying for a construction permit. Finally, the Building Control Act does not impose obligations only when constructing or renovating a building. Since 2007, the Building Control Act also demands periodic inspections of certain types of buildings. Among the buildings requiring inspection are high-rise buildings (more than 23 meters high), very large buildings (areas of 10,000 sqm) hotels with 80 or more rooms, public buildings (buildings used for the public of more than 1,000 sqm or capacities of 500 people), condominiums of more than 2000 sqm and factories of more than 5000 sqm.

Chapter 33   The Environmental Impact Assessment and

Energy Conservation

In addition to zoning and building related rules, construction regulations in Thailand also include the National Environmental Quality Act in. The authority in charge of the application of the act is the Office of Natural Resources and Environmental Policy and Planning (ONEP). One of the tools introduced by this act is the Environmental Impact Assessment (EIA).

The EIA is a process used for the screening of certain types of real estate projects as described on the next page. Note that in our table we do not mention industrial projects, which are also subjected to EIA and other constitutional requirements (such as the new Health Impact Assessment imposed by the Constitution). Industrial related investments are not within the scope of this book.

Note that the content of the table next takes into account the latest notification of Thailand Ministry of Natural Resources and Environment which came into effect on 29 December 2009.

TABLE 26: ENVIRONMENTAL IMPACT ASSESSMENT

Types of Projects or Activities	Size
Buildings that may affect the area's environmental quality in areas adjacent to rivers, coastal areas, lakes or beaches, or in the vicinity of National Parks or Historical Parks, or used for wholesale or retail business	Height of 23 meters or more. Total floor area or individual floor area in the building of 10,000 square meters or more.
Residential buildings as defined by the Building Control Act.	80 Rooms up or 4,000 SQM useable area.
Land allocation for residential or commercial purposes.	500 land plots or more. Total developed area exceeds 100 rai (16 hectares).
Ports	With a capacity for vessels of more than 500 gross tons up or with quay length of 100 meters up or with total area of 1,000 sqm up.
Marinas	With a capacity of 50 more vessels up or an area of 1,000 sqm up
Hotel or resort facilities.	80 rooms up or 4,000 SQM useable area.
Hospital locations. (a) Areas adjacent to rivers, coastal areas, lakes or beaches.	30 in-patient beds or more.
(b) Areas other than (a).	60 in-patient beds or more.

In the early stages of the application of the act, developers were able to commence the construction of their projects prior to the completion of the EIA. However, they've had to wait for the completion of the EIA prior to commencing the construction of their projects for the past two years.

There are several problems with the application of the EIA. Firstly, the process takes time. Secondly, it is costly, thirdly, while public participation is one of the cornerstones of the EIA, actual public participation has been nominal up to now. The public does not participate due to either ignorance of the hearing or failure to realize the potential effects of the project.

Finally, and despite the legal requirements, there were still developers trying to circumvent the EIA requirement by breaking their projects into multiple phases.

For example, if a developer makes two separate projects of 70 units each instead of a single project of 140 condominiums, then the developer won't need to go through the process of the EIA. Another practice to circumvent the EIA is for a developer to start a project with 70 big units and break part of the 70 units down into smaller apartments during the construction project increasing after the fact the number of the project units above the 80-unit limit.

However the ONEP is aware of this situation and the Secretary General of the ONEP has recently warned developers who are breaking the law that this practice will not be tolerated anymore and that the Land Department will not allow anymore the transfer of the additional units to their buyers.

Several new regulations have been issued during the past two years to improve the environment. For example in December 2007, the ONEP issued in a new regulation pursuant to which developers will have to plant a tree higher than 5 meters for every air conditioning unit between 12,000 to 24,000 BTU in the building from now on. This new regulation has not been well received by developers, who are concerned it will increase their costs.

In a recent development to improve energy conservation the Thai Ministry of Energy has issued a Ministerial Regulation (in effect since the 20 June 2009) aimed at reducing energy costs and promoting a greener environment.

The purpose of this regulation is to implement new design requirements for certain types of buildings. Energy conserving measures includes limiting overall thermal transfer value, limiting maximum electrical power for lighting systems, imposing maximum efficiency values for air conditioners, water heating consumption and limiting overall energy consumption limits in the building.

This new standards are applicable only to any new buildings or existing building to be constructed or modified and for which plans have been filed after 20 June 2009 as listed below:

TABLE 27: ENERGY CONSERVATION IN BUILDINGS

Types of Buildings	Size
Medical Establishment	
Educational Establishment	
Offices	
Condominium	Total Floor Area of the Building is equal or superior to 2,000 SQM
Halls	
Entertainment Establishments	
Hotels	
Service Establishments	

While this new regulation will certainly increase the costs of construction, long terms benefits such as reduced energy costs and a better environment should outweigh these increased costs.

Chapter 34   Land Appropriation

Land appropriation also known as land allotment consists of dividing land into smaller plots[117] for resale as undeveloped land or within the context of a land development project. The Land Appropriation[118] Act was promulgated in 2000 to protect buyers purchasing in housing projects and *"...to specify measures to protect the appropriate land buyer"* regulates land appropriation in Thailand... (Government Gazette Volume 117 Part 45 A).

The scope of the land appropriation act is as follows: *"Land Appropriation means disposition of land which is allotted in many small plots altogether from over 10 plots, notwithstanding allotment from a sole plot or many plots in successive area with assets or benefit acquired as remuneration. It also means allotment of less than ten small plots with the addition of former plots later on within three years totaling over ten small plots".* Pursuant to Section 21 of the Land Appropriation Act, *"Anybody is forbidden to perform land appropriation, [119]unless permission*

---

[117] 10 or more
[118] Sometimes also referred to as Land Allotment Act
[119] That is to say to divide a land for resale in 10 or more pieces.

is given by the board." Also note that the act only applies to land divided with the intent of resale.

Once a developer has received a land appropriation license, the developer may only sell the allotted land and cannot lease it. If you ever wondered why Top Developers of housing projects in Thailand, such as Sansiri or Golden Land, do not offer leasehold options to foreign buyers in their projects, this is the reason. As they only develop projects under land allocation licenses, those developers cannot legally accommodate foreign buyers with a lease option because they may only sell and/or transfer the allotted land plots.

The developer of a project who divides the land for lease only should not be subjected to the Land Appropriation Act. Note that small developers often try to avoid and circumvent the Land Appropriation Act by setting up several legal entities, each of which owns a part of the land which will be later divided into less than 9 pieces each. If you purchase or have purchased from a developer who has used this method to divide the project land instead of applying for a land allotment license, note that the Land Department does not punish the buyers who have purchased within such projects. The current policy is only to sanction the developers.

The main purpose of the Land Appropriation Act, however, is not to regulate how to divide land, but to set minimum standards applicable to development of the infrastructure and utilities of housing projects. For example, the Land Appropriation Act and subsequent Ministry regulations have imposed standards, such as the size of the common areas, the size of the green area, the minimum width of project roads, and so on. Furthermore, in order to obtain a land allotment license, the developer will have to first submit the electricity installation drawings to the Electricity Authority of Thailand for approval, etc. All of those standards have been implemented for the benefit of the buyers. Projects with areas of less than 20 rai of land must have internal roads with minimum widths of 8 meters, with 6-meter widths reserved for condominium traffic and at least 2 meters on each side for the sidewalks. Projects developed on more than 20 rai of land must have roads that are 12 meters in width, with at least 8 meters reserved for car circulation and at least 2 meters on each side for the sidewalks.

As too many small developers[120] are currently operating outside the law and trying to avoid the Land Appropriation Act, the Land Department is expected to modify the content of the Land Appropriation Act and to introduce several exemptions to facilitate the application by small developers for land appropriation licenses.

If those modifications are adopted and enforced, Developers of small projects; (1) located in Bangkok or within municipal areas offering no more than 20 plots with a total saleable area of no more than 2 rai *or* (2) located in Tambon administrative areas and offering no more than 30 plots with a total saleable area of no more than 4 rai; will be exempted from the need to provide 5% of the project's area for public use such as green areas or other public facility such as club houses for common use.

The reason for the exemption is that if fewer developers try to avoid the law it will ultimately benefits buyers who will be better protected. It will be interesting to see whether the exemption offered by the land department will be enough to convince more small developers' to develop their projects under the Land Appropriation Act.

---

[120] Note that not all small developers are First Time Developers.

PART II

RIGHTS TO LAND, BUILDINGS AND CONDOMINIUMS AND

OTHER LEGAL ISSUES

Chapter 35 Land Rights Classifications: Minor Claims

In this part, we'll review the land rights people may acquire in Thailand. The issue of the rights available to foreigners will be discussed in the next part of Book II.

As previously discussed, private land is any land to which private persons or companies have legally claimed ownership as attested by a document. Now what rights can a person legally obtain on private land?

The Thai Civil and Commercial Code recognizes possessory rights and/or ownership rights and there are several kinds of documents to evidence various levels of rights to land, ranging from documents evidencing mere squatters' or occupation rights to full ownership rights.

The classification of the various types of claims or rights to land available in Thailand is no easy task, because there are many categories and it's not always easy to determine the exact rights a particular document will confer upon its holder. In addition, the rights attached to certain types of documents may have evolved over time.

Note that land rights in Thailand's land classification system (NS-3, NS-3K and NS-4) are based on the Australian Torrens title system. Furthermore, land is measured in "rai", "ngan", and "wah" rather than acres or hectares. For reference, one rai is equal to 1600 sqm or four ngan, one ngan is equal to 400 sqm or 100 square wah and one square wah is equal to 4 sqm

Now let's take a look at the classifications of Thai land rights from the lesser rights up to full ownership rights. The lesser rights on land are as follows:

✓ *The Por. Tor. Bor. 5:* At the bottom rung of the ladder is the Por. Tor. Bor. 5[121], a document providing no actual evidence for a claim to land, but merely serving to establish that a person occupying a piece of land has been issued a tax number and has paid taxes for utilizing the land. The issuance of a Por. Tor. Bor. 5 is done without any survey by the authorities and grants no claim to the occupant. The document can be used as evidence towards proving possession against other private individuals, but not against the State. The tax number may be transferred to another person along with the physical possession of the land, but this transfer grants no rights to the transferee on the land against the State.

✓ *The "Pre-emption Certificate" (NS-2):* Then there is the *"Pre-emption Certificate"* (NS-2) or a *"Bai Jong"* which is a transitional document created under the 1936 Land Code Act. The pre-emption certificate simply serves to establish that the beneficiary has temporary rights to occupy the land. Pre-emption certificates were issued on a transitional basis with the understanding that they would eventually be transformed into a certificate of use or full title ownership. In theory, these documents are non-transferable, except by inheritance.

---

[121] The Por. Tor. Bor. 6 isn't a land ownership document, either, but a document issued for any land (whether represented by a Sor. Kor. 1, Nor. Sor. 3, Nor. Sor. 3 Kor.) to attest the land can be assessed for taxes.

✓ *The "claim certificate" (SK-1) or Sor. Kor. 1:* Another transitional document is the claim certificate" (SK-1) or *"Sor. Kor. 1"* created by the 1954 Land Code. This document serves to notify possession of a land to maintain actual existing rights. Farmers who had occupied a vacant plot of land for at least six months could obtain this document after a 30-day publication providing there was no opposition. The acquisition of an SK-1 was deemed the first step toward the issuance of a certificate of use or a title deed. The Thai Supreme Court has judged the SK-1 as only a claim of ownership and not a right to ownership.

To upgrade a SK-1, the beneficiary must prove the claimant has possessed the land legally and put the land the good use. The right to the upgrade is not associated with or inherent to the SK-1.

The main problem with this type of land is that Sor. Kor. 1 were distributed based upon a *"metes and bounds"* description of the property. Metes and bounds is a method used to measure land through the description of the boundaries in a prose style. The author of the description simply walks the reader around the parcel of land, from a starting point and returning back to the same point[122]. The survey covers only the specified piece of land without reference to a grid or a master map covering adjacent property. In other words, the survey process may not always be very accurate regarding the location and size of the land. Because of their inaccuracy, S.K-1 documents issued for specific lands have been used by unscrupulous businessmen to make claims for lands at other locations or as the basis for making claims to several pieces lands. SK-1 documents used to make claims to other lands or many pieces of lands are known as *"flying"* SK-1. If a flying SK-1 has been used to issue a Certificate of Use or a NS-4, then the title has been

---

[122] A typical description for a small parcel of land would be: *"beginning with a corner at the intersection of two stone walls near an apple tree on the north side of Muddy Creek Road one mile above the junction of Muddy and Indian Creeks, north for 150 rods to the end of the stone wall bordering the road, then northwest along a line to a large standing rock on the corner of John Smith's place, thence west 150 rods to the corner of a barn near a large oak tree, thence south to Muddy Creek road, thence down the side of the creek road to the starting point."* Source: *http://en.wikipedia.org/wiki/Metes_and_bounds*

unlawfully issued and may be revoked by the government at any time (please see previous chapter).

Lesser claims have in common that no official permission to build a house may be granted on such land. While it's common practice for Thai people to build homes on Por. Tor. Bor. 5 or SK-1 land, those houses are built without any official permission. In theory, none of those documents are transferable except by inheritance. In practice, a person in possession of an SK-1 may transfer physical possession of the land and the new possessor may apply for a new pre-emption certificate or certificate of possession. Finally, SK-1 cannot legally be used as security against a loan or mortgage and it's impossible to register rights or liens of any sort on the land. For example, it's impossible to register a long-term lease on land represented by a pre-emption certificate or claim certificate[123].

---

[123] As already explained above and despite the legal prohibitions on alienation of land held under the lesser claims, all types of land are sold in Thailand and only the price varies depending upon the nature of the claim. As previously discussed, although the Thai legal system is very formal, Thai people are not. A Thai person trying to sell a lesser claim is not trying to cheat the buyer, but just doing what everyone else does.

Chapter 36   Land Right Classifications: Major Claims

The highest claims on land are the Nor Sor Sam or Certificate of Use (NS-3), the Nor Sor Sam Gor or Confirmed Certificate of Use (NS-3K) and the Chanote (NS-4) claims.

The NS-3 and NS-3K evidence possession and the NS-4 shows full ownership rights. In 2005, there were 1.66 million NS-3 claims representing 14.79 million rai; 6.03 million NS-3K claims representing 32.42 million rai; and 22.11 million NS-4 claims representing 78.20 million rai.

NS-3 and NS-3K are *"a document from a competent official certifying that land has already been put to use"*[124]. They are recognizable by the green Garuda symbols on the top of the front page. The NS-4, also known as Chanote, is a full title deed i.e. *"the document showing ownership of the land and including the land title deed with map, pre-emption title deed and pre-emption certificate stamped "Already put to use"*"[125]. The NS-4 is recognizable by the red Garuda symbol on the top of the front page.

---

[124] Land Code Act B.E 2497 (1954) Section 1.
[125] Land Code Act B.E 2497 (1954) Section 1.

The front page of an NS-3, NS-3K or an NS-4 shows the legal information pertaining to the document, such as the document number, land number, survey number, book page, etc. It also includes a diagram of the parcel, the size of the parcel and the name and address of the first holder of the document with the signatures of the officers and official seals. The back page of the document shows the details of all the dealing pertaining to the land represented by the document (liens, charges, mortgages, leases). NS-3 and NS-3K records are kept at the local District Land Departments and NS-4 records are kept at the Provincial Land Departments. The original is always kept at the Land Department and one duplicate given to the holder. In case of discrepancies between the original at the Land Department and the duplicate, the original of the Land Department prevails. If many transactions have been registered on a piece of land, then several leaves will be bound together. All those documents also have in common that they are fully negotiable subject to the Land Code and can be used as a surety for a commercial loan.

As discussed in the previous chapter, private property rights are not absolute and land rights may be lost to the State under certain circumstances. In addition, the owner of an NS-3, NS-3K or NS-4 may also lose his rights to another private party through the mechanism of hostile possession. Hostile possession is the claim of a person settled upon the landowner's absence from the plot. If the owner does not act and allows the squatter to settle peacefully upon the land for an uninterrupted period, the squatter may have a valid claim on the land after a certain period. If a Chanote represents the land plot, the landowner will have 10 years to remove the unlawful settler. If an NS-3 or NS-3K represents the land, the owner of the certificate will only have one year to take action and file an action for the removal of the disturbance with the local competent court in order to remove the unlawful settler. If the landowner does not act within the legal period, the landowner will lose his land to the settler.

As explained in a previous chapter, the transfer of land rights, mortgaging of land and registration of any liens or charges are carried out at the Land Department Office in Thailand. All transactions on NS-3 and NS-3K titles are done at the district Land Department, while transactions on NS-4 are done at the provincial land office.

The transaction is quite straightforward and may be accomplished in only a few hours. The parties to the transaction may either attend in person or be represented by power of attorney. The parties will be required to fill out the appropriate government forms[126] and pay the required fees and taxes. In order for the transaction to take place, the owner of the land must bring his duplicate copy of the document to the Land Department on the day of the transaction and the Land Department officer will amend both the original title and the duplicate immediately. On average, the transfer of a title takes less than a day. In terms of payment, the buyer will generally have paid a deposit on the date of reservation. The payment of the balance due by the buyer will be made by cashier's check or bank draft[127]. The buyer will purchase the cashier's check or bank draft one day in advance and provide copies to the seller to affirm the authenticity of the check. On the day of the transaction, the buyer will show the cashier's check to the seller who will then file the documents for the amendment of the title. The officer will process the amendment and inform the parties when the amendment is complete. The buyer will then give the check to the seller and collect the amended title.

In the following section, we'll review the differences between the three higher claims from the lowest to the highest.

✓ *The Certificate of Utilization, or Nor. Sor. Sam (NS-3)*. The NS-3 is a certificate providing evidence of possession. The NS-3 shows that the owner has fulfilled certain conditions, particularly relating to occupation and utilization of the land, and has been

---

[126] Please see some of the forms applicable in List of Appendixes at the end of this book

[127] Note that a cashier's check cashed at a bank located in the same province as the issuing bank will be cleared in 24 hours, but can take up to 6 days if the issuing bank and clearing bank are in different provinces. For inter-provincial transactions, the use of a bank draft is recommended.

granted the right to possess the land and obtain benefit from the land as an owner, but these rights still have to be confirmed by the authorities. Despite the fact that the right is not yet confirmed, the law recognizes the right of possession of the NS-3 holder and the NS-3 may be used as evidence toward proving possession in any disputes against other private individuals and against the State. It can also be freely transferred and juristic acts may be registered on it. However, as the right of possession evidenced by a NS-3 is not yet confirmed, any transaction or legal acts registered on a NS-3 must be published for 30 days to allow third parties to oppose the transaction. NS-3 documents are kept at the local District Land Office.

The main difference between a NS-3 and a NS-3K is that the NS-3 has been less accurately surveyed. Their boundaries were recorded in relation to the adjacent plots and survey errors in length of boundaries or total area of the plot are not unusual. The map of a NS-3 is a floating map with no parcel points issued for a specific plot of land and not connected to other land plots. If the land evidenced by an NS-3 has no clear physical boundaries, then the limits have to be staked out and confirmed by the surrounding landowners. Buyers are always recommended to request an official survey of land boundaries before purchasing land evidenced by an NS-3. The difference between the size recorded in the NS-3 and actual size of the land may vary up to 20%.

✓ *Certified Certificate of Use, Nor. Sor. Sam Kor*[128]. *(NS-3K).* An NS-3K is also a certificate of possession. Like an NS-3, this document evidences the holder's right to possess the land and obtain benefit from the land as an owner. In addition, the NS-3K also evidences that the holder's rights have been confirmed and certified by the authorities. As the right of use is confirmed, legal acts or transactions concerning the land do not need to be published. NS-3K claims have been more accurately surveyed than NS-3 and each plot of land is cross referenced with a master survey of the area and a corresponding aerial photograph with

---

[128] Or Nor Sor Sam Gor

points of reference on the map. Despite the fact that the NS3-K is more accurately surveyed, a geometrical survey is also recommended prior to any purchase.

✓ *Nor. Sor. See, Chanote (NS-4).* The NS-4 is the only true title deed[129] that serves to evidence unrestricted ownership rights. Chanotes are issued by the Provincial Land Office and based upon a geometrically accurate survey of the land made by the Land Department geometer. The exact boundaries are marked by concrete or metal plot markers and the map is charted in relation to a national survey grid with an overall land plot map. At the time of the geometrical survey, the presence of the surrounding landowners is required and they will be requested to sign a document attesting to the size and boundaries of the plot being measured. The land map on a Chanote document is depicted with the measurements and a detailed drawing showing the round posts at each corner of the plot and also with a view of neighboring land plots or public roads.

Please see the illustration on the next page:

---

[129] The Sor. Bor. Kor. is an allotment of land issued by the Land Reformative Committee. While this land has been accurately surveyed (like a Chanote), it cannot be sold or leased and may only be transferred under last will and testament. There are those who would assert that the Sor. Bor. Kor. are true title deeds like Chanotes. My understanding, however, is that they are a right of usufruct granted on a land.

On the front page of a Chanote will appear the:

Title number

Land number

Survey number

Book number

Page number

Location

Name and address of the first owner

Map of the land, including the land area, boundaries and markings

Date of issue

Officer signature and stamp

Ngor.Sor.4 Jor.

-Garuda-

LOCATION		TITLE DEED	
Position		No.	
Land Number		Issue .... Page	
Surveying		Amphur	
Tambon	LAND TITLE DEED	Province	

is the Ownership Certificate
be Issued under a title of the Land Code

For .... Nationality .... Address .... Moo .... Road ....
Soi .... Tambon .... Amphur .... Province ....

This plot of land has space ___ rai, ___ ngarn and ___ Tarang wa.

Position Scale 1 :   **MAP**   Scale 1 :

N

Issued on

( )
The Land Officer

Writer	Map Draftsman
Reader	Map Proof Reader
Proof Reader	Section Head

On the back of the Chanote is recorded the history of all transactions concerning the land, e.g. transfer of ownership, liens or charges, right of superficies, lease agreements or mortgages.

INDEX OF REGISTRATION

Date of registration	Type of registration	Offer	Acceptance	The magnitude of contract	Remaining of area	New certificate	The officer sign with position seal affixed

Chapter 37   **How Are Rights to Houses and Buildings**

Evidenced[130]?

Land documents such as NS-4 (Chanote), NS-3K (Nor. Sor. Sam Kor.) or NS-3 (Nor. Sor. Sam), which we discussed in the previous chapter, only serve to evidence rights to land and contain no mention of the structures built on the land (if any) and may not serve as evidence of ownership of the buildings built on the land.

A legal principle called *"accession"* states that the accessory follows the principal. Applied to real estate, this principle means, among other things, that the ownership of a building follows "*in principle*" the ownership of the land on which this building is build. In Thailand, this principle is mentioned by section 139 of the Thai Civil and Commercial Code, which stipulates, *"Immovable property denotes land and things fixed permanently to land forming a body therewith. It includes real rights connected with land or things fixed to*

---

[130] In this chapter, we will discuss the issue of the ownership of buildings and houses with the exception of condominium titles, which shall be discussed in the following chapter.

or forming a body with land." Does the principle of accession mean the owner of the land rights is always the owner of the building?

Unfortunately no, because the principle of accession is not absolute; to the contrary, section 146 of the Thai Civil and Commercial code also states that *"Things temporarily fixed to land or to a building do not become component parts of the land or building. The same rule applies to a building or other structure which, in the exercise of a right over another person's land, has been fixed to the land by the person who has such right."*

Furthermore, the Thai Supreme Court has long ago acknowledged that buildings are a form of immovable property that can be owned separately from the land. Therefore, a careful buyer who wants to purchase both land and building should not assume the owner of the land is also the owner of the house built on that land, because it is possible to dissociate the ownership of land and any buildings constructed on the land.

Finally, if a person who constructed a building on another person's land had no right to do so, but acted in good faith at the time he or she did it , then it is Section 1310 of the TCCC, which will apply to the situation: *"If a person has, in good faith, constructed a building upon another person's land, the owner of the land becomes the owner of the building, but he must pay the constructor for any increase of value accruing to the land by reason of the building."* [131]

If there are no specific documents providing evidence of building ownership, and if it's possible to dissociate land ownership from building ownership, then how do we establish the ownership of a building?

The first method is to do complete due diligence, including not only the review of the title deed itself but also of the documents attached to the land title deed. For example, at the time of any land sale, the parties must execute the sale and purchase agreement

---

[131] See 1311 TCCC to determine whether the person who built the building has no rights and was of bad faith.

attached to the title deed at the Land Department. Then it will suffice to verify the sale and purchase agreement pertaining to the latest sale recorded on the land title. If the previous buyer has purchased the ownership of the land along with the building, then a mention of the transfer of the ownership of the building will generally be made in the sale and purchase form executed by the parties at the Land Department. Therefore, the first thing a buyer could do is to check the content of the sale and purchase agreement form attached to the title deed at the Land Department[132] to clarify this issue. If the building existed at the time of the latest recorded transaction, then the sale of the building along with the land should be mentioned in the sale and purchase agreement form.

In the same way, if the land is sold undeveloped, it should be specified in the land purchase agreement that *"this land is sold without any building"*.

If the latest land purchase agreement recorded at the Land Department shows that the current owner has purchased the house along with the land, then it's more than likely by application of the accession principle that the current owner of the land is also the owner of the building. If further confirmation is needed, it would suffice to check in the public records to determine whether the ownership of the house was transferred separately from the ownership of the land. Indeed, in order to transfer the ownership of a building separately from the ownership of land, it's necessary to publish the transaction at the Land Department for a 30-day period.

The house or building located on the land may also have been built by a person who was not at the time the owner of the land. If this is the case, then there should normally be a record of the transaction. When a person builds a building on someone else's land, the agreement of the landowner is usually sought. For example, the landowner may have granted a third party the right of superficies. A right of superficies is a real right pursuant wherein *"The owner of a*

---

132 Please see appendixes 5 and 6 at the end of the book to see the difference between an agreement executed for the sale of a land together with a building and without a building.

piece of land may create a right of superficies in favor of another person by giving that person the right to own, upon or under the land, buildings, structures or plantations."[133]. If a landowner has granted a right of superficies to a third party allowing this person to own any building constructed on the land, this transaction will be registered at the Land Department as the registration is one of the conditions of validity for a right of superficies.

Another option to dissociate the ownership of building and land is through the execution and registration of a long-term lease agreement. However, the lease agreement must contain a clause expressly stipulating that the lessee will own any building built on the land, because Section 564 and subsequent sections of the TCCC[134] that are applicable to the right of lease do not contain any disposition granting to a lessee the right of ownership on the building the lessee constructed on the leased land. If the lease agreement does not expressly mention the lessee as the owner of the house constructed on the land, then Sections 139, 146, 1310 or 1311 of the TCCC would apply to the situation instead. Depending upon whether the lessee acted in good or bad faith, the landowner may choose to become the owner of the building. In this case, the landowner will have to pay an indemnity to the lessee for the increase of value; or require the lessee to restore the land to its former condition.

Therefore, if a third party has constructed a building on someone else's land, there should be evidence of an agreement in public records, such as the registration of a right of superficies, or a lease agreement. Although this evidence should be available, it doesn't always exist. As we explained earlier, Thai people are very informal when they do business among themselves and they will not always take all of the necessary legal steps when executing a transaction. One of our clients who wanted to purchase a hotel in a Thai resort city asked us to do due diligence on the property.

---

[133] Thai Civil and Commercial Code, Section 1410.
[134] Section 564 and subsequent sections in the TCCC regulate the agreement to hire property (leasehold).

During the course of our task, we discovered that the owner of the land has granted, 20 years ago, a 30-year lease agreement to a Thai lessee for the purpose of building and operating a hotel on the land 20 years previously. As already explained, in Thailand a long-term lease agreement is valid beyond three years only if it is registered at the Land Department. Now in this particular case our due diligence showed that the landowner and the original lessee never bothered to register the 30-year lease agreement in the first place. In other words, as the contract was not registered, the lessee had not had any enforceable right to use the land for the past 17 years.

Furthermore, the parties had used a standard form lease agreement, which expressly prohibited the lessee to sublet the property without the written agreement of the landowner. Now, 10 years into the contract, the original lessee had sublet the property to another Thai who later granted the management of the hotel to a third Thai person. Of course, none of those transactions were ever formally approved in writing by the landowner. As a consequence, neither the lessee, nor the sub-lessee or the person managing the property had actual rights on it. The most surprising in this case was not the legal failings of the transaction but the fact that despites those failings all parties involved have fulfilled their obligations towards each other as if all the documents were valid and enforceable. Of course this is an extreme case and most transactions are done by the book and documented in such a way that it's possible to clearly establish who owns what, there are always exceptions.

Another issue that must be taken into consideration when purchasing a building from a person who is not the owner of the land is that the dissociation between the ownership of the building and the ownership of the land may not be permanent, but only for the duration of the agreement. If a buyer purchases a building owned by the beneficiary of a right of superficies, or from a person who leases the land pursuant to a lease agreement, then it's important to address what will happen at the end of the agreement. If you purchase the building from the beneficiary of a right of superficies, and if nothing is mentioned in the superficies agreement, then this matter shall be solved by the application of Section 1416 of the TCCC. Pursuant to Section 1416 TCCC, *"When the right of superficies is extinguished, the superficiary may take away his buildings, structures or plantations, provided he restores the land to its former condition. If, instead of permitting the removal of the buildings, structures or plantations, the owner of the land notifies his intention to buy them at market value, the superficiary may not refuse the offer, except on reasonable grounds."*

There are no equivalent dispositions in the TCCC applicable to the lease agreement. Therefore, if the agreement itself addresses this issue, Sections 139, 146, 1310 or 1311 of the TCCC, which we mentioned above, should be applicable. The building construction permit is another document that may be used in order to establish ownership to a building.

Contrary to a popular belief, the *"Tabian Baan"* or *"Census Registration"*, also known as the *"Blue Book*[135]*"*, is not a direct proof of ownership to a building. The *"Tabian Baan"* is an official document issued by the government. It is evidence of a household and of the registered address of the persons living in a building. It will also contain information, such as house location, house configuration, house number; details of the people living in the house i.e. name, surname, ID card number, original domicile, mother's name, father's name, and date of birth. The *"Tabian Baan"* also indicates who the chief of the household is. There are two types of *"Tabian Baan"*. The census registration (Tor. Ror. 14) blue book is used to record the details of persons of Thai nationality or foreigners who have resident permits. The yellow census registration (Tor. Ror. 13) book is used to record the details of foreigners who legally reside in Thailand, but do not yet have residency[136] permit status. In other words, the *"Tabian Baan"* may create a presumption that the chief of a household is the owner of a building, but is not absolute proof of ownership.

---

[135] Most official documents in Thailand are blue, but the Tabian Baan may be yellow if issued to a foreigner
[136] Resident means resident status under the Immigration Act

PART III
WHAT RIGHTS CAN FOREIGNERS LEGALLY ACQUIRE ON LAND AND BUILDINGS?

Chapter 38   What Are the Options Available to Foreign

Buyers of Real Estate in Thailand?

The most straightforward option for a foreign buyer wishing to purchase real estate in Thailand is to purchase a condominium. The process is, as you will see later, simple, safe (in terms of legal ownership) and allows the buyer to own the property freehold.

What of those who simply cannot stand the idea of spending their retirement in a condominium building, but wish to fulfill their dreams of a house and swimming pool with an exotic garden?

There are numerous other options available to these buyers, as Thai laws do allow foreign buyers to acquire several kinds of land rights. Among other choices, foreign individuals may lease land or be granted a right of superficies on a long-term basis without any restriction. They may also acquire other land rights, such as usufruct or mortgage. Thai laws further allow foreigners to own buildings or register a right of habitation for a building. We've already detailed the key issues applicable to the leasehold or right of superficies agreement and will not discuss them again, other than to remind to those who wish to purchase a house of this essential truth:

At the time of the house purchase, your developer will offer you a lease agreement with a clause of renewal to execute along with the purchase of your house. The renewal clause will require the landowners to grant you one or two renewals, or even a perpetual renewal in some cases. Be aware that your rights will be guaranteed for the initial period of 30 years, but whether or not your agreement will be renewed at the end of the initial period is anyone's guess, because there are too many variables to consider. As explained, the issue of the renewal clause is a legal minefield full of potential hazards or dangers. Therefore, purchase under leasehold only if you do not mind the uncertainty attached to the renewal clause.

Until recently, foreign companies were also able to lease land without any restrictions, but, as previously mentioned, the Circular of the Ministry of Interior dated 21 July 2008 has brought changes to the registration of long-term leases or rights of superficies in favor of foreign companies.

From now on Land Department officers may no longer accept registrations of a long-term leases or rights of superficies on land in favor of a foreign company without further examination of the transaction purpose. In order to register a long-term lease, the foreign company will have to provide evidence the company is not registering a long-term lease or right of superficies for the purpose of carrying out a business, which would amount to holding land on behalf of foreigners and constitute a breach of the Land Act and/or Foreign Business Act of 1999. For example, a foreign company seeking to lease land in order to sublet the land out to other foreigners would be in breach of the Foreign Business Act, because the landlord's business is a service business that may be operated by foreigners only if they have obtained a foreign business license and the acquisition of this license is impossible.

It is not yet clear whether foreign companies seeking to register long-term leases will be required to provide actual evidence of their purpose. The alternative would be for the land officer to request the company sign a form certifying that the company does not lease the land with the intention to breach the Land Code Act or the Foreign Business Act. This form would be signed under penalty of criminal prosecution if the company falsely declares its purpose. It is also not clear whether a foreign company leasing land will be deemed as holding the land on behalf of foreigners. Could a company leasing land for 30 years with an option of renewal be considered as holding the land on behalf of foreigners? Furthermore, will a company leasing land and house for the use of its directors or shareholders be deemed as performing landlord activities in breach of the FBA?

Are there any other options available to those who would rather not purchase a condominium and are left cold by the restrictions pertaining to leasehold purchases? This brings us to the next issue: Who can own land freehold in Thailand?

Chapter 39   Can a Foreign Company or Individual Own Land

Freehold?

A great deal of confusion reigns in people's minds regarding who may or may not own land in Thailand, especially when it comes to the rights of freehold ownership by companies (foreign or Thai), foreign individuals , their Thai spouses, and Thai children of foreign citizens. Each of these issues will be addressed in this chapter and the next.

Now, Thailand is often criticized for not allowing foreign land ownership. Therefore, I think that before discussing the Thai legal framework we should review and compare the policies of Asian countries regarding foreign land ownership.

As you will see, Thailand's policy toward foreign land ownership is not so different from its neighbors', and in some regards is even better. In the table that follows I use either the term "Possible" instead of "Yes" when answering the question whether foreign land ownership is allowed in a given country, for reasons I will discuss after the table.

TABLE 28: COMPARING FOREIGN LAND OWNERSHIP REGULATIONS IN ASIA

Rank	Country	Foreign Land ownership	Remarks
1	Malaysia	Possible	No approval needed for unit under MYR 500,000 (USD 145,000). Purchase of unit costing more than this does not require government approval if under "Malaysia My Second Home" program or other programs as specified by authorities
2	Korea	Possible	Foreigners from countries that do not allow Koreans to own land may be prohibited from acquiring land. Additional formalities such as notice or prior approval may be required
3	Taiwan	Possible	Only if foreigner is from a country that allows Taiwanese reciprocity. Freehold ownership is limited to certain types of land, zones and purposes only (including residential)
4	Singapore	Possible	Need prior government approval if restricted property such as: Vacant Residential Land, Landed Property (house, town house, terrace house), or property in strata development other than condominiums.
5	*Thailand*	*Possible*	Foreign Commercial, Industrial ownership allowed for limited purposes and subjected to prior approval by the BOI or IEAT. Foreign Residential ownership allowed but subject to minimum investment requirement and limited in size (1 rai), zoning and requires prior approval Minority shareholding (49%) allowed in company that owns land
6	Cambodia	No	Minority foreign shareholding (49%) allowed in Cambodian Company that own land is allowed
7	Philippines	No	Minority foreign shareholding (40%) allowed in company that owns land
8	Indonesia	No	
9	China	No	Private freehold land ownership not available
	Laos	No	Private freehold land ownership not available
	Hong Kong	No	Private freehold land ownership not available
	Myanmar	No	Private freehold land ownership not available
	Vietnam	No	Private freehold land ownership is not available

Overall the situation is as follows:

✓ Out of 13 countries surveyed, 5 countries do not allow private freehold land ownership at all because this legal concept does not exist there. Those countries are China, Laos, Hong Kong, Myanmar and Vietnam. (//NOTE: sounds odd to call HK a country)

✓ Out of the 7 countries where the principle of freehold ownership exists, 3 countries do not allow foreign freehold land ownership at all. Those countries are Cambodia, Indonesia and Philippines.

✓ Foreign freehold land ownership is *possible* only in five Asian countries: Korea, Malaysia, Taiwan, Singapore and Thailand.

To rank Asian countries policies with respect to to foreign landownership was actually a difficult exercise. In the first draft of the above table, I answered "Yes" to the question *"Is foreign landownership allowed in this country"* for Korea, Malaysia, Taiwan and Singapore, and *No* for Thailand. However, I subsequently realized that:

✓ None of the four countries to which I was giving a *Yes* mark were actually offering an option of unconditional and unrestricted foreign land ownership, *and*

✓ While foreign land ownership is in principle prohibited in Thailand, Thailand laws contain many exceptions to this principle. Therefore, to give a *No* mark to Thailand was not only incorrect, but unfair.

I therefore concluded that the most accurate term for ranking Asian countries in terms of foreign land ownership was the word *"possible"*, because possible *means that something is likely to happen given the right set of circumstances*. This is exactly the purpose of the policies of Asian countries in relation to foreign land ownership: to make it possible providing that a certain set of conditions is fulfilled.

I ranked Malaysia at the top because Malaysian foreign land ownership policy does not call for reciprocity. For example, a Chinese citizen could buy land in Malaysia even if a Malaysian citizen could not do so in China. But the same Chinese could not do so in Korea or Taiwan because China does not offer reciprocity to Korean and Taiwanese citizens. The fact that Singapore only ranked 4th must come as a surprise for many readers. Yes, Singapore allows foreign ownership, but if you read the fine print (i.e. the remarks) then you will notice that Singapore requests prior government approval for foreign buyers that want to purchase *"restricted properties"*. If you look at the definition of *"restricted properties"*, it covers all residential properties but condominiums.

To sum up, the question of how to rank Asia countries by foreign land ownership laws is a little bit like the conundrum of the glass of wine. There are only conjectural answers to the question of whether the glass is half full or half empty.

As to Thailand's policy, it is in comparison to its neighbors, not as bad as critics would like you to believe. Should the foreign community in Thailand push the Government to allow unrestricted foreign residential land ownership? I do not believe so. First, because this idea is not popular at all among Thai people; second, in the current political context, now is not the right time for such a move. The issue would become politicized and a balanced debate would not take place. I believe that the right move at this point is to push for an extension of the leasehold period, as I already explained in chapters 10 and 11.

As to the situation in Thailand, it is true that Thailand prohibits foreign land ownership in principle. Pursuant to the Land Code of B.E. 2497 (1954), foreign individuals and foreign-owned companies *are not allowed* to own land *unless an exception* to the general rule applies.

For the time being most exceptions to the foreign land ownership prohibition are in relation to specific commercial or industrial purposes and subject to prior approval by Thai authorities.

To date, the privilege of freehold land ownership is mostly given to foreign companies investing in commercial or industrial sectors, mining, oil exploration and other specifically targeted business activities, and only to the extent necessary to allow the company to run its business. Practically, the permission to own land freehold for a specific purpose is granted by the BOI (Board of Investment) in relation to certain promoted activities, or by the Industrial Estate Authority of Thailand (IEAT).

Note that a foreign company allowed to purchase land freehold for industrial purposes may also be allowed by the BOI upon certain conditions to own land for residential purposes, but only to the extent that this is related to its main activity. For example, a factory owned by a foreign company may be allowed to purchase a limited amount of land freehold for constructing residential buildings for its employees. This privilege is linked to the main activities of the company and the company will be required to sell the land on which the employee residences are located if the company ever ceases its business activities.

Foreign individuals may not own residential land freehold but for one exception provided by Section 96 of the Land Code, which was enacted on 19 January 2002. Pursuant to Section 96 of the Land Code, foreign buyers who have invested over 40 million baht in Thailand may be allowed to own freehold up to one rai[137] of land for residential purposes only. This exemption is subject to fulfillment of the following conditions:

- ✓ First, the foreign buyer must have invested at least 40 million THB in Thailand, exclusive of the purchase price of the land and house.
- ✓ Second, the money invested must constitute an investment beneficial to the Thai economy, promoting social welfare, or promoted by the BOI.

---

[137] Reminder: 1 rai = 1,600 Square meters

✓ Finally, the money must be invested in Thailand for a minimum of 3 years.

Buyers who fulfill those three conditions will be allowed to purchase up to one rai of land freehold in designated areas, such as in Bangkok, Pattaya, municipal areas of all provinces and areas designated as residential under the City Planning Act.

Now what about the other exceptions contained in Land Code Act allowing in theory for foreigners to own residential land freehold? As a matter of fact, none of those other exemptions are actually applicable.

For example, Section 86 of the Land Code stipulates that *"Aliens may acquire land by virtue of the provisions of a treaty granting the right to own immovable properties and subject to the provisions of this Code".* Do not bother to check, Thailand does not have any treaty with any country that would allow foreigners to acquire land by virtue of a Treaty.

Another example is Section 93 of the Land Code that stipulates: *"A foreigner who acquires land by inheritance as statutory heir can have an ownership in such land upon the permission of the Minister of Interior. However, the total plots of land shall not be exceed those specified in Section 87".*

As a result, many foreigners who have Thai spouses believe they will be allowed to inherit their Thai spouse's land in the event of death. However, the truth is that Section 93 of the Land Code must be read along with Section 86 mentioned in the previous paragraph. In other words, a foreign citizen could inherit land only if there is a Treaty that would provide for it (they are none). In the absence of a Treaty he could inherit land only subject to the approval of the Ministry of Interior.

What then would happen if a foreign husband was bequeathed land, despite those restrictions? In my opinion, the will would still be valid, but a delay would be granted for the foreign heir to resell the land to a Thai national. The foreign heir would then be allowed to inherit the sales price of the land.

Chapter 40   Can a Thai Company Own Land Freehold?

In this chapter, we will review the conditions pursuant to which a Thai company may purchase land freehold.

A Thai company may own land providing it fulfills the two following criteria:

1. 51% of the shareholders are Thai; and
2. The Thai shareholders own a total of 51% of the company shares.

A Thai company fulfilling those two criteria may own land for industrial or residential purposes without any restrictions. At least this was the situation up to early 2006. In other words foreign investors may legally and without any problem own up to 49% of the share capital of a company owning or developing land. Up to three years ago, Thai companies that had foreign shareholders owning 49% of their shares and foreign authorized directors could without any problem and without any special requirements but the one mentioned above under number 1 and 2. This changed in April 2006 for the following reasons.

For the past thirty years, many foreign buyers have taken advantage of legal loopholes to purchase land using companies with Thai shareholders who could be deemed nominees[138]. For nearly 30 years the successive Thai governments did not take any actions to stop foreign buyers from circumventing the law. Everything changed in 2006 and the first thing readers may wonder is if what happened in 2006 compelled the Thai Government to finally act. I believe that two events incited the Ministry of Interior to issue new regulations to start addressing this issue. The first was political; Prime Minister Taksin Shinawatra family had just sold their telecommunication empire to Singapore Temasek (Singapore Sovereign Fund). This sale was very unpopular because the Shin group was also the owner of Shin Satellite the jewel of Thai companies. Also it was suspected that Temasek did not only purchase a minority interest of 49% in the Shin group but that they also purchased the Thai shares through Thai holding companies owned on its behalf by Thai nominees (an inquiry is still ongoing). Therefore we had at the time kind of an anti-foreigner climate. In addition the Ministry of Interior received a letter from the Governor of Prachuabkirikhan province complaining of foreign land investments in the province, especially in Hua Hin.

Now Hua Hin is a Thai Sea Resort that happens to be the place of residence of the King of Thailand as well as the preferred destination of Thai high-society. In this context, the Ministry of Interior had to act on the complaint. I believe that this explain why after years of inaction the Thai government started, in early 2006 to issue new regulations including the disclosure requirement applicable to the Thai shareholders of Thai companies purchasing land. The purpose of the right to disclosure is to restrict foreign buyers from using Thai companies when purchasing land.

This disclosure requirement is the result of a series of guidelines and circulars issued by the Ministry of Interior and the Land Department starting on 23 May and 21 July 2006, with the most recent in July of 2008, for the purpose of imposing a disclosure

---

[138] See Book 1 for the discussion of the nominee issue.

requirement upon the Thai shareholders of companies purchasing land.

This regulation impress a duty to disclose the source of their investment upon the Thai shareholders of any legal entity wishing to acquire land to operate an immovable property business, such as purchasing and sales, leasing, hotel operations and vacation homes. The duty to disclose the source of the investment applies to any shareholders of any Thai company that has:

i.   foreign director(s); *or*
ii. foreign shareholder(s); *or*
iii. Thai shareholders and directors only, but there are reasonable grounds to suspect the Thai shareholders are nominees holding shares on behalf of a foreigner.

The evidence requirement varies depending on whether the Thai shareholder is an individual or a company. If the Thai shareholder of the company that purchases land is an individual, he/she will have to provide the following evidence:

- Evidence of employment, such as salary and salary affirmation, certificate of employment, period of employment; and

- Other credible evidence of funds, such as savings accounts, money received from previous land sales, inheritance, and loans along with documentary evidence, such as bank saving books or land sale agreements, inheritance certificates, or loan agreements.

Finally, the individual Thai shareholders of a company which acquire land to operate immovable property businesses will also be required to sign a form certifying the truth of the information provided to the Land Department about the source of their income. The form individual Thai shareholders will be required to sign also includes a declaration that the shareholder:

1. is not holding the shares as a nominee for a foreigner or foreign juristic person,
2. is aware that holding land on behalf of a foreigner or foreign juristic person is an illegal practice in violation of Section 113 of the Land Code,
3. is aware that charges of providing any false information to any official according to Section 137 of the Penal Code may apply and
4. is aware that the General Director of the Land Department has the power to dispose the land in the event of violation of Section 113 of the Land Code.

Note that a new circular was issued on 21 July 2008 requiring the Land Department to use new forms with greater detail regarding the content of the criminal violation and applicable sanctions.

Corporate shareholders of companies purchasing land to operate immovable property businesses shall be requested to provide evidence proving the monetary sources used to purchase shares of the company purchasing the land, such as:

- The company balance sheet, or
- The loan agreement and minutes of meetings accepting the loan when the source of the fund is a loan.

Furthermore, the director of the Thai corporate shareholder of a company who purchases land for operating an immovable property business will be required to sign a form pursuant to which the director swears to certify the truth of the information provided to the Land Department. The content of this form is the same as the content individual shareholders are required to sign and lists the potential violations of the law and potential sanctions applicable to the violator.

If a company purchases land at a higher price than its registered capital and do so without applying for a mortgage, the purchasing company will also be required to provide evidence about the source of money used to pay for the land. For example, if the company received a loan, then it needs to provide a copy of the loan agreement and the minutes of meeting of the company approving the loan. If the company used a loan from a foreign person, then evidence such as transfer receipt(s) or withdrawal(s) from a savings account must be provided for the source of money. If the loan comes from a Thai person, or Thai Juristic Person, evidence such as the company balance sheet, withdrawal receipt(s) from savings accounts and minutes of the meeting of the debtor and creditor must be provided for the source of money.

Until 21 July 2008, companies purchasing land and house solely for residential purposes[139] were requested to fulfill a lighter version of the disclosure requirement. This lighter requirement was applicable to companies wishing to:

i. purchase land to build or own company offices, or a house for the use of the company directors; *and*
ii. purchase less than one rai in total land area.

Until recently, the shareholders of these companies were not required to provide information about the sources of their monies. Instead, the director of the company was requested to sign a form at the Land Department to certify that:

- The acquisition of the land is for the company's office or residential purposes, not for commercial or leasing purposes; *and*
- If the company later changes the purpose of the acquisition and uses the land for operating an immovable property business, the Thai shareholders must present evidence of the monetary source for buying the shares in order to prove they do not hold shares as nominees for foreigners or foreign juristic persons.

---

[139] And companies with foreign director(s); or foreign shareholder(s); or Thai shareholders and directors when there are reasonable grounds to suspect the Thai Shareholders are nominees holding shares on behalf of a foreigner.

Furthermore, the form the directors or authorized representatives of the company were requested to sign also included mention they:

1. swore the company was not a substitute for a foreigner or foreign juristic person to hold the land and
2. were aware that acting as a substitute for a foreigner or foreign juristic person to hold the land is an illegal practice in violation of Section 113 of the Land Code and
3. were aware of potential charges by providing any false information to any official according to Section 137 of the Penal Code and
4. were aware the General Director of the Land Department has the power to dispose of the land. Note that, according to Land Department practice at the time, the Director signing this form could be a foreign director.

On 21 July 2008, the Ministry of Interior issued a new circular for the purpose of confirming and completing the previous circulars and standardizing the application of the previous circulars by local Land Departments regarding the disclosure by Thai shareholders of their investment in companies purchasing land. This new circular confirmed the Land Department officers' duties to examine the sources of the monies used by Thai shareholders in purchasing shares of companies with foreign shareholders and directors purchasing land for operating real estate businesses.

But the new circular had the additional purpose of extending the disclosure duty of Thai shareholders of companies purchasing land which did not have the objective of carrying out real property business (that is to say, companies purchasing less than one rai of land for the use of the directors or shareholders of the company). *"With regard to limited companies, limited partnerships or registered ordinary partnerships applying to receive transfer of ownership in land without the objective of carrying out a real property business but with reason to believe there are Thai persons as shareholders on behalf of foreigners, or foreigners are authorized to sign on behalf of the company, or foreigners are the promoters of the company, or foreigners hold preference shares with majority voting rights, Thai holders with substantial shares have a profession which is not directly related to the business of investing e.g. attorney at law or estate agent, to examine the source of monies of shareholders with Thai nationality who purchased shares.*"[140]

Since the enactment of this latest circular, Thai shareholders of companies who purchase land, but have no objective of carrying out a real property business, are also subjected to the disclosure requirement if certain conditions apply. Among the criteria that would trigger the application of the disclosure requirement are companies with foreign shareholders, promoters or directors, or preference shares granting preferential votes to the foreign shareholders, or companies with shareholders who are not normally investors, such as real estate agents or lawyers.

Finally, the new circular of the Ministry of Interior also precisely set forth the timeframe granted to companies in violation of the law and owning land on behalf of foreigners. The delay granted will be no less than 180 days and no more than one year. Note that this circular also deals with the matter of foreign companies leasing land on a long-term basis, a matter we'll discuss later.

While Thai companies may purchase land freehold without any restriction, the guidelines and circulars issued by the Ministry of Interior over the past two years have been more effective than the measures taken in the past and should effectively dissuade foreign buyers from purchasing land using Thai companies. Please also see my comments on the nominee issue in Chapter 9.

---

[140] Unofficial translation.

Chapter 41   **Can the Thai Spouse or Thai Child of a Foreign**

National Own Land Freehold?

Contrary to popular belief, a ministerial regulation issued following the enactment of the now defunct 1997 Constitution allows Thai wife's married to foreigners to buy land, providing that the Thai wife can prove the money used for the purchase of the freehold land is legally and solely her own.

The catch is that, in order for the Thai spouse to be allowed to purchase the land, the foreign spouse must sign a declaration at the Land Department stating the funds used for the land purchase belonged to the Thai spouse prior to marriage.

If the money used for the land purchase is deemed the Thai spouse's prior to the wedding, then the land bought with this money is not the common property of the couple, but solely the property of the Thai spouse and the foreign spouse will have no right to the land, or its value, in the event of a divorce or the death of the Thai spouse. Note that once you have signed and filed with the administration, a declaration stating that the funds used for the purchase of property belonged to the Thai spouse prior to marriage, there is no way back. If in a subsequent divorce you tried to make the claim that the money was actually yours, then you would face the risk of criminal charges for having lied to a government official at the time of the purchase.

A Thai minor born to a foreign parent can also acquire land, providing that *the land acquisition is not done for the purpose of circumventing or evading the law.* If parents wish to give a piece of land to their Thai-born child, the authorities will inquire about the reason for the gift to the minor and into the relations between the parents and the minor. If the property to be given as a gift was acquired by purchasing, the monetary source used for the acquisition must be determined (the Thai or the foreign parent).

Unfortunately, parents seldom realize several drawbacks to transferring land to a minor. The main drawback is that the power of the child's parents will be severely restricted regarding the use of the land.

Pursuant to Section 1574 of the TCCC, the rights of a person exercising parental power are severely restricted with regards to the immovable property of the minor.

For example, and unless they have Court permission, parents may not sell, exchange, sell with right of redemption, let out property on hire purchase, mortgage, release a mortgage to a mortgagor or transfer the right of mortgage on an immovable property or on a mortgageable movable property; extinguish the whole or a part of the real rights of the minor on immovable property; create servitude, right of inhabitation, right of superficies, usufruct or any charges on immovable property; or lease immovable property for more than three years.

Therefore, transferring land to a minor is full of drawbacks, because all those restrictions are not viable options for people who intend to develop the land.

Note that once a child reaches legal adulthood, he/she can own or acquire land and no special inquiry applies in the case of a Thai adult born to a foreign parent.

Chapter 42   What Are the Key Features of the Right to Lease

under Thai Law?

As already explained, the lease contract is regulated by Section 537 and subsequent sections in the Thai Commercial Code ("TCCC") under the title "Hire of Property". Pursuant to Section 537 of the TCCC, hire of property is a contract whereby: *"A person, called the letter ("Lessor"), agrees to let another person, called the hirer ("Lessee"), have the use or benefit of a property for a limited period of time, and the hirer agrees to pay a rent".*

Lease agreements may be executed either for the life of the Lessor (the owner of the land) or the life of the Lessee (the tenant); or for a limited period. If made for a limited period, the duration of a lease on immovable property cannot exceed 30 years for residential property[141], or 50 years for commercial leases. Note that even when a residential lease is made for the life of the parties, the current practice of the Land Department is to register the lease for a 30-year period.

---

[141] Please see Chapter 11 the comparative table of lease periods in Asia

Finally, a lease agreement made for a limited period can be renewed, but the renewal period must not exceed 30 years from the time of renewal. However, please see comments in Chapters 10 and 11 in relation to the issues applicable to the renewal clause.

A formal lease agreement is enforceable only if it has been drafted in writing and duly executed. In addition, a lease agreement made for a period of more than 3 years or the life of the Lessor or Lessee must be registered at the Land Department. Unless registered at the Land Department, the lease can only be enforceable for three years. Beyond three years, the unregistered lease becomes a natural obligation only and the parties cannot request the protection of the courts for enforcement.

Upon registration of a lease agreement at the Land Department, a government fee equivalent to 1% of the assessed rental value or declared rental value for the entire duration of the lease must be paid. In doing so, always verify that you rent from the owner of the building. In Thailand, it's not uncommon for the person offering you the land or building for rent not to be the owner. If the Lessor is not the owner, request a duly executed power of attorney or proof of the Lessor's rights to the property. As explained in Chapter 10, sub-leasing a property is not authorized by law without the written consent of the owner. This is the reason why most standard lease agreement forms used in Thailand prohibit subleasing. So if you are offered to sublet a property, do confirm that your Lessor does indeed has the right to sublet the property or that the owner is ready to approve the sub-lease in writing.

As previously discussed, it's not a sign of dishonesty for Thai people to offer to sublet property when they do not have the right to do so. It's just a result of the fact that Thai people are so *"informal"* when it comes to doing business. In addition, Thai owners are often reticent to register lease agreements, because one of the effects of a lease registration is to inform the tax administration that the land and/or buildings are leased out. When Thai people do business among themselves, they will rarely register long-term lease agreements, but will generally honor the terms of duration of the lease, despite the fact the lease is not formally valid beyond three years.

Do not be surprised if your landowner requests the execution of two agreements. The first lease will have the real rental value and will be kept by the parties only. The second lease agreement will have a lower rental value and will be executed and registered with the Land Department.

Should you accept such a deal? I can understand that people want to save costs and taxes. From a lessee point of view, however, under-declaring the value of the rental may become a source of problems in the long run. For example, imagine the case of an investor who incorporates a company that leases premises on a property to establish a restaurant business. The agreement is registered for a period of 10 years and, while the monthly rent is actually THB 300,000, the parties only declare THB 30,000 per month of rent at the time of the lease registration. Now, from the lessee's point of view, problems are encountered in the declaration of the corporate income tax return every year. Although THB 3,600,000 has been paid in rental tax-deductible expenses, the lessee will only be able to claim THB 360,000 per year as deductible expenses. Furthermore, the information about the existence of the actual rent the lessee is paying to the lessor every month will have to be kept hidden from the tax administration for the next 10 years. Not only is this practice complicated over the long term, but there is a potential tax liability attached to it. Indeed, when a company is renting premises, the company has to deduct a 5% withholding tax from the actual rent paid every month to the lessor and the company is liable for paying this amount to the tax administration. If the tax administration finds out, the lessee company may face a potential tax liability of several million baht.

Finally, when you lease a building with the intention of using the leased premises as your company office, never forget to secure the owner's agreement. Lots of Thai people remain reluctant to see their property used for office purposes by a company, because the company will have to register itself with the tax administration at this address. If you aren't able to obtain your landowner's authorization to use the leased premises as a company office, you won't be able to run your business.

Chapter 43   **What are the Key Features of the Right of**

Superficies under Thai Law?

The right of superficies is a real right recognized by most civil law countries. In the 1970s and 1980s, foreign buyers were prohibited from purchasing land freehold in Switzerland and the right of superficies was used as an alternative. Foreign land ownership is also prohibited in most East European countries; thus, the right of superficies is the preferred alternative used by foreign buyers.

Oddly, foreign buyers in Thailand prefer to use leasehold, despite the fact that the right of superficies gives them better protection. One of the reasons must be that most buyers of real estate in Thailand come from common law countries where the right of superficies is unknown. Another reason is agents' attitudes. Many developers have to switch to the leasehold after originally choosing to offer rights of superficies to buyers due to pressure from agencies which wanted the project to be sold in leasehold, because leasehold is better known.

What, then, are the key features of lease and right of superficies agreements?

Pursuant to Section 1410 and subsequent sections of the TCCC, the right of superficies is defined as follows: *"The owner of a piece of land may create a right of superficies in favor of another person by giving the person the right to own, upon or under the land, buildings, structures or plantations."* In other words, the law grants the right to the beneficiary of a right of superficies to own any construction or structures built upon that land.

A right of superficies can be created either for the life of the grantor (the owner of the land) or of the beneficiary (the tenant); or for a limited period of 30 years. If made for a limited period, the duration of the right of superficies cannot exceed 30 years.

The right of superficies, can be renewed, but the renewal period must not exceed 30 years from the time of renewal. A right of superficies must also be registered at the Land Department. Upon registration of a right of superficies, a government fee of 1% of the rental value for the entire duration must be paid.

In contrast to a right to lease, the right of superficies is transmissible to heirs by law. Pursuant to Section 1411 of the TCCC, *"Unless otherwise provided in the act creating it, the right of superficies is transferable and transmissible by way of inheritance"*

Finally, and in contrast to a lease, the right of superficies is not terminated by the destruction of the buildings, structures or plantations, even if caused by force majeure (Section 1415 of the TCCC).

Both lease agreements and rights of superficies are valid options for foreign buyers interested in purchasing a house and land in Thailand, as long as buyers understand the limitations inherent to the duration of the lease agreement and the right of superficies.

The right of superficies has a few features to make it more interesting than the leasehold from a buyer's point of view. Firstly, the law provides for the dissociation between the ownership of the land and the ownership of the buildings constructed on the land. Secondly, the right of superficies is legally transmissible by inheritance. The right of superficies suffers from the same limitations as the lease agreement only in terms of the limited duration of 30 years.

For the time being and despite the claims made by many first time developers, it's impossible to guarantee to a lessee or the beneficiary of a right of superficies that the lease or right of superficies will be renewed without problems at the end of the initial 30-year period. As already explained before, there are too many variables entering into consideration to do so. Any claims of perpetual renewal made by developers are not only false, but preposterous.

PART IV

WHAT IS A CONDOMINIUM AND WHAT RIGHTS MAY FOREIGN BUYERS ACQUIRE ON CONDOMINIUMS?

Chapter 44   **What is the Difference between an Apartment**

Building and a Condominium Building?

Before discussing the Condominium Act, I believe it is necessary to explain the difference between a condominium and an apartment building. To do this I need first to clarify what the term *"condominium"* means.

In this chapter I will present the general definition of the term *"condominium"*. I will not only refer to the Thai legal definition, but I will discuss what the term means under the laws of other countries as well.

Most people in Thailand commonly associate the term *"condominium"* with the concept of an *"individual unit"* located in a *"multiple unit building"*, generally a high rise that may only be sold freehold. While this an accurate definition of a condominium in Thailand, the concept of condominium actually refers to far more than this.

The first thing to understand is that the term *"condominium"* does not describe what a property *"looks like"*, but defines the *"physical rights"* attached to the property.

The second is that "condominium" may refer not only to a high rise building divided into units (generally called a vertical condominium) but as also to horizontal condominiums that may be detached or not.

Finally, while most condominium units happen to be of the residential type, any kind of immovable property may be sold as *"condominium"*, including residential buildings, office buildings, parking garages and housing projects.

Now that we have defined the concept of *"condominium"*, what is the difference between a condominium and an apartment unit?

What really sets condominiums apart are the physical rights associated with the purchase of a condominium unit.

What makes condominiums different from apartment projects is that a condominium is *"an estate in real property consisting of (1) an undivided interest in common in a portion of a parcel or real property <u>together with</u> (2) a separate interest (in Thailand an Or Chor 2 Deed) in space (such as an apartment, a store, an office) in a residential, industrial or commercial building"*.

A condominium is the sum of an individual interest (freehold or leasehold) in a determined unit and of a collective interest in an undetermined common property.

In other words the buyer of a condominium unit will receive two sets of rights:

> (1) a separate interest (whether freehold or leasehold) in a separate unit; *and*

(2) a share percentage of the deed or leasehold interest that encompasses the whole common property

As a result of their interest in the common property, condominium buyers will have the right to become members of the juristic person (co-owner association) that manages their building and they may also choose to become active members (if elected) of the juristic person committee that supervises the work of the property manager. In other words, condominium buyers have a right to participate in their building's management. Depending on how involved they want to be in the affairs of their condominium, they may also simply exercise their voting rights during the juristic person meetings (minimum once a year).

In contrast, buyers of apartment units will have no say in the way the building is managed[142]. The management of the building will be the exclusive responsibility of the landowner or of the developer/lessor[143]. The landowner will set the management fees to be paid by the buyers every year without any oversight from the buyers/tenants, and will decide by himself the level and the quality of the building maintenance.

What really distinguish a condominium from an apartment is the rights granted to the buyer, the fact that in a condominium the buyer will not only own a separate interest on a determined unit but that he will also have a collective interest into the common property. On the other hand in an apartment building the buyer will only receive an interest in the separate unit but will have no collective interest in the common area.

Many buyers believe that another criterion distinguishing a condominium from an apartment building is that condominium units are only sold freehold while apartment units are only sold leasehold.

---

[142] Of course they can still complain or sue the developer but they do not have an actual participation right in the management of the common property.
[143] The Developer/Lessor may not be the owner of the land on which the building is built. This is the case on most buildings built on Crown Property Bureau land (please see chapter 10)

These belief is for the time being true in Thailand, where a developer may only apply for a condominium license if the developer is the freehold owner of the land and of the building, but this is not the case in many other countries.

In the US, for example, condominium projects may be developed on freehold land or on leasehold land. If the condominium is developed on leasehold land the condominium project is referred to as a leasehold condominium. Condominium rights *"(...) may, with respect to the duration of its enjoyment, be either (1) an estate of inheritance or perpetual estate, (2) an estate for life, or (3) an estate for years, such as a leasehold or sublease hold. California Civil Code 783"*. [144]

Therefore the nature of the interest the project owner/developer will have in the land or the type of interest the buyer will have in the unit is not always a reliable criterion to distinguish condominium projects from apartment projects.

Finally, the fact is also that a condominium project may be run like an apartment building and an apartment building may in theory be converted into a condominium. For example a single investor could purchase all the individual units in a condominium project and then lease them out and operate the condominium building in the same manner as an apartment building. Conversely, it is possible for a developer to purchase an apartment building and to convert the individual units to condominium units by bringing the building up to the standards required by the Condominium Act and then offering them for sale as condominium units.

Now if you are about to purchase a property in Thailand and are offered the choice between purchasing a condominium unit or leasing an apartment units what should you do?

---

[144] Black's Law Dictionary Vol.1 page 267: Henry Campbell

My recommendation would be to purchase into the condominium project whenever possible. The first reason is that your rights are more secured in the long term (perpetual freehold ownership), and that 20 years down the road it will be easier to sell a condominium freehold than an apartment unit with 10 years left on the lease agreement[145]. The second reason is that in Thailand (as in many countries) the laws that regulate the construction, sale and management of condominium projects are more elaborate than those relating to apartment buildings. Condominium laws have often specific regulations to protect buyers' rights, but those regulations will not benefit apartment buyers.

However it is not always possible to do so, and in Thailand there are many reasons why a high rise project may be developed in the form of an apartment building instead of a condominium. One reason we have already discussed in Chapter 10 (a building developed on Crown Property Bureau land). Another reason why a developer may chose to develop a project as an apartment building instead of a condominium is that apartment buildings are not subject to the 49% foreign quota in the Condominium Act. An apartment building may have up to 100% foreign tenants, as opposed to a condominium building, which is limited to 49% foreign buyers. This will rarely happen in Bangkok where the ratio of foreign buyers rarely reaches 49% but often be the case in beach resorts (especially Pattaya, Phuket and Koh Samui) where potential foreign buyers outnumber Thai buyers.

---

[145] Reminder: lease may only be registered for 30 years in Thailand for the time being

Chapter 45   How are Rights to Condominium Units

                    Evidenced?

In Thailand a condominium is defined as *"A building that can have its separate portions sold to individuals or groups for personal property ownership"*. For the time being, the Thai Condominium Act provides only for vertical condominiums, and the concept of horizontal condominiums is not yet mentioned in the law. However, in ruling Number NorRor 0601/1466 the Council of State of Thailand stated that a condominium under the Condominium Act can be a group of buildings situated under the same title deed. According to this ruling, it is possible to design a condominium in the form of low rise buildings.

The area of a condominium building is divided into two distinct areas: the private area, which may include residential as well as commercial space and common area consisting of the facilities, parking area, utilities and land[146] on which the condominium is built.

---

[146] Condominium law prohibits foreigners from owning more than 49% of a condominium building, because the Condominium Juristic Person owns the

The commercial area is defined as the part of a condominium building directed toward business. Since the enforcement of the amendment of the Condominium Act (No. 4) on 4 July 2008, the commercial area of a condominium building is limited to specified areas of the building and must have an independent entrance. Furthermore, the business operations of the commercial area must not disrupt the peaceful living of residents.

When the building is more than 90% complete, the developer will file an application for a condominium license. Upon completion of the condominium project and approval of the application, the Land Department will issue the condominium titles for the private areas (residential and commercial), while the common areas become the property of the Condominium Juristic Person.

Once the condominium is completed and ready for transfer, the Condominium Act requires developers to register the Condominium Juristic Person, the legal entity established to own, manage and maintain the common property. The Condominium Juristic Person will have articles of association that must be registered with the Land Department. The articles must conform to the Condominium Act and set the Condominium Juristic Person's objectives, the rights and duties of the board and procedures for holding co-owners' meetings, etc. The Condominium Juristic Person must have a manager to handle day-to-day affairs and act as the Condominium Juristic Person's representative. The manager must act within the framework of the law, the Condominium Juristic Person by-laws, the resolutions of the co-owners' meetings and under the supervision of the board of directors, which is elected by the co-owners annually.

From a financial point of view, the Condominium Juristic Person will have at its disposition two sources of funds. First, the Condominium Juristic Person will receive the sinking fund. This is a

---

land upon which a condominium is built and each unit owner owns a fraction of the land.

reserve fund established with contributions made by condominium buyers to the Condominium Juristic Person at the time when the developer first transfers the condominium units to buyers. The Condominium Juristic Person has the duty of maintaining the sinking fund for the duration of the condominium and the money may be used only under very specific circumstances, such as special maintenance or replacement in the common areas. The board of directors has very limited powers over how to invest the sinking fund and may either choose to put the money into a long-term savings account or purchase government bonds.

The Condominium Juristic Person will also receive maintenance fees. These are the monthly fees paid by each private unit's owner to the Condominium Juristic Person in order to ensure the day-to-day operation of the common areas. In general, maintenance fees must be paid once per year in advance.

The Or. Chor. 2 or Condominium Title is the document serving to evidence freehold ownership rights to a private unit in a condominium building. The Or. Chor. 2[147] title is issued by the Land Department. Note that the title only represents ownership rights to the unit volume (height, length and width area) and of the interior partitions included in this volume. Private ownership rights do not extend to the external walls or to the structure of the condominium building, which are owned by the co-owners and managed by the Condominium Juristic Person. An Or.Chor 2 title will state the exact floor area of the private unit. In addition, the title will also mention the ground area of the common land and the percentage interest of the common property held by that particular unit (including, land, building structure, stairwells, lobby, swimming pool and recreation areas). This percentage also represents the value of the voting interest in the Condominium Juristic Person or owners' association.

The front page of a condominium title contains information about the location of the unit, the details of the property and the name of the first owner. The back page of a condominium title is

---

[147] Please see Appendixes 9 and 10 for a representation of an actual Or.Chor.2

similar to the Chanote and contains a record of all transactions registered on the title.

Chapter 46 Foreign Freehold Ownership of Condominiums

As previously discussed, purchasing a condominium is a straightforward process, because Thai laws do allow foreign buyers to own condominiums freehold with only one limitation.

Because the units buyers in a condominium building also receive in addition to the ownership of their individual unit a percentage interest into the common property that includes the land on which the condominium building is erected, the ratio of foreign ownership in any condominium building is limited to 49% of the total private area of any condominium building at any one time, because foreigners may not own land freehold[148] for residential use in Thailand. Note that the 49% quota is calculated based on the surface of the private sellable area, not the number of units. If you are purchasing a condominium in Bangkok, the 49% foreign ownership quota is generally not a problem as Thai buyers are heavily represented among purchasers.

---

[148] Foreigners who invest THB 40 million in Thailand may be authorized to own 1 rai of residential land freehold to build a private residence.

However, if you are purchasing a condominium in Phuket or Pattaya, there are generally more foreign buyers than the 49% foreign quota may accommodate. If you wish to buy a condominium freehold in a resort area in Thailand, you'll have no option other than to purchase off plan at the time of the project launch if you want a guarantee your unit will be in the foreign quota. If you're purchasing in a building that is already completed, check the ratio of foreign ownership in this building before paying a deposit to your seller. Information about the level of foreign ownership in a particular condominium may be requested at the condominium juristic person[149] office in the building.

Foreign buyers must fulfill the following legal requirements in order to be eligible to purchase a condominium:

- Ability to enter Thailand legally; *and*
- Proof that the funds used to purchase the condominium were remitted from overseas in foreign currency. Without such proof, the Land Department will not permit the transfer of ownership of a condominium to a foreign buyer.

Foreigners who have resident status[150] (Blue Resident Book) are exempted from the obligation to remit foreign currency from overseas. Legal residents are also allowed to buy in baht and even to borrow money from a Thai bank to finance their purchase.

When transferring foreign currency from overseas, you should follow the following rules. The foreign currency:

- must be of an amount at least equivalent to the purchase price of the condominium, or the condominium appraisal price; *and*
- remitted from overseas; *and*
- brought into Thailand; *and*
- exchanged in Thailand; *and*

---

[149] The Juristic Person is the Co-Owners association
[150] Residents in the sense of the Thai Immigration Act only

- either be from a bank account in the name of the foreign buyer; *or* transferred to a bank account in Thailand in the name of the foreign buyer.

When requesting your bank to initiate the transfer, have them add the following details to the part of the wire transfer form reserved for remarks: *"as payment due on the purchase price of condominium unit no. [000] in the [000] Condominium"*. The number of the unit and the name of the condominium are not mandatory, but recommended.

If you are purchasing in co-ownership with a foreign spouse and the money is not sent from a joint account in the names of both spouses, mention that the transfer is also made on *"behalf of the [first name] and[surname] of the spouse"*. Here again, this remark is not mandatory, but recommended.

If a foreign buyer purchases a condominium in co-ownership with a Thai person, such as a Thai spouse, *and* if the condominium unit title deed is to be transferred and registered to both co-owners names[151], then the foreign buyer will only need to remit half of the purchase price of the condominium in foreign currency.

The other half of the condominium price may be paid in Thai baht, because it is the Thai buyer's contribution to the purchase of the Thai share of co-ownership. Note that the Thai co-owner could apply for a loan with a Thai bank to finance the payment of his/her share of the condominium unit purchase price. In this case, however, the bank will want the mortgage to apply to the whole condominium unit.

The document the foreign condominium buyer will have to use in order to prove the transfer of the purchase money in foreign currency is called the Foreign Exchange Transaction

---

[151] The names of the foreign and Thai co-owners are both registered on the back of the condominium title as co-owners of the unit.

Form[152] (FETF) and replaces the Tor. Tor. Sam. If you transfer the foreign currency directly into the bank account of the developer, the developer will request that its bank issue an FETF for each transfer. The same will happen if you transfer the money via your lawyer's account with the lawyer being responsible for applying on your behalf for the FETF. If you transfer the foreign currency into your personal account in Thailand, you will have to apply for the FETF yourself. Be careful to do it upon each transfer and don't wait until the last minute, because banks need an average of 24 to 48 hours to issue an FETF.

Nowadays, minimum amounts are no longer applicable when purchasing condominium. If you have made transfers below the amount of USD 20,000 per transfer you may request your bank to issue a Foreign Currency Exchange Advice for any small amounts (including small monthly installments of 500 or 1000 Euro). Banks will charge a fee for this service of around THB 200 per certificate.

If you lose your FETF or your Foreign Currency Exchange Advices before the transaction at the Land Department, you may request that the bank re-issue duplicates, as long as you still have the reference for the transaction. In general, the bank will request that you declare the loss of the original documents with the police before issuing duplicates. If the transfer took place more than two years ago, some banks will not issue duplicates, but others will. This process will take from 10 days to a month or more if the documents to be duplicated are older than 2 years, and the bank might charge you for the service.

If you lose your copy of the FETF after the transfer of the condominium at the Land Department, you may go to the Land Department anytime and request a copy of the FETF that the Land Department will have on file. Here again, you will be asked to pay a small government fee for the service.

The following must be strictly avoided when transferring your money:

---

[152] Please see Chapter 21 for more information on the FETF

- Do not exchange your foreign currency for Thai baht on the international market, because you will not qualify to purchase a condominium freehold.
- If you transfer directly to the account of the developer in Thailand or through the account of a lawyer, do not send the money from an account that's not under your own name (company account, pension fund, trust fund, etc.). Your name simply appears at one end of the transaction or the other.

If you are married, you have two options when buying the condominium. Firstly, you may wish to buy the condominium in co-ownership with your foreign or Thai spouse. You can do this even if the name of your spouse was not included in the original purchase and sale agreement executed with the developer, as long as you decide upon this matter before the registration of the transfer at the Land Department.

In cases where both spouses are foreigners, the foreign currency for the condominium purchase does not necessarily need to be transferred from a joint account under both names. However, if you transfer from your own personal account, you'll need to request that your bank add the remark that the transfer was made on behalf of you and your spouse (it's not mandatory, but it's recommended). In order to register the condominium under both names, you'll need to produce a certified copy of your marriage certificate and a certified translation of this certificate if it's in a language other than English.

Note that if you are married, you need to declare your status to the developer, or to your lawyer, or to the government official at the time of the purchase. Forgetting to provide this information prior to the registration of the transaction at the Land Department in order to avoid the formalities mentioned above is a bad idea, because failure to disclose information is deemed a false statement to a government official, which is a criminal offence. If you'd rather not share the ownership of the condominium with your spouse, then you must require your spouse to sign a form authorizing you to purchase the condominium solely in your name.

For those of you who are considering placing your purchase through an offshore company, there are definite benefits to such a method of purchase. The first advantage of purchasing your condominium freehold through an offshore company is visible in the event of resale to another foreign buyer who is not a tax resident in Thailand. In this case, you might choose either to sell the condominium unit or to transfer the ownership of the company to your buyer instead. In this last case, the transaction will consist of the sale of the shares of a foreign company to a foreign buyer. If neither the seller nor buyer is a tax resident of Thailand, the transaction will happen offshore and the resulting profits will not be taxable in Thailand. Furthermore, if you choose your offshore jurisdiction carefully, the amount won't be taxable overseas, either. The second advantage is that it makes your succession easier to manage, because your estate will consist of movable property (i.e. the shares of the company owing the condominium), not immovable property (the condominium itself). But as always no solution is perfect and there will also be drawback, such as the fact that the offshore company will be subjected to the Land and House Tax. Also if the offshore company is renting out the property then there will be the issue of corporate income tax and withholding tax.

Can a Thai company purchase a condominium? Of course it can, but the issue of Thai nominee shareholders must be carefully considered. Can you ask a Thai person to purchase a condominium on your behalf? Here you need to be careful and be aware of a new amendment introduced by the Condominium Act (4) in 2008. Any person who owns a condominium unit on behalf of a foreigner, regardless of whether the foreigner is entitled to own a condominium unit or not, may face imprisonment of no more than 2 years or a maximum fine of no more than THB 20,000, or both.

A foreign or Thai investor purchasing a condominium using a company (whether a foreign company or a Thai one) should be aware of the following drawbacks.

The company will have to pay both house and land taxes at a rate of 12.5% per year based on the condominium unit's annually appraised lease value or the actual rental value if the unit is rented out, whichever is higher. The tax is due even if the company does not rent out the property, or if a director or shareholder of the company is living in the unit rent-free, because the land and house tax exemption applies only to individual owners using the condominium unit as a principal residence. It does not, however, apply to companies because companies don't *"live"* in condominiums.

Note that the land and house tax may soon be repealed to be replaced by a real property tax. Once this new property tax is enforced, any condominium will be subject to a yearly tax that should be calculated as follows: Residential Assets = 0.1% of the assessed value and Commercial Assets = 0.5% of the assessed value. In the absence of more details, we assume that a condominium unit owned by a company will be deemed a commercial asset and taxed at the 0.5% rate.

One issue requiring serious consideration by foreign buyers is the following: while foreign citizens can legally purchase as many condominium units as they wish or can afford to purchase, they may not rent out those condominium units. Indeed, renting out immovable property is a service business (landlord service). Now the problem is that all services businesses are controlled under the Foreign Business Act, List 3. Therefore, a foreign buyer who has purchased several condominium units to rent out may not do so without first applying for a Foreign Business License to provide property owner services.

The catch is that the Business Development Department does not for the time being grant foreign business licenses to foreign investors for property owner services, because this activity does not bring any technological transfer.

Chapter 47   **Contractual Requirements Applicable when**

Purchasing a Condominium

What are the minimal contractual requirements applicable to the sale of a condominium? The sale of a condominium is void unless drafted in writing and registered with a government official. Similarly, agreements to buy, sell or promises to buy or sell immovable property are not enforceable unless drafted in writing.

The minimal contractual requirements applicable when purchasing a condominium will depend upon whether the buyer is purchasing the unit from a private individual or directly from the developer.

When a buyer purchases a condominium on the resale market, the parties are free to use any contract form they wish and no special requirements are applicable except for the requirements mentioned above. However, buyers who purchase from a developer are subject to additional requirements set forth by the government to protect buyers.

The Ministry of Interior has drafted and issued a Standard Contract Form (hereinafter referred to as the *"MI Standard Form"*). In the past, developers were free to choose whether or not to use this form with their customers. They were also free to modify the content of the agreement even in disfavor of the buyer whenever they chose to use the form.

One of the most remarkable features of the newly Amended Condominium Act dated 4 July 2008 is the establishment of the MI Standard Form as the benchmark against which all developers' agreements will be examined and compared. According to the Condominium Act, if developers use a different contract form with different content from the MI Standard Form containing any provisions:

- contrary to, *or* different from the provisions of the MI Standard Form, *and*
- to the disadvantage of the buyer,

Then those provisions shall be null and void and not enforceable. In addition, developers who use a contract deemed as unfair to their buyers may be subject to a fine. Although this amendment is certainly welcome news for buyers, I can't help but wonder why the government didn't simply make the use of the MI Standard Form mandatory, which would have made things easier.

Another welcome development for buyers since the enforcement of the new Condominium Act is that developers are now legally bound by the commercial documents used to market or commercialize their projects. Developers are now liable to abide by their advertising claims and must retain copies of all condominium advertisements, whether in the form of text, photos, or any other format, until all the condominium units are sold.

Upon transferring the common area to the Condominium Juristic Person, the developer will submit at least one set of all advertising documents to the Condominium Juristic Person, including all images, pictures, and information the developer submitted to the Land Department at the time of the condominium registration. Furthermore, the documents submitted by the developer at the time of the condominium registration must be the same as the documents the developer used in all advertisements or contractual documents.

All advertising materials and all information used by a developer to commercialize the project are now deemed part of the condominium sale and purchase agreement. In cases of discrepancies between the commercial documents and the finished condominium, buyers will be entitled to claim damages from their developers. In addition, developers who violate this regulation shall also be subject to fines.

The new Condominium Act also puts an end to the established practice of developers charging administrative fees in cases of transfer or assignment of the condominium sale and purchase agreement. While buyers of condominiums could transfer their condominium units prior to completion and transfer at the Land Department if they wished to do so, developers have consistently requested their buyers to pay an administrative fee (from THB 100,000 to THB 200,000, depending upon the developer) in order to do so.

Now that the MI Standard Form has become the benchmark, developers may not claim these fees anymore. Pursuant to Section 4.5, *"the Buyer has the right to transfer his/her rights according to this contract to another person by sending a written document to the Seller. And the Seller has agreed not to request any additional expenses"*. As a result, developers will no longer be allowed to charge administrative fees or any other additional expenses from condominium buyers who transfer their agreements to third-party buyers prior to the transfer of the condominium at the Land Department.

Depending on the interpretation of the Land Department officer, buyers who have executed a condominium sale and purchase agreement with a developer prior to 4 July 2008 may still be required to pay the administrative fee in cases of assignment of their contract prior to the transfer of the unit. Buyers who executed their agreement with a developer after 4 July 2008, however, can no longer be required to pay the administrative fee

Another controversial practice that will have to stop is the inconsiderate use of the construction extension clause by developers. Briefly, the construction extension period is a contractual clause allowing developers to delay the delivery of a condominium past the initial construction date without being in default and without being liable to pay damages or interest to the buyers.

Until now, developers' agreements have been very liberal as to the use of the extension period and developers have been used to delay the delivery of their projects by one or two years without having to pay any indemnity to their buyers. Here again, the MI Standard Form has set strict requirements as to the criteria to be fulfilled for a developer to claim the use of the construction extension period.

Firstly, Section 5.3 of the MI Standard Form regulates this matter by limiting the maximum duration of the extension of the construction period to one year.

Secondly, Section 5.3 of the MI Standard Form further limits the duration of the construction extension period by stipulating it must be no longer than the period of time during which the construction has been stopped or delayed.

In other words, developers will no longer be able to claim construction extension periods any longer than the duration of the actual work suspension. This also means developers will have to provide their buyers with detailed explanations as to the cause of the suspension of work and the duration of the suspension of. In addition, Section 5.3 of the MI Standard Form requires developers to inform buyers of the work suspension in writing within seven days from the date when the work suspension has ended, and developers who fail to do so will be deemed as having forfeited the right to extend the construction period.

In a nutshell, developers will no longer be able to claim the extension of the construction period globally as they have been doing up to now. Nor will developers be able to send to their buyers a letter at the end of the initial construction period to claim a single extension period covering all work suspension periods affecting the project. From now on, developers will have to send a notice to their buyers in relation to each work suspension for which they intend to claim an extension of the construction period. Note that this interpretation of Section 5.3 in the MI Standard Form has been confirmed by the Land Department.

Finally, developers can only claim the benefit of an extension of the construction period if the construction was suspended or delayed by no fault of the developer. Unfortunately, the MI Standard Form does not define the concept of "fault of the developer".

The last interesting point is Section 5.3 of the MI Standard Form's provision that a developer may not claim an extension of the construction period if the developer has agreed to the buyer's moving in and occupancy of the condominium unit on a specific date. Although I've never seen a developer agreement containing a *"ready to move in on the..."* clause, developers have frequently made such promises in their publicity is the past and this publicity is now deemed a part of the sales and purchase agreement.

What happens if a buyer is in default or late with his payments? Can the developer request default buyers to pay interest? If you are in default of payment, the developer may certainly request you to pay interest. Default buyers, however, need to confirm that the interest required of them conforms to the rates stipulated by the MI Standard Form. Pursuant to Section 7.1 of the MI Standard Form, interest rates applicable to a buyer in default may not exceed 15% per year. Furthermore, the total amount of interest paid by the buyer in default to the developer may not exceed 10% of the condominium unit purchase price. When reviewing your sale and purchase agreement, always verify that the amount of interest your developer requests you to pay conforms to the standards of the MI Standard

Form. Also verify that the amount of interest you would have to pay to the developer if in default does not exceed the amount the developer would have to pay you if in default. Indeed, the MI Standard Form also stipulates that the interest to be paid by the buyer may not exceed the interest the developer would pay to the buyer if the developer were in default.

When can a developer terminate a buyer's agreement? According to the MI Standard Form, the developer may only terminate the agreement with the buyer in the following three cases:

1. When the condominium purchase and sales agreement requires buyers to pay the full purchase price of the unit in one installment and the buyer is late with the payment of this installment and fails to clear the default within 30 days after receipt of the developer's notification letter.[153]

2. When the condominium purchase and sales agreement requires the buyer to pay the purchase price in less than 24 installments and the buyer is late in paying an installment representing more than 12.5% of the purchase price and fails to clear the default within 30 days after receipt of the developer's notification letter[154].

3. When the condominium purchase and sales agreement requires the buyer to pay the purchase price in 24 or more installments and the buyer is late in paying three consecutive installments due on the purchase price and fails to clear the default within 30 days after receipt of the developer's notification letter[155].

One problem in the current version of Section 7.2.2 of the MI Standard Form is that it doesn't appear to allow a developer to terminate a condominium purchase and sales agreement providing 24 or more installments in the event that a buyer fails to pay one

---

[153] MI Standard Form, Section 7.2.1
[154] MI Standard Form, Section 7.2.3
[155] MI Standard Form, Section 7.2.2

installment only even if it is the last installment that represents 60 or 70% of the unit purchase price. One suggestion would be for developers to modify section 7.2.2 as follows: "*...when the buyer is in default for payment of three consecutive installments, or <u>one installment equivalent or in excess of three installments</u>*". That clause should not be deemed as putting the buyer at a disadvantage as its purpose is to clarify the agreement and break a potential deadlock.

What are the buyer's options when the developer is in default? A developer is in default when:

1. The developer is unable to complete the condominium and transfer the units to the buyer within the contractual period for the completion; *and*

2. The developer cannot claim the benefit of the construction extension period.

If the developer is in default, the buyers first option is to terminate the agreement and request the developer to refund all of the buyer's payments with interest at the rate agreed upon in the agreement.

The rate of the interest due to the buyer may not be inferior to the rate of interest that the buyer would have to pay to the developer if the buyer were in default. The maximum rate applicable is 15%, but the total interest due the buyer may not exceed 10% of the condominium purchase price. In addition and pursuant to Section 7.3.1 of the MI Standard Form, the buyer may claim other damages.

If the buyer does not wish to terminate the agreement, Section 7.3.2 allows the option of requesting the developer to pay a daily fine. This daily fine will be as agreed upon with the developer but may not be less than 0.1% or more than 10% of the purchase price of the buyer's condominium unit. The total maximum fine to be paid by the developer may not exceed 10% of the purchase price of the condominium unit.

The MI Standard Form does not expressly permit developers to offset the daily fine against the payment of the balance due by the buyer on the purchase price of the condominium unit. Nor does it expressly require the developer to commence daily payment of the fine upon receipt of notification from the buyer or stipulate whether the developer may pay the fine upon transfer of the unit to the buyer.

According to the Land Department, the developer does not need to pay the daily fine immediately and may chose to make payment by offsetting the amount of the daily fine against the balance due by the buyer on the purchase price.

Once the amount of the daily fine due by the developer has reached 10% of the purchase price of the condominium unit, and if, at this time, the developer has not yet completed the condominium, then the buyer may once again choose to terminate the agreement and claim the refund of all payments made to the developer with interest. In this case, and if the developer has already paid a daily fine to the buyer, the developer is authorized to deduct the payment made as a daily fine from the interest due to the buyer.

What are the benchmarks set by the MI Standard Form in relation to warranty for defects? The minimum period of warranty for the structural components of the condominium is set at five years. The minimum period of warranty for other parts of the condominium is set at two years. These defects must be repaired within no more than 30 days from receipt of the buyer's written notice, or immediately after the receipt of the buyer's notice if the defects are high priority defects. If the developers fail to repair the defects, the buyer may hire a third-party contractor to perform the work and request the developer to reimburse the price paid to the contractor.

Chapter 48   Solving the 49% Foreign Quota Issue

One of the legal headaches limiting foreign buyers' access to the Thai real estate market is that Thai laws currently limit foreign freehold purchases of condominium units to a percentage of the total privately-owned area of a condominium building.

While this limitation is rarely a problem in Bangkok, it has become a serious handicap for condominium developers in resort areas, such as Koh Samui, Pattaya and Phuket, where foreign buyers often outnumber Thai ones. As a result of this restriction, developers in resort areas are building up a stock of unsold units that Thai buyers are not interested in purchasing and that foreign buyers cannot purchase because of the current legal restrictions.

Why the 49% quota? The logic behind these restrictions on foreign ownership is that any buyer (Thai or foreign) who purchases a condominium will receive:

(1) the freehold ownership of their unit, and
(2) a *"ratio of ownership in the common property* _____% _in 10,000"._

The common property of a condominium, collectively owned by the co-owners (all the condominium unit owners), includes:

(1) The land on which the building is situated,
(2) The land for mutual benefit,
(3) The structures of the building,
(4) Part of the building for mutual benefit,
(5) Tools and utilities for mutual benefit,
(6) Places for common services, and
(7) Other properties for mutual benefit. Act No. 4 adds the following properties as common property of a condominium including
(8) The office of the condominium juristic person,
(9) Immovable properties with obligations,
(10) Structures or systems for security or environmental purposes in the condominium (i.e. electricity, ventilation, air-conditioning, drainage and disposal and fire prevention systems etc.), and
(11) Other assets maintained by the common expenses collected from the co-owners, the condominium building itself, all the facilities and also the land on which the condominium is built

If the Government was to authorize a quota of more than 49% foreign ownership in condominium buildings (for example 70% foreign quota) then this measure would have the immediate consequence of giving foreigners a majority interest in the Common Property, which includes the land on which the condominium is built this would conflict with Thai legal prohibition on foreign freehold land ownership

Also, the ownership of a condominium unit also includes the right to become a member of the juristic person (or the co-owners' association) that manages the common property on behalf of the co-owners. This comes with the right of vote attached to the ratio of ownership of the common property and the right to be elected as a member of the committee of the juristic person, which may create more problems under Thai laws.

Of course, increase or simply lift the foreign quota would be the easiest solution but things are not always so easy in Thailand, especially in a political context where the Thai press delights in sensationalizing the *"foreign menace"* to Thai land.

How then can we resolve this conflict in a way that would permit foreign buyers to purchase condominiums beyond the 49 percent foreign quota, without gaining control of the land?

A simple solution to this problem would be to allow foreign purchasers to buy units beyond the 49 percent quota, providing they agree to have their Common Property co-ownership rights suspended.

If a foreign buyer were to purchase a condominium unit in excess of the foreign quota, the buyer could be required to sign prior to the transfer of the unit a Letter of Affirmation at the Land Department. The content of the letter could be as follows:

Pre-Purchase Letter of Affirmation
For Foreign Buyers Purchasing Condominium Units in Excess of 49%
Ratio of Foreign Ownership

At_____
Date_____ Month_____ Year_____
I, Mr./Mrs./Ms._____ and Mr./Mrs./Ms._____ ,
the foreign Buyer of the Condominium Unit No._____,
Floor_____,
Condominium Name_____ ,
Soi_____, Street/Road_____, District____
_____,
Province _____, do hereby confirm that I/we have been notified by a competent officer that the abovementioned condominium unit is being sold and transferred in excess of the 49% ratio of foreign ownership in this building and I/we understand and accept that, as a result of this sale, the exercise of the rights attached to the ratio of Common Property ownership in the aforementioned condominium unit shall be suspended for as long as the condominium unit I/we purchased is in excess of the maximum foreign ownership ratio set forth in Section 19 bis. I/We understand that I/we shall not have any rights of co-ownership of the Common Property and shall not be

allowed to exercise the right to vote associated with our ratio of Common Property co-ownership and that I/we shall furthermore not be allowed to become a member of the Juristic Person Committee or hold any other rights resulting from our share of co-ownership of the Common Property for as long as our condominium unit is in excess of the aforementioned maximum ratio.

I/We further understand and agree that while the exercise of my/our rights are suspended I/we shall still be bound to exercise the resulting duties attached to our co-ownership of the Common Property ratio such as, but not limited to, payment of the annual common management fees, obey the Juristic Person rules and regulations and so on...

In addition, mention would be made on the Condominium Title stipulating that this unit is transferred in excess of the maximum foreign ratio and that the right of a share of the co-ownership of the common property is suspended and without effect for as long as this unit is in excess of the quota. Of course, a few articles of the Condominium Act would also have to be modified if such a change were to be introduced.

In this way, foreign buyers could be allowed to purchase condominium units in excess of the current limitations on foreign ownership without taking majority control of the common property that includes the land owned by the co-owners, as their rights of co-ownership of the common property would have been suspended along with their right to participate in the management of the juristic person.

The pitfall of the proposed solution is that it would create two classes of freehold owners. On the one hand, we would have foreign and Thai buyers with co-ownership rights in the common property and the right of participation in the affairs of the juristic person, including voting rights and right to become member of the committee. On the other hand, we would have foreign buyers without co-ownership rights (or which rights are temporarily freeze or suspended).

It is a matter of fact, however, that many condominium owners (Thais and foreigners) are more concerned about the rights attached to their units than by the rights of co-ownership attached to the common property and the right to participate in the activities of the condominium building juristic person. In any case, buyers rarely attend condominium juristic person meetings. This is especially true for condominiums located in resort areas. The fact that the proceedings take place in Thai is another deterrent for foreign buyers.

Therefore, I believe that most foreign buyers who purchase units with suspended rights would not object to these restrictions.

Note that the restrictions would not be permanent, but only for as long as there are foreign owners in excess of the 49 percent limit. If foreign ownership were to fall below the 49 percent limit, the exercise of the rights attached to the unit would be reinstated. And if the unit were sold on to a Thai buyer, the rights attached to the common property ownership would be immediately reinstated.

While imperfect, this solution would certainly be preferable to the status quo.

PART V

SELECTED TAX ISSUES PERTAINING TO IMMOVABLE PROPERTY

Chapter 49   **Taxes and Government Fees Applicable to the**

Sale of Immovable Property

In this section, we'll review the taxes and government fees applicable at the Land Department when purchasing or reselling an immovable property.

The first tax applicable in cases involving the sale of a condominium is the Special Business Tax ("SBT"). The SBT is a tax collected from income generated by specific businesses as specified in the Revenue Code including the sale of immovable property (land, condominiums, or houses). The SBT applies only to the transfer of immovable property made within the first 5 years of ownership.

The SBT no longer applies beyond 5 years. Therefore, when you purchase from a developer, the developer will be liable for the payment of the SBT. The SBT rate is 3% or 3.3% when local taxes are included. For the time being (until 28 March 2010[156]) this rate has been reduced to 0.1% or 0.11% with the inclusion of the local tax on

---

[156] Originally the tax break was granted until 28 March 2009 but the measure has been extended until 2010 due to difficult economical situation

specific transactions. The amount of the SBT is calculated on the basis of the registered sale and purchase price (i.e. the sale and purchase price declared by the parties at the Land Department).

Another tax is the withholding tax. The withholding tax represents a prepayment of the income tax of the developer or the seller (in cases of resale) to be paid at the Land Department at the time of the transfer and is calculated on the basis of the registered sale price or the government assessed value, whichever is the highest. The rate is 1% if the seller is a company, and calculated at a progressive rate if the seller is an individual. When purchasing from a developer, the developer will be liable for the cost of the withholding tax. When purchasing in a resale transaction, however, the payment of this tax will depend upon the agreement of the parties.

There are also government fees (or transfer duties) which are calculated on the basis of the official assessed value as tax due upon the transfer of immovable property. Government fees are normally 2% of the assessed value, but have been temporarily reduced to 0.01% until 28 March 2010 for certain transactions. For example, the government fee reductions do not apply to the transfer of undeveloped land.

Finally, there are the stamp duties, payable only if the SBT does not apply.

When you purchase from a developer, the developer will generally absorb the cost of the Special Business Tax and of the withholding tax. If you buy from a developer, the government fees and stamp duty costs will be shared by the buyer and seller at the rate of 50% each[157]. When you purchase from an individual, the seller will want the buyer to absorb the cost of all taxes.

---

[157] These rates are the standard rates applicable as per the Ministry of Interior contract form. If a developer agreement contains provisions contrary to the Ministry's standard form and to the disadvantage of the buyer, then those provisions will be null and void and unenforceable.

Chapter 50   Examples of Taxation at the Land Department

In this chapter, we'll review a few examples of the taxes and fees payable at the Land Department upon the sale and purchase of a condominium.

Note the following:

- The method and principles of calculation are in general the same whether the object of the transaction is a condominium, house, building or land.
- The temporarily reduced government fees are not applicable to all transactions. For example, they do not apply to undeveloped land transactions.
- The seller is an individual in the first two examples and a company in examples three and four.

First Example
Condominium

Seller	*= Individual*	
Years of Ownership	*= 3 years*	
Assessed value	*= THB 9,000,000*	
Sale Price	*= THB 13,000,000*	

A.
TRANSACTION OCCURS
BEFORE END OF MARCH 2010

Government Fees		
Transfer fee before March 2010 = 0.01%	Assessed Value	THB 900
Stamp duty (1/200 sale price)	Not Applicable	--------------
Taxes		
Special Business Tax before March 2010 = 0.11%	Sale Price	THB 14,300
Withholding tax = progressive tax rate	Assessed Value Mitigated	THB 249,000
TOTAL		THB 264,200

B.
TRANSACTION OCCURS
AFTER END OF MARCH 2010

Government Fees		
Transfer fee after March 2010 = 2%	Assessed Value	THB 180,000
Stamp duty (1/200 sale price)	Not Applicable	--------------
Taxes		
Special Business Tax after March 2010 = 3.3%	Sale Price	THB 429,000
Withholding tax = progressive tax rate	Assessed Value Mitigated	THB 249,000
TOTAL		THB 858,000

Second Example

Seller	*= Individual*
Years of Ownership	*= 6 years*
Assessed value	*= THB 9,000,000*
Sale Price	*= THB 13,000,000*

C.
TRANSACTION OCCURS
BEFORE END OF MARCH 2010

Government Fees		
Transfer fee before March of 2010 = *0.01%*	Assessed Value	THB 900
Stamp duty (1/200 sale price)	Sale Price	THB 65,000
Taxes		
Special Business Tax before March 2010 = *0.11%*	Not Applicable	---------------
Withholding tax = progressive tax rate	Assessed Value Mitigated	THB 390,000
TOTAL		THB 455,900

D.
TRANSACTION OCCURS
AFTER END OF MARCH 2010

Government Fees		
Transfer fee after March of 2010 = 2%	Assessed Value	THB 180,000
Stamp duty (1/200 sale price)	Sale Price	THB 65,000
Taxes		
Special Business Tax after March 2010 = *3.3%*	Not Applicable	---------------
Withholding tax = progressive tax rate	Assessed Value Mitigated	THB 390,000
TOTAL		THB 635,000

Next are the taxes and governments fees to be paid at the Land Department when the seller is a company Here again we envisage a sale before and after end of March 2010.

Third Example

Seller	*= Company*
Years of Ownership	*= 3 years*
Assessed value	*= THB 9,000,000*
Sale Price	*= THB 13,000,000*

E.
TRANSACTION OCCURS
BEFORE END OF MARCH 2010

Government Fees		
Transfer fee before March of 2010 = 0.01%	Assessed Value	THB 900
Stamp duty (1/200 sale price)	Not Applicable	-------------
Taxes		
Special Business Tax before March 2010 = 0.11%	Sale Price	THB 14,300
Withholding tax = 1%	Assessed Price or Sale Price, whichever is higher	THB 130,000
TOTAL		THB 145,200

F.
TRANSACTION OCCURS
AFTER END OF MARCH 2010

Government Fees		
Transfer fee after March 2010 = 2%	Assessed Value	THB 180,000
Stamp duty (1/200 sale price)	Not Applicable	-------------
Taxes		
Special Business Tax after March 2010 = 3.3%	Sale Price	THB 429,000
Withholding tax = 1%	Assessed Price or Sale Price, whichever is higher	THB 130,000
TOTAL		THB 739,000

Fourth Example
Condominium

Seller	*= Company*	
Years of Ownership	*= 6 years*	
Assessed value	*= THB 9,000,000*	
Sale Price	*= THB 13,000,000*	

G.
TRANSACTION OCCURS
BEFORE END OF MARCH, 2010

Government Fees		
Transfer fee before March 2010 = 0.01%	Assessed Value	THB 900
Stamp (1/200 sale price)	Sale Price	THB 65,000
Taxes		
Special business tax before March 2010 = 0.11%	Not Applicable	---------------
Withholding tax = 1%	Assessed Price or Sale Price, whichever is higher	THB 130,000
TOTAL		THB 195,900

H.
TRANSACTION OCCURS
AFTER END OF MARCH, 2010

Government Fees		
Transfer fee _after March 2010_ = 2%	Assessed Value	THB 180,000
Stamp duty (1/200 sale price)	Sale Price	THB 65,000
Taxes		
Special business tax _after March 2010_ = 3.3%	Not Applicable	---------------
Withholding tax = 1%	Assessed Price or Sale Price, whichever is higher	THB 130,000
TOTAL		THB 375,000

Note that individual sellers will (with exceptions) pay their final tax on the sale at the Land Department. In contrast, companies will have to declare the sale of the condominium in their corporate income tax returns.

Chapter 51   Understanding How the Withholding Tax

Payable by an Individual Seller is Calculated

How does the Land Department actually calculate the withholding tax payable by individuals? The calculation of the withholding tax payable at the close of a condominium sale is complicated, because individuals are allowed to make lump sum deduction, wherein rates depend upon the years of ownership. In other words, the calculation of the withholding tax for individuals is a two-step exercise.

Firstly, the Land Department will calculate the Net Assessable Income based upon the following formula:

Assessed Value – Lump Sum Expenses per year of ownership ÷ Years of Ownership = Net Assessable Income per year.

It will then apply the lump sum expenses mitigation factor.

The mitigation factor will be as follows:

- 92% for up to one year of ownership,
- 84% for more than two years of ownership,
- 77% for more than three years of ownership,
- 71% for more than four years of ownership,
- 65% for more than five years of ownership,
- 60% for more than six years of ownership,
- 55% for more than seven years of ownership and
- 50% for more than eight years of ownership.

In the example shown in Table 1B above, the assessed value was THB 9,000,000 and the seller had owned the condominium for 3 years; therefore, the mitigation factor was 77%.

The Net Assessable Income = 9,000,000[158] - 6,930,000 (9,000,000 x 77%) = 2,070,000: 3 = THB 690,000 per year.

Once the Net Assessable Income has been determined, the amount of the tax to be paid will be determined by applying the following Progressive Tax rates.

- From 0 to THB 100,000 = 5%;
- From THB 101,000 up to THB 500,000 = 10%;
- From THB 500,001 up to THB 1,000,000 = 20%;
- From THB 1,000,001 up to THB 4,000,000 = 30%;
- From THB 4,000,001 and up = 37%.

Note that the Land Department does not use the Revenue Department's new income tax table that provides for an income tax exemption of THB 0 to 150,000. According to the explanation provided by the Land Department officer, this is because the Revenue Department already grants buyers a lump sum deduction.

In our example, the seller will pay tax on the net assessable yearly income of THB 690,000 as follows:

---

[158] Assessed Value – Mitigation Factor: by years of ownership

THB 5,000 tax on the first THB 100,000 (5%),
THB 40,000 on the next THB 400,000 (10%) and
THB 38,000 on the balance.

The total taxes to be paid by the seller on the yearly assessable income will be THB 83,000 per year. Multiplying this amount by the number of years of ownership, then, is sufficient to determine the total tax to be paid at the Land Department.

The yearly income tax due is THB 83,000. Next, we multiply the yearly income tax by the number of years of ownership to obtain the final number. In this example, the amount was THB 83,000 x 3 = THB 249,000, which was the total withholding tax to be paid at the Land Department.

As explained above, the withholding tax paid at the Land Department by an individual seller may be final[159], while a company will still have to declare the sale in its corporate income tax return. This is how companies and individuals are treated differently.

---

[159] Individual sellers have the choice between: (1) considering the withholding tax paid at the land department as their final tax payment. In this case they do not need to declare the income resulting of the sale in their personal income tax. (2) Declaring the product of the sale in their personal income tax return in which case the withholding tax is a tax credit to be applied against final income tax. Check with an accountant which option is more favorable.

Chapter 52   Is There a Property Tax?

Thailand does not have a real property tax system and, for the time being, there are two local taxes applicable to people who own immovable property.

The first tax is the Local Development Tax imposed upon people who either own or possess land. This tax rate varies according to the estimated land value as appraised by the local authorities. Allowances may be granted if the owner utilizes the land for personal dwellings, animal husbandry and/or the cultivation of crops. The extent of these allowances depends upon the location of the land. It is said that the rates are so low that officials don't usually bother to collect on a yearly basis. This tax is also levied on houses, buildings or any other improvements built on the land.

Then there is the House and Land Tax, which applies to the owner of a house, building, structure or land that is either rented or put to commercial use. Taxable property under the House and Land Tax includes houses not occupied by the owner, industrial and commercial buildings and land used in connection therewith. The tax rate is 12.5% of the estimated annual rental value of the property or the actual rental value, whichever is the highest. Owner occupied residences are exempt from this tax. Note, however, that this exemption applies only to individuals, not to juristic persons, because juristic persons are deemed to use their property commercially. In other words, a company that purchases an office has to pay the tax, even if the company uses the premises to serve its own offices.

There is a project to replace the House and Land Tax with a real property tax within 2 years, wherein the rate would be from 0.01% up to 1% of the estimated value of the property, depending upon the property type. The rate would be 0.01% on agricultural land, 0.1% on personal residences; 0.5% on commercial buildings and 1% on undeveloped land. We understand that this property tax will be payable in 1 to 12 installments.

Note that it is possible to mitigate the cost of the House and Land Tax. If, for example, you rent your condominium fully furnished, you may choose to execute two agreements with your lessee. The first agreement will be for the rental of the condominium unit and the second agreement will be for the rental of the furniture and/or additional services (if any are provided). This will reduce the cost of the House and Land tax because the tax only applies to the yearly rent received from renting out the property, but not on the rental income received from renting out the furniture, etc.

If the rental agreements are executed between two individuals, there is no VAT applicable on the furniture or service agreements. If, however, the owner of the condominium is a company and if the company is registered for the VAT, then the VAT will apply at 7% on the furniture or service agreements executed between the lessor and the lessee.

For example, if you rent out your condominium fully furnished for a rental fee of THB 60,000 per month and only make one agreement with your Lessee, then you'll have to pay a yearly House and Land Tax as follows: 60,000 x 12 x 12.5% = THB 90,000.

You can save on taxes legally by simply breaking the rental fee down into two agreements. For example, the rental fees may be THB 35,000 per month for renting out the condominium and THB 25,000 for renting out the furniture. If you break the rent down in this way, the Land and House Tax will be only THB 35,000 x 12 x 12.5%= THB 52,500. If, however, the owner of the condominium is a company registered for VAT, then it will have to apply the VAT to the furniture lease agreement. Even so, the company owning the property will save money on taxes, because the Lessee supports the cost of the VAT.

The matter of the withholding tax also applies when renting out. If an individual leases a property to another individual in Thailand, the payment of the rent is not subject to withholding taxes. However, when a company is renting a property, then the company will have to deduct a withholding tax from the amount of the rent paid to the owner (whether an individual or a company). The amount withheld must be paid to the tax administration on behalf of the owner who will use the withholding tax as a tax credit against the yearly income tax. The rate of the withholding tax is 5% in Thailand. Note that when a rental fee is paid outside Thailand, the amount of the tax to be withheld from the payment is 15%. Furthermore, if you are a non-resident offered a rental guarantee by a developer, never forget to take the withholding tax into account when calculating your potential income.

Chapter 53   Did the 2008 Financial Crisis Affect Thailand as

Severely as the 1997 Crisis?

While I'm not an economist by trade, I simply cannot conclude this book without mentioning the current financial crisis, because its repercussions have been felt everywhere around the world.

As we all know, Thailand was one of the victims hit hardest by the 1997 crisis, and many of Thailand's top developers and financial institutions were bankrupted by the crisis. Earlier in 2009 I was asking whether the 2008 financial crisis would see Thailand revisiting the troubles of 1997.

My answer at the time was that 2008 found Thailand as one of the few countries in the world most likely to resist the effects of this crisis, mostly because the Bank of Thailand, other Thai banks and top Thai developers have all learned from their mistakes of the past. Thailand's impressive comparative ranking in 2008 as an investment destination (see table below) was sufficient evidence at the time that, despite a two-year political crisis, the economic fundamentals for Thailand remained positive.

Thailand A Top-ranked Investment Destination		
Category	Ranking	Source
Most Attractive Economy for Direct Foreign Investment	11/141	UNCTAD 2007-09
Most Ease in Doing Business	12/181	WB 2009/2010
Global Competitiveness Index (GCI)	28/137	WEF 2008
Cost of Living Expenses (from most to least expensive)	105/144	Mercer 2008
Best Long-term Economic Fundamentals	8/51	OCBC 2008
© Rene Philippe & Partners Ltd.		www.renephilippe.com

Not only did Thailand score well economically at the time, but it also ranked eighth (Singapore is no. 1) out of more than 50 economies most likely to overcome the economic crisis triggered by the 2008 global financial meltdown, according to a report by OCBC Bank dated 18 October 2008. Other countries listed as low-risk were Denmark (2), Norway (3), Sweden (4), Switzerland (5), South Korea (6) and Russia (7), while the United States (45), and the United Kingdom (50) were at the bottom of the list.

Thailand was passing the "seven economical indicators test" without problems. The seven economic indicators used to determine a country's long-term economic fundamentals – criteria economists believe to be the most important gauges of a country's ability to survive 'severe economic adversity' that include among other savings/GDP ratio, usable reserves, fiscal performance, and net debt/GDP. So did Thailand do as well as foretold in the various surveys?

Thai banks were indeed nearly unaffected by the 2008 financial crisis, as the direct exposure of Thai banks to subprime mortgages represented less than 0.3% of their capital.

As for developers, the fact is that none of the Thai SET listed developers went into bankruptcy, and that they completed or are about to complete projects that they started before the crisis. In 1997 you could see the physical effects of the crisis on the real estate sector in Bangkok, where hundreds building projects were abandoned and their structures left to rot. Since then, most of the abandoned sites have been taken over and construction completed, but you still have a few ghost structures left over from the 1997 crisis that are still uncompleted. This did not happen in 2008.

It did not happen in 2008 because of course Thai banks and developers have learned the lessons of the 1997 crisis and have become more careful in their business endeavors. Currently Thai banks do not grant loans to developers who have not presold at least 40 to 50% of their projects. But what really seems to have saved the real estate market is Thailand's political crisis. As a result of the political crisis, Thai listed developers had started as early as the end of 2007 to reduce the number of new projects launched in 2008 and 2009, while many medium-sized developers had already folded their projects (often before launching) by the time the global crisis started.

As a result, and in contrast to what happened in other countries, all Thai SET listed developers showed better than expected sales in 2009. Several housing and condominium projects launched in 2009 were snapped up in a few days by buyers (mostly Thais). One of the paradoxes of this crisis is that the rejection rate of individuals' loans in 2009 was lower than ever, with an average rejection rate of 8% versus 23% in normal years. The result of this is that Thai buyers have money.

However, this does not mean that the Thai real estate sector is healthy. While Thai listed developers are doing well in Bangkok, Hua Hin and Pattaya, medium and small developers are not doing as well. In particular, the small and medium developers that cater to foreign buyers are still in a lot of trouble, and my best guess is that a lot of small housing projects that target foreign customers in seaside resorts will go uncompleted.

While the real estate and banking sectors have done relatively well, other sectors of the Thai economy could not completely escape the effects of the 2008 global crisis, because it happened at a time when the country had already been suffering endemic political strife for two years. Among the sectors that have suffered most are tourism and services. Hardest hit were service businesses whose turnover depends of a constant influx of foreign investors or tourism. These sectors had already been in trouble for the past two years, and the 2008 crisis was just one more nail in the coffin.

The real victims in Thailand of the 2008 crisis were the few sectors that had been left unaffected by the political crisis, such as manufacturing and manufacturing related services. During the past 12 months we have seen many factories closing down or reducing their capacity and laying off workers.

What next? While the Thai banking and real estate sectors weathered this crisis better than the 1997 one, 2009 was a year of negative growth, with Thailand's GDP shrinking 3.2%. Most countries in the region expect a growth rate between +6 to +8% in 2010.

According to the experts, we have reached bottom. The global economy seems to be improving and Asia is on the verge of recovery. Will Thailand benefit from the recovery? This is still uncertain because the political conflict is still not resolved, the current Democrat-led government may collapse at any time, and the chances of the current coalition winning the next election is nil. Several protests will take place during the next few months and each protest has the potential to turn violent. Because the political situation in Thailand is still volatile, experts believe the Thai economy will not fully benefit from the Asian recovery and grow only about 3%.

It is not too much to hope that Thai political figures will finally recover their good sense and realize what they have done to the country. Hopefully this day will come soon and we will finally be out of the current mess. One can always dream.

CONCLUSION

While I've discussed the numerous pitfalls to purchasing offshore real estate in this book, the fact remains that, when all is said and done, purchasing real estate offshore can be a safe transaction as long as the buyer helps to make it so. To draw a parallel, I would say Thailand is a safe country to live in and the average tourist doesn't need to be afraid about getting attacked or robbed on any street corner. Despite Thailand's relatively safe environment, however, we've all heard stories of tourists who have fallen victim to one scam or another. Although it may seem harsh to say so, the most common observance I hear is, "People who fall victim to such scams were looking for trouble in the first place". The unfortunate fact, however, is that too many victims lose their common sense and perspective at some point in the game, and that's the largest contributor to whatever harm befalls them.

Most people who purchase real estate offshore are realizing a dream. In their anticipation of fulfilling the goal of a lifetime, buyers will often toss caution to the wind, lose all common sense and ignore some simple precautions aimed at minimizing the chance of becoming what I've called in this book an "Unfortunate Buyer".

For those of you considering an offshore real estate purchase, the best advice I can offer is to be careful and don't allow reality to spoil your dreams. Most importantly, don't let your hard-earned life savings go to waste when simple measures may prevent you from the pitfalls awaiting the unwary buyer.

The best way to use my book is to pay less attention to my answers and more attention to the questions I've presented. Wherever you decide to purchase your offshore property, keep an inquisitive mind and never hesitate to ask questions about any and all the issues I've raised within this book. Make good use of the due diligence forms I've included. The tables and forms included in this book can be downloaded for free at our website: www.renephilippe.com

While I've put my best effort into covering as many issues as possible, I'm aware that this book is not an exhaustive treatment of this subject, and there's more to the topic than is discussed here. The information in this book is not intended to constitute a legal opinion, or to be relied upon as the sole basis for any decision potentially affecting you or your investment. Please do not hesitate to consult a local lawyer or expert to assist you in handling your purchase.

Finally, I believe in learning by example. Therefore, if any reader (buyer or professional) has had any experiences similar to the one I discussed in the chapter "Buyer Beware", don't hesitate to send me your story at contact@renephilippe.com and I'll try to include it in the next edition of this book.

Bangkok, 15 January, 2010

BIBLIOGRAPHY

- *"Land Ownership and Foreigners: A comparative analysis of regulatory approaches to the acquisition and use of land by foreigners"* by Stephan Hodgson, Cormac Culligan and Karen Campbell FAO Legal Papers
- *"Public Policy for the Private Sector: Land Market WorldBank Note No 300"* by Russel Muir and Xiaofang Shen
- *"Report and Recommendations by the panel of experts regarding land ownership by foreigners in South Africa"*
- *Land Planning Law System, Land Acquisition and Compulsory Purchase Law: The case of Thailand"* by Eathipol Srisawaluck in *"Taking Land: Compulsory Purchase and Regulation in Asian-Pacific Countries"* Tsuyoshi Kotaka*
- *"FAO-Land Reform Report 2006/1: Land tenure data in Thailand"* O. Nabangchang- Srisawalak
- *"The law and development movement: a case study on land law in Thailand."* Philip von Mehren, Tim Sawers
- *"Cadastral Survey Techniques in Developing Countries with Particular Reference to Thailand."* P. Williamson
- *"Thailand's 20-year program to title rural land 2004"*: Antony Burns
- *"Trends in forest ownership, forest resource tenure and institutional arrangements: are they contributing to better forest management and poverty reduction? A case study from Thailand"* Sureeratna LAKANAVICHIAN
- *"Thailand National Report on Protected Areas and Development-2003"*: Lower Mekong Region Organization
- *"Thailand Forests Policies, plantation sector and commodity exports links with China"*: Keith Barney
- *"Regional Study on Land Administration, Land Markets, and Collateralized Lending East Asia and Pacific Region 2004"*: World Bank
- *The Civil and Commercial Code, Books 1-6 (Thai-English)[160]"* compiled and translated by Prof. Kamol Sandhikshetrin.

---

[160] All citations of the TCCC in this book are from this source.

APPENDIX TABLE	
Circular	**Land Department dated of 26 April 2006**
Circular	**Ministry of Interior dated of 21 July 2006**
Circular	**Ministry of Interior dated of 21 July 2008**
Appendix 1	Chanote Front Page
Appendix 2	Chanote Front and Back Page *-Unofficial Translation Appendix 3-*
Appendix 3	Land Department Form Power of Attorney for Land Transaction *-Unofficial Translation -*
Appendix 4	Land Department Form Letter of Confirmation to be signed by the husband of a Thai wife prior to the purchase of land by the Thai wife *-Unofficial Translation*
Appendix 5	Land Department Form Land Sale and Purchase Agreement *-Unofficial Translation-*
Appendix 6	Land Department Form- Land Sale and Purchase Agreement *-Unofficial Translation-*
Appendix 7	Confirmed Certificate of Utilization Nor Sor 3 Kor
Appendix 8	Land Department Form - Form for the Sale & Purchase of Land*-Unofficial Translation -*
Appendix 9	Or.Chor.2 Condominium Unit Title
Appendix 10	Condominium Title Deed *-Unofficial Translation -*
Appendix 11	Form of Power of Attorney for Condominium Transaction - *Unofficial Translation-*
Appendix 12	Form to authorize the other spouse to purchase a condominium under its own name *-Unofficial Translation –*
Appendix 13	Form for the registration of the Sale and Purchase of Condominium at the Land Department
Appendix 14	Condominium Title and Sale and Purchase Agreement and Tabien Baan
Appendix 15	Land Department Form Registration of a Long Term Lease Agreement *-Unofficial Translation -*
Appendix 16	Land Department Form Long Term Lease Agreement - *Unofficial Translation -*
Appendix 17	Land Department Form Registration of a Long Term Right of Superficies *Unofficial Translation -*
Appendix 18	Land Department Form Rights of Superficies Agreement - *Unofficial Translation-*
Appendix 19	Example of agreement to create a right of habitation - *Unofficial Translation -*
Appendix 20	Building Construction, Modification and Removal License- *Unofficial Translation-*
Appendix 21	-Application for Blocking Land-*Unofficial Translation-*
Appendix 22	Acceptation of Application for Blocking Land *-Unofficial Translation-*

Remarks: The following pages contain selections of the most commonly translated Land Department forms as well as a few less common forms I've deemed interesting for the lectors.

We also inserted the three circulars of the land department and the Ministry of interior in relation to the matter of circumventing foreign prohibition of landownership.

Unofficial Translations are not certified translations but have been translated by Thai lawyers.

The language might sound a little bit strange to the reader, but this is a result of the translation. Thai language structure differs from English, so the translation of Thai legal documents is always a daunting task. When translating these documents, the lawyers tried to retain the formatting of the actual forms in order to give some reality to the translations.

Finally, the forms used at the Land Department are short. In general, parties to a transaction will first draft a more detailed and complete agreement that will be binding upon the day of the transaction when they file the Land Department's form.

-Circular 1-
Land Department dated of 26 April 2006
- *Unofficial Translation* –

Mor. Tor. 0515/ Vor 12013 Land Department

Dated 26 April 2006 (Published on 19th June 2006)

Subject : Request for acquisition of land by foreigners

To : Provincial Governor.

Section 97 and 98 of the Land Code state that any juristic person, which foreigner are holding shares more than 49% or have majority number of foreign shareholders, cannot acquire land in Thailand. Thus, there have been various attempts to evade such law by transferring the land while the Companies was not considered as foreign company under Section 97 or 98. However, the Companies, thereafter, increased their share capital so that the shareholding ratio of foreign shareholders was more than 49% or changed the shareholding structure so that the company had more foreign shareholders than Thai. As a consequence, the Companies held land without any additional approval of the Director-General of the Land Department, although this was actually only possible upon approval of the Director-General of the Land Department and in the amount approved by him. Otherwise the law states that the land shall be disposed within the time as specified by the Director-General which shall not less than 180days and not exceeding 1 year. In the event that the Company fails to dispose such land within the time limitation, the Director-General shall have a power to order the disposal of such land.

However, since the Land Department does not have the information of the Company after acquisition of land whether the company will change its shareholding's structure or not, the Land Department is currently unable to control such juristic person. After consideration, the Land Department has approved that - in order to allow the Government authority to investigate the juristic person status after the acquisition of Land whether the Company has increased the capital or has changed its shareholder structure - the following procedure shall be performed:

1)   Collecting the information regarding Limited Companies, Partnerships and Ordinary Partnerships having foreigners as a shareholder or director which has registered the acquisition of Land (except the juristic person which acquire land according to the law, such as Section 27 of the Investment Promotion Act B.E 2520, the section 44 of the Industrial Estate Authority of Thailand Act B.E 2522, or property funds or financial institutions organized by a specific law of Thailand, and insurance companies).

2)   Within the month of June in every calendar year, the Land office in Bangkok and other provinces shall deliver the list of such juristic person to the Department of Business Development requesting for investigation whether the juristic person has changed its shareholding structure to be subjected to Section 97 (1) or (2) or Section 98 of the Land Code.

3)   After receiving the report from the Department of Business Development, if such Juristic person is subjected to section 97(1) or (2) or Section 98 of the Land Code, the Land Office shall order to dispose the amount of Land exceeding the amount approved by the Director General of the Land Department as specified under Section 87. Moreover, Section 87, 94, 95, 100 and 112 of the Land Code shall be further proceeded.

Notify for the acknowledgement and instruct the officer to abide this instruction.

Mr Kanthachai Vichakana

The deputy permanent secretary of Land Department

-Circular 2-
Ministry of Interior dated of 21 July 2006
- Unofficial Translation –

VERY URGENT

At Mor Tor 1515/Wor   2430   Ministry of Interior

Assadang Road Bangkok 10200

July 21st 2006

Subject   Acquisition of Land of juristic Person that has Aliens Shareholders
To   All Provincial Governors
Reference The Ministry of Interior Letter very urgent at Mor Tor 1515/Wor 1562 dated
                        May 15th 2006
Attachment   3 Samples of Memorandum of Words

        Following that the Ministry of Interior has set up the practice for the acquisition of land for limited company, limited partnership, and registered ordinary partnership (except for public limited company or juristic person that is permitted to acquire land by other law) with the purpose to operate immovable property business and has alien shareholders or directors, or has a sound reason to have Thai nominee shareholders for aliens by which indicating to have revenue inspection of the Thai shareholders,
        The Ministry of Interior has considered the issue and in order to regulate the investigation of the officer in the same manner, additional understanding and practice shall be informed as follows:

1.   The Practice as referred in the letter shall apply to juristic person who wishes to acquire the land with the objective to operate immovable property business such as sale and purchase, lease, hotel operation, and vacation home
2.   The supporting evidence in the investigation of the Thai shareholders is for occupation, salary, such as organization certificate of position, from which period, and what is monthly income or other credible evidence and the shareholders shall be investigated the source of the fund used to purchase the shares such as saving money, land sale, inheritance, loan, by which evidence is required such as Bank Saving Book or Land Sale Agreement, Inheritance Certificate, or Loan Agreement.
3.   In case the shareholder is a Thai juristic person (although that juristic person has no alien shareholders or directors), the source of money used to purchase shares shall be inspected by investigating the representative of the shareholding juristic person

for the source of fund and the evidence shall be declared such as the Company Balance Sheet and if it is claimed as loan, the evidence shall be declared such as Loan Agreement and Minutes of Meeting about such issue.

4. In case the juristic person purchase land for the price higher than its registered capital; for example, the registered capital is 500,000 Baht but the land purchased is 10,000,000 Baht without any mortgage of the land, the investigation shall be about the source of money used to purchase the land with supporting evidence declared and if it is from loan the Minutes of Meeting shall be declared with loan evidence document and related document as follows:

    4.1. In case of the loan from alien person or alien juristic person, the evidence for source of money such as transfer from foreign or withdrawal from saving account as well as the debtor's Minutes of Meeting shall be declared

    4.2. In case of the loan from Thai person or Thai juristic person (although that juristic person has no alien shareholders or directors), the evidence for source of money such as the Company Balance Sheet, withdrawal from saving account as well as the Minutes of Meeting of the debtor shall be declared

    Please be informed and have the officers comply with such. The samples of the Memorandum of Words are attached for the officers to use in conduction.

Yours Sincerely,

-Signature-

(Mr. Sura-at Thongniramon)

Deputy Undersecretary of the

Ministry of Interior

Head of Internal Security Duty

Mission Group

Land Department
Land Registration Office
Tel. 0 2221 9189
Fax 0 2222 0623
Tel (Mor Tor) 50801-12 ext. 237

-Circular 3-
Ministry of Interior dated of 21 July 2008
- *Unofficial Translation* -

EXTREMELY URGENT

Ref: Mor. Thor. 0515/Wor. 2227   The Interior Ministry
Atsadang Road Bkk 10200

Date: 21 July 2008

Ref: Application for acquisition of land by juristic person with foreign shareholders
To: All Provincial Governors
Re: Extremely Urgent Circular of Interior Ministry Ref: Mor. Thor. 0515/Wor. 2430
dated 21 July 2006
Encl: Specimen forms for recording Statements - 3 copies

Pursuant to the practice directive of the Interior Ministry relating to applications for the acquisition of land by limited companies, limited partnerships or registered ordinary partnerships (save for public limited companies or juristic persons which have received authorizations to legally acquire land under other laws) which has the objective of carrying out real property business and has foreign shareholders or directors or there is reason to believe has Thai persons as shareholders on behalf of foreigners, there must be examination of the source of monies of the shareholders who are of Thai nationality, to purchase shares and the source of the monies for the company to acquire the land.

The Interior Ministry has deliberated and is of the view that to standardize the examination by officials and prevent avoidance of laws or purchasing land for the benefit of foreigners, it should reinforce understanding and lay down additional practice directives for officials to comply with as follows:

(1)   in respect of limited companies, limited partnerships or registered ordinary partnerships applying to receive transfer of ownership in land, which has the objective of carrying out real property business and has foreign shareholders or directors, to examine the source of monies of shareholders with Thai nationality, to purchase shares;

(2)   in respect of limited companies, limited partnerships or registered ordinary partnerships applying to receive transfer of ownership in land, which does not have the objective of carrying out real property business but there is reason to believe that it has Thai persons as shareholders on behalf of foreigners for example foreigners are authorized to sign on behalf of the company, foreigners are the promoters of the company, foreigners hold preference shares with majority voting rights, the Thai holder of substantial shares has a profession which is not directly related to the business of investing for example attorney at law or estate agent, to examine the source of monies of shareholders with Thai nationality, to purchase shares;

(3)   in a situation where a juristic person purchases land at a price higher than its registered capital without having a mortgage over the land, to examine in detail the source of monies of the juristic person to purchase to the land.

The examination of the source of monies pursuant to (1), (2) and (3) must be carried out strictly pursuant to the practice directives in the documents referred to.

(4)   in respect of receiving transfer of ownership in land by public limited companies or juristic persons which have received authorizations to legally acquire land under other laws for example pursuant to the Promotion of Investments Act 1977 or the Industrial Estate Authority of Thailand Act 1979, there is no need to comply with (1), (2) and (3) in any way.

(5)   in respect of a foreign juristic person leasing land or receiving a right for a long term, to examine whether or not it has the objective of leasing land for the purpose of carrying out a business which amounts to holding of land on behalf of foreigners or in breach of the Foreign Business Act 1999;

(6)   each province must notify all officials involved in public relations that anyone holding land on behalf of foreigners are in breach of Section 113 of the Land Code i.e. giving false information to officials and causing officials to record false information in government documents according to Sections 137 and 267 of the Criminal Code. As for the foreigners and the juristic persons, they are in breach of Sections 111 and 112(1) of the Land Code and must dispose of the land within the timeframe set by the Head of the Land Department which shall not be less than One Hundred and Eighty days and shall not exceed One year. As the current specimen forms for recording statements of shareholders and representatives of juristic persons which purchase land as referred to have incomplete references to the breach of criminal laws and are not inline with what is to be notified to the public, the use of the said forms shall cease and the specimen forms enclose hereto shall be used in their place.

In closing, in examining anyone if there is reason to believe that the application for the registration of rights or dealings is a breach of law or amounts to purchase of land for the benefit of foreigners according to Section 74 Second Paragraph of the Land Code, the official must examine the facts in detail and then send the matter to the Land Department and await further instructions of the Minister.

Please be notified accordingly and instruct all officials to henceforth comply strictly.

Yours respectfully

- Signature Illegible -

(Mr. Phirapol Trithasavit)
Deputy Permanent Secretary for Interior

Land Department, Bureau of Land Registry Standards
Tel. 0 2221 9189
Fax 0 2222 0623
Tel (Mor. Thor.) 50801-12 ext 237

- Appendix 1 -
Chanote Front Page

- Appendix 2 -
Chanote Front and Back Page
- *Unofficial Translation* -

Nor.Sor.4 Jor.

LOCATION   TITLE
DEED
              TOR
Position   No.
Land Number   Issue   Page
Surveying   **TITLE DEED**   Amper
Tambon   **is the Ownership Certificate**   Province
               be Issued under a title of the Land Code

For_____._____Nationality _____Address_____Moo____-
Road_____-_____Tambon_____-_____Amphoe___-_____Province___

This plot of land has space _____ rai, ____ngan and _____Tarang wa

Position Scale 1: 2000   **MAP**   Scale 1: 8000

Issued on 20th January B.E. 2532

(Mr. Prasert Poopong)
The Land Officer

Writer   Map Draftsman
Reader   Map Proof Reader
Proof Reader   Section Head

INDEX OF THE REGISTRATION

Date	Type of registration	Offer	Acceptance	Magnitude of contract	Remaining area	New certificate	The officer sign + Seal
D/M/Y	Mortgage	[000] Ltd	. [XXX] Ltd	94 Rai 3 Ngan 53 2/10 Tarang wa	-	-	[000]
D/M/Y	Second Mortgage	[000] Ltd	[XXX] Ltd	94 Rai 3 Ngan 53 2/10 Tarang wa	-	-	[000]
D/M/Y	Revocation of Mortgage	[XXX] Ltd	[000] Ltd	94 Rai 3 Ngan 53 2/10 Tarang wa	[XXX]Co. Ltd has changed its name to be [ZZZ]Plc		[000]
D/M/Y	Revocation of Mortgage	[ZZZ] Plc	[000] Ltd	94 Rai 3 Ngan 53 2/10 Tarang wa	-	-	[000]
D/M/Y	Sale	[000] Ltd	Mr. A	94 Rai 3 Ngan 53 2/10 Tarang wa	-	-	[000]
D/M/Y	Mortgage	Mr. A	[ZZZ] Plc	94 Rai 3 Ngan 53 2/10 Tarang wa	-	-	[000]
D/M/Y	Transfer the right of Mortgage	[ZZZ]Plc	[YYY] Plc (Transfere)	94 Rai 3 Ngan 53 2/10 Tarang wa	-	-	[000]

INDEX OF THE REGISTRATION (Attachment)   Page Kor

Date	Type of registration	Offer	Acceptance	The magnitude of contract	Remaining of area	New certificate	The officer sign + Seal
D/M/Y	Revocation of Mortgage	[YYY] Plc (Mortgag or)	Mr. A (Mortgagee)	94 Rai 3 Ngan 53 2/10 Tarang wa	-	-	[000]
	Mortgage	Mr.A	Mr.B	94 Rai 3 Ngan 53 2/10 Tarang wa	-	-	[000]
	Subdivide the Land in the owner name (Extended Mortgage)	Mr. A	Mr. A	9 Rai 1 Ngan 87 5/10 Tarang wa	85 Rai 1 Ngan 65 7/10 Tarang wa	[oo]TOR [oo]AOR /	[000]
				Mortgage is still effective on subdivided land according to the Mortgage Agreement on the date of April 10, B.E. 2546			

Remarks: The list of registration above is interesting because it shows a few of the juristic acts that may be registered on a title deed. In this particular case, most of the transactions recorded above were made over a one-year period. This translation is not actually the complete record of the transactions made on this title deed.

- Appendix 3 -
Land Department Form
Power of Attorney for Land Transaction
- *Unofficial Translation* -

POWER OF ATTORNEY

Land

Scale..Subdistrict...........................
No..District...............................
Survey Page....................................Province.............................
Title Deed No. ....

Subject...
....

Written at...
Date....Month..........B.E.............................
With this letter I,..
Age....-....Race.........-....Nationality...................Child of.........-..........
Living at No.........Road..............................Moo..........................-...........
Subdistrict..District..
............Province...
Authorize ....Age....................Race........Nationality.......
Child of ....Living at No.......................Moo-...........
............Subdictrict...District.......................
Province............................
To...on behalf of myself until finish.

      In Witness Whereof, I hereby set my signature hereto in the presence of
witnesses   ....
                      (Grantor)

      I hereby certify that it is true signature of the grantor and the grantor
signed in the presence of myself.

      ....Witness
      ....Witness

- Appendix 4 -
Land Department Form
Letter of Confirmation to be signed by the husband of a Thai wife prior to the purchase of land by the Thai wife
- *Unofficial Translation* -

หนังสือรับรอง
Letter of Confirmation

เขียนที่...

At

วันที่.............เดือน...........................ปี..............

Date   Month   Year

ข้าพเจ้า นาย/นาง...........................และนาย/นาง...

I, Mr./Mrs   and Mr./Mrs

เป็นคู่สมรสโดยชอบด้วยกฎหมาย   ขอให้ถ้อยคำยืนยันร่วมกันว่าเงินที่นาย/นาย............

....

are registered both spouses.   We together confirm that the money which Mr./Mrs

นำมาซื้อที่ดิน ตามโฉนดที่ดิน / น.ส 3.ก/.น.ส 3 .เลขที่ ....ตำบล...........

Shall expend on the purchase of land title deed/ N.S. 3 K/N.S. 3 no   Sub-district

อำเภอ..จังหวัด..............................

District   Province

พร้อมสิ่งปลูกสร้าง..............................ตำบล.............................

With the construction   Sub-district

อำเภอ..จังหวัด..............................

District   Province

หรือห้องชุดเลขที่.........................ชั้นที่...........ชื่ออาคารชุด.................

or Condominium unit no   Floor   Name of Condominium

ตำบล.....................อำเภอ.........................จังหวัด................

Sub-district   District

          Province

เป็นสินส่วนตัวหรือทรัพย์ส่วนตัวของ นาย/นาง...

is wholly Sin Suan Tua of the personal property of Mr./Mrs

แต่เพียงผู้ฝ่ายเดียว มิใช่สินสมรส หรือทรัพย์ที่ทำมาหาได้ร่วมกัน

alone, not Sin Som Ros or the matrimonial property between husband and wife.

การรับรอง	) ลงชื่อ(_____	สามี/ภริยา ผู้รับรอง
Confirmation	(Signature)	Certified spouse

)ลงชื่อ(_____ สามี/ภริยา ผู้รับรอง
(Signature) Certified spouse

)ลงชื่อ(_____ พยาน
(Signature) Witness

ลงชื่อ(_____ พยาน
(Signature) Witness

Remarks: The **Sin Suan Tua** of a spouse consists of: (1) property belonging to either spouse prior to the marriage; (2) property for personal use such as clothing or accessories suitable for the person's station in life, or tools necessary for carrying on the profession of either spouse; (3) property acquired by either spouse during the marriage by means of a will or gift; (4) Khongman, or property purchased in replacement of a Sin Suan Tua. Each spouse is the owner and manager of his or her **Sin Suan Tua.** By declaring the land as Sin Suan Tua, the foreign spouse loses any right to the land or its value in the event of a divorce.

- Appendix 5 -
Land Department Form
Land Sale and Purchase Agreement
- Unofficial Translation -

(Tor.Dor. 13)

Land Purchase Agreement

Land

Title Deed No. [00000]   Land No. [00000]   Surveying [00000]
Tambon ___[00000]   ___Amphoe [00000]   Province___[00000] _____

This Agreement is made on the date of __[00000]   _month_____[00000]   B.E.
[00000] at Provincial Land Office__ Province___Bangkok _____

between { _[00000] Co.,Ltd. _Represented By_ Mr._[00000] } aged { _____ - _____ _____ } Nationality _Thai_

child of ___-____ residing in _____ No. _____ Moo_ -____

Tambon_____Amphoe _____ Province___Bangkok___

And { [00000] Co.,Ltd. _Represented By_ Mr._[00000] } aged { _____ - _____ } Nationality _Thai_

child of _____-____residing in _____No._____ Moo_ -____

Tambon_____Amphoe _____Province__Bangkok__

Both parties hereby agree with the terms and conditions as follows:

No. 1 The Seller agrees to sell the land to the Purchaser indicated hereinabove at the amount of[00000].- Baht ([00000] Only) . . . .

No. 2 The Purchaser agrees to purchase the land stated in No. 1 from the Seller and the Seller has already received the purchase sum by Cashier's Cheque No. [00000] and in cash

No. 3 The land is sold with a [00000] - storey building at No. [00000] Soi[00000], Bangkok with an area of [00000] Square Meters.

This Agreement has been drafted in duplicate with identical content with one copy for the Land Department and the other for the Purchaser. (This copy is for the Purchaser) Both parties having read and understood the whole content of this Agreement hereby affix their respective signatures.

(Signature of the Seller) _____

(Signature of the Purchaser) _____

(Signature of the Witness) _____

(Signature of the Witness) _____

In witness whereof, Signature_____

Authorized Officer

Stamp

_____writer

_____reviser

Remarks: This is a translation of the Land Department form for the sale and purchase of land and house. An example for a sale of undeveloped land can be viewed below.

- Appendix 6 -
Land Department Form
Land Sale and Purchase Agreement
- Unofficial Translation -

(Tor.Dor. 13)

Land Purchase Agreement

Land

Title Deed No. [00000]   Land No. [00000]   Surveying [00000]
Tambon ___[00000]   ___Amphoe [00000]   Province__[00000] _____

This Agreement is made on the date of __[00000] _month_____[00000] B.E.
[00000] at Provincial Land Office__Province___Bangkok_____

between { [00000] Co.,Ltd. / Represented By / Mr. [00000] } aged { ___-___ } Nationality Thai

child of ____-____residing in _____No._____Moo__-___
Tambon_____Amphoe _____Province__Bangkok___

And { [00000] Co.,Ltd. / Represented By / Mr. [00000] } aged { ___-___ } Nationality Thai

child of ____-____residing in _____No._____Moo__-___
Tambon_____Amphoe _____Province__Bangkok__

Both parties hereby agree with the terms and conditions as follows:

No. 1 The Seller agrees to sell the land to the Purchaser indicated hereinabove at the amount of [00000].- Baht ([00000] Only).

No. 2 The Purchaser agrees to purchase the land stated in No. 1 from the Seller and the Seller already received the purchase sum.

No. 3 The Seller obtained this land by the purchase on [00000]B.E. [00000].

No. 4 This is the land without buildings which is a plantation in area, without lease, nor unpaid tax.

No. 5 Payment is made completely.

No. 6 This land is purchased for building branch office, house for director / official and warehouse.

This Agreement has been drafted in duplicate with identical content with one copy for the Land Department and the other for the Purchaser. (This copy is for the Purchaser)

Both parties having read and understood the whole content of this Agreement hereby affix their respective signatures.

(Signature of the Seller)   _____

(Signature of the Purchaser)   _____

(Signature of the Witness)   _____

(Signature of the Witness)   _____

In witness whereof, Signature_____

Authorized Officer

Stamp

_____writer

_____reviser

- Appendix 7 -
Confirmed Certificate of Utilization Nor Sor 3 Kor

- Appendix 8 -
Land Department Form
Form for the Sale & Purchase of Land
- *Unofficial Translation* -

(Tor.Or. 5)

Land Purchase Agreement totaling 2 Nor.Sor. 3 Kor.

Land   **Register**

Tambon _____ Moo _____ Vol. __ Kor., _____ Kor.

Amphoe _____ Page _____

Changwat _____ No.

Total Area __ Rai_ _____ Ngan _____ Wa

_____

This Agreement is made on the date of __ month _____ B.E. ___

at Provincial Land Office Province_____

between { _____ } the Seller, aged { _____ } Nationality __Thai

child of ____ residing in _____ No. _____ Moo _____

Tambol_____ Amphoe _____ Province_____

between { .... } the Purchaser, aged { .... } Nationality Thai .

child of .... - .... residing in .... No. ...... Moo ...-...
Tambol .... Province ....

Both parties hereby agree with the terms and conditions as follows:

No. 1 The Seller agrees to sell the land to the Purchaser indicated hereinabove at the amount of ....- Baht (.....) ....
....

No. 2 The Purchaser agrees to purchase the land stated in No. 1 from the Seller and the Seller already received the purchase sum in full. ....
....

No. 3 There is no construction in the land which is for the residential purpose. The Land was acquired by inheritance more than 10 years. The purpose of the land purchase is to construct a resort which is the business of the company. ....
....
....

This Agreement is made in duplicate with identical content; one for Amphoe Office and the other one for the Purchaser. (This copy is for the Purchaser)

Both parties having read and understood the whole content in this Agreement hereby affix their respective signatures.

(Signature of the Seller) ....

(Signature of the Purchaser) ....

(Signature of the Witness) ....

(Signature of the Witness) ....

Signed .... Land Officer, registration or right department

      Position   -seal-   Writer

                                                Reviewer

- Appendix 9 -
Or.Chor.2 Condominium Unit Title

- Appendix 10 -
Condominium Title Deed
- *Unofficial Translation* -

LOCATION OF LAND

Title Deed no.
Tambol
Amphur
Province
Area of ___Rai_Ngan_Sq.War_

LOCATION OF CONDOMINIUM UNIT

Unit no.
Floor
Building no.
Condominium Unit name
Condo Unit Registration No.

DEED OF CONDOMINIUM UNIT

Issued under the power of Condominium Unit Act B.E. 2522

This Deed is issued in favor of

Name_____ Company Limited[161] Nationality _Thai_ Address no.___ Moo___-_Road_
Trok/Soi_-_Tambol/Sub-District_____Amphur/District_____Province Bangkok

Plan of Condominium Unit

Scale: 1:125
Area of   Sq.m.   Esq. Height   m.

The ratio of ownership in common property   _____ in 10,000
Issued on   May

(Mr. Prakit Sirichareon)
Official

---

[161] Condominium titles are first issued to the developer who transfers them to the buyers.

INDEX OF THE REGISTRATION

Date of Registration	Type of Registration	Offer	Acceptance	The official signs with position seal affixed
Day/Month/Year	Mortgage	[000]Co. Ltd	[000]Bank Plc - Mortgager - According to Mortgage Agreement on the	[000]
Day/Month/Year	Transfer right of mortgage	[000]Bank Plc - Transferor -	[xxx]Bank Plc - Transferee -	[000]
Day/Month/Year	Removal of Mortgage	[xxx]Bank Plc	[000]Co. Ltd	[000]
Day/Month/Year	Sale	[000]Co. Ltd	Mr. [000]	[000]

- Appendix 11 -
Form of Power of Attorney for Condominium Transaction
- *Unofficial Translation* -

POWER OF ATTORNEY

Land	**Condo**
Title Deed No. _____	Unit _____Floor _____ Building no. _____
Subdistrict _____	Name of Condominium _____
District _____	Registration of Condominium no. _____
Province _____	Area _____ Square Meters

Subject_____

Written at _____

Date_____Month_____ B.E._____

With this letter I,_____
Age_____Race_____Nationality_____Child of_____
Living at No._____Road_____Moo_____
Sub-district_____District_____Province_____
Authorize_____Age_____Race_____Nationality_____
Child of _____Living at No._____Moo_____
Sub-district_____District_____Province_____
To_____
_____on behalf of
myself until finish.

In Witness Whereof, I hereby set my signature hereto in the presence of witnesses

_____Grantor

I hereby certify that it is true signature of the grantor, and the grantor signed in the presence of me.

_____Witness

_____Witness

- Appendix 12 -
Form to authorize the other spouse to purchase a condominium under its own name
- *Unofficial Translation* -

Permission Letter

At Rene Philippe and Partners Ltd.
82/9 Langsuan Rd., Lumpini
Patumwan, Bangkok

Date

I, Mrs. [000000] ep. [000000]; Nationality [000000], hold passport no. [000000] issue at [000000] on [000000] and valid until [000000], I' am the registered spouse of Mr. [000000]. I consent to let Mr. [000000] to purchase solely a Condominium unit [000000], Floor [000000], name of the condominium is [000000] at Soi [000000], Sukhumvit Rd., [000000], Bangkok with [000000] Properties Co., Ltd.

I hereby certify true content and thereby affixed their respective signature in the presence of the witnesses on the date month and year first above written.

Signature _____ Certified Spouse
Signature
Signature _____ Witness
Signature _____ Witness

- Appendix 13 -
Form for the Registration of the Sale and Purchase of Condominium at the
Land Department
Condominium Title Deed
- Unofficial Translation -

Sale and purchase of condominium agreement

Location of land   Location of condominium

The title deed no....................   Unit Number ......Floor....Building number.....

Sub district...........................   Name of condominium.....................

District................................   Registration number..........................

Province.............................   The amount of the area.......square meter

This contract has been made on the date of .... at the land registration office   of

.... Between

..................................Nationality............. Name of father/mother...................Which reside

at..Tel. number............... Identification card

number................. And hereinafter in this agreement shall be called "The Seller" and

. ...Nationality.................Name of father/mother.................... which reside

at...........................Tel. number...............Identification card number................. And

hereinafter in this agreement shall be called "The Buyer"

    Both parties have an agreement as follows:

1.   The (Seller/The Buyer) agreed to buy .... Condominium as mentioned
      above to.................for the amount price of.........bath(......)

2.   The (Seller/The Buyer) agreed to sale .... Condominium for the
      amount price as mentioned in article 1.

3.   The seller will be responsible for any damages which causes from the
      defection of the condominium unit within not less than 5 years from the

condominium registered the date and the Seller shall fix for the defect within 30 days since he/she get the notice from the Buyer. Except if such defect has a high priority to be fixed, The Seller shall fix the defect immediately as soon as he/she got a notice from The Buyer. If The Seller refuses to take an action, The Buyer may hire a contractor to fix the defect and The Seller shall compensate for the price which The Buyer already paid to the contractor.

4.   Both parties agreed not to refuse to make any payment regard to section 18 of Condominium Act B.E.2522. And has a certification of dept free from the condominium representative.

This agreement is made in duplicate for……. set with all text identical. For the land department 1 duplicate. For……………………………. 1 duplicate and ……………………………. 1 duplicate (This duplicate is for………………..)

Both parties have aware and understand the entire context in this contract, so they made a signature in front of authorized officer.

Signature of The Seller_____ Signature of The Buyer_____
Signature of witness_____ Signature of witness_____
                                                       Signature_____
                                                                     Authorized Officer
                                                                                    Stamp
                                                       _____writer
                                                       _____reviser

- Appendix 14 -
Condominium Title and Sale and Purchase Agreement and
Tabian Baan

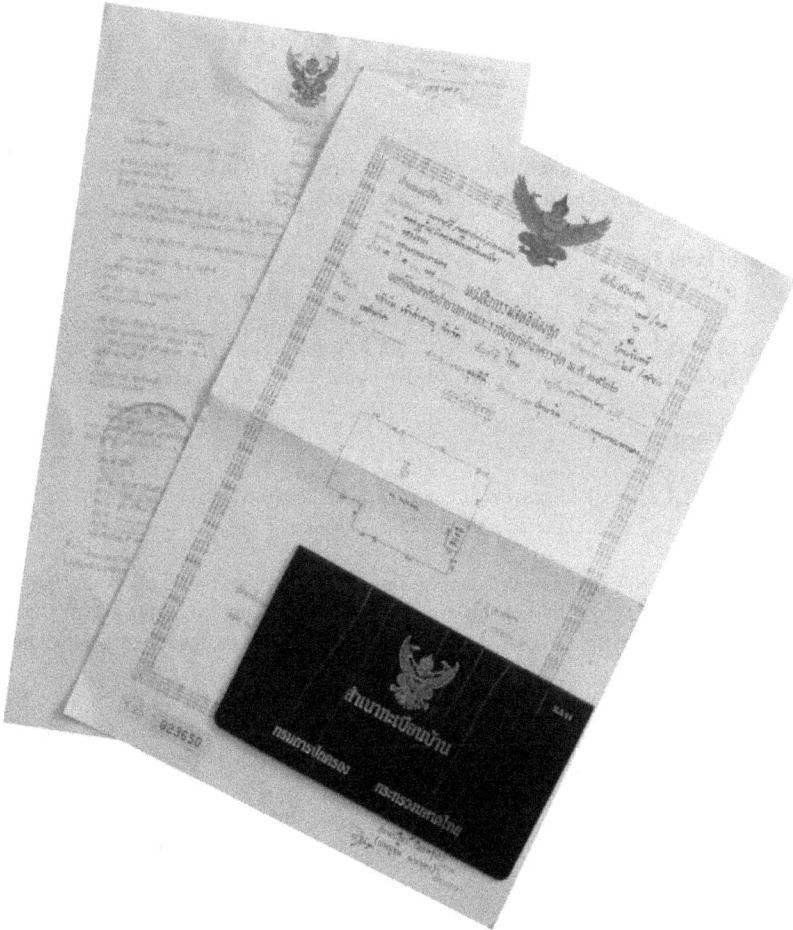

- Appendix 15 -
Land Department Form
Registration of a Long Term Lease Agreement
- *Unofficial Translation* -

(Tor.Dor. 1)
...(Land Type)...

An application form for registration of right and juristic act and for investigation of right on the land in category of lease for the period of 10 years.

Position of Land Plot

Section...Tumbol.........................
Number of Land Plot No......................................Amphoe...
Survey Page...Province..

Land Title Deed

No. ....Book No. ....Page No. ....
Area of Land...........................Rai.............................Ngan.............................Tarang Wah

      1. I, the undersigned would like to request for registration of right and juristic act related to the immoveable property as mentioned above. I affirm that my statement is true. If I give false statement it can be used as evidence against me in criminal charge.

ID. Card No.

      2. I, ... , ..., the Lessor
Age...........................years, Nationality.............. Father/Mother Name...........................
...... Single ...... Divorce .... Name of spouse.......................Nationality...........................
Residing in House/Village............No. ......Soi......................Rd. ....Moo.................
Tumbol/Sub-district.................Amphoe/District..............Province.......Tel No. ....

ID. Card No.

      3. I, ... , ..., the Lessee
Age...........................years, Nationality.............. Father/Mother Name...........................
...... Single ...... Divorce .... Name of spouse.......................Nationality...........................
Residing in House/Village............No. ......Soi......................Rd. ....Moo.................
Tumbol/Sub-district.................Amphoe/District..............Province.................
Tel No. ....

4. I would like to declare the cost of property to perform this juristic act in amount of ………………………Baht…………………Satang.

5. I hereby certify that
(1)   The transfer of property I made is not for foreigner or in foreigner's favors.
(2)   The cost of property declared in 4. is true.
(3)   The lease term is fixed for 10 years from the date of execution this agreement. The rental shall be annually paid in amount of 10,000 baht per year.
(4)   The rental shall be paid within March 2nd of each year/upon the expiration of the lease term, any constructions on the land made by the Lessee shall belong to the Lessor.

(5)   The Lessee shall not be permitted to sub-lease the land to the third party.
(6)   (6) In case any party dies during the lease term, an heir of such party shall be bound by the rights and obligations of this agreement

On ………(Date/Month/year)………
    Signature…………………………Lessor applicant
        Signature…………………………Lessee applicant
            Signature……………………………Investigator

For the officer
1) Appraisal value of Property……………………………Baht……………………………………Satang
2) New Title Deed: section…………Land Plot No. …………………Survey Page…………………
Land Title Deed no. …………………………Book no. ……………………………Page no.
……………………………
    Land's area……………………………Rai…………………………Gnan…………………………Tarang Wah
    Balanced……………………………Rai……………………………Gnan…………………………Tarang Wah
3) The registration made on ……………………(Date/Month/year)………………………
                Signature ……………………………………………………
                (……………………………………………………)

Land Officer

Remarks: This is a translation from an example of a standard Land Department form. The lease may be for more than 10 years

- Appendix 16 -
Land Department Form
Long Term Lease Agreement
- *Unofficial Translation* -

(Tor.Dor.36)

<u>Land Lease Agreement</u> for the period of ....years

Land

Title Deed No. ....Land Plot No. .... Survey Page................
Tumbol...................................... Amphoe.............................. Province.......................
This agreement is made on this day .... of Month.....................B.E. ....

At Provincial Land Office ....

ID.Card No.

Between ⎰ .... ⎱ .... ⎰ Lessor Age ⎰ .... ⎱
         ⎱ .... ⎰   ⎱   ⎱ .... ⎰

Nationality....................................... Child of..
Residing in House/Village................. No. .... Soi....................Rd. ......Moo...........
Tumbol/Sub-district.................Amphoe/ District.............Province...............
Tel No. ....

ID Card No.

Between ⎰ .... ⎱ .... ⎰ Lessee Age ⎰ .... ⎱
         ⎱ .... ⎰   ⎱   ⎱ .... ⎰

Nationality....................................... Child of..
Residing in House/Village................. No. .... Soi....................Rd. ......Moo...........
Tumbol/Sub-district.................Amphoe/ District.............Province...............
Tel No. ....

ID Card No.

The Parties do hereby agrees with the terms and conditions as follows:

No. 1 The Lessor agrees to lease the Lessee the land s mentioned above for the purpose of .... (specify the purpose of lease) ....
....for period of years .... months from the date of execution of this agreement onward.

No. 2 The Lessee agrees to pay the Lessor the rental in amount of Baht . The rental shall be paid in amount of Baht 10,000.- (Ten Thousand Baht only) per annual within March 2nd in each year ....

No. 3 The construction on the land; upon the expiration of the lease term, any constructions on the land made by the Lessee shall belong to the Lessor. To sub-lease this land to the third party shall not be permitted.

No. 4 In case any party dies during the lease term an heir of such party shall be bound by the rights and obligations of this agreement.....................

This Agreement has been executed by the Parties in triplicate; one copy is kept by Land Department. Each the Lessor and the Lessee kept another copies. (This copy is for the ....)

The Parties have reviewed and fully understood all content of this Agreement do hereby affixed their signatures or fingerprint in the presence of witnesses and land officer.

   (Signature of the Lessor)............ Signature ....
   (Signature of the Lessee)............ Signature ....
   (Signature of the witness)........... Signature ....
   (Signature of the witness)........... Signature ....

In the presence of
   .... Signature .... Land Officer Land Officer's seal
          .... Writer
          ....Checker

- Appendix 17 -
Land Department Form
Registration of a Long Term Right of Superficies
-Unofficial Translation -

(Tor.Dor. 1)
...(Land Type)...

An application form for registration of right and juristic act and for investigation of right on the land for the period of 10 years.

Position of Land Plot

Section..Tumbol..........................
Number of Land Plot No..Amphoe...
Survey Page..Province...

Land Title Deed

No. ....Book No. ....Page No. ....
Area of Land............................Rai............................Ngan............................Tarang Wah

      1. I, the undersigned would like to request for registration of right and juristic act related to the immoveable property as mentioned above. I affirm that my statement is true. If I give false statement it can be used as evidence against me in criminal charge.

ID. Card No.

      2. I, ... , ..., the Lessor
Age.........................years, Nationality.............. Father/Mother Name.............................
...... Single ...... Divorce .... Name of spouse........................Nationality..........................
Residing in House/Village............No. ......Soi......................Rd. ....Moo...................
Tumbol/Sub-district................Amphoe/District..............Province.......Tel No. ....
ID. Card No.

      3. I, ... , ..., the Lessee
Age.........................years, Nationality.............. Father/Mother Name.............................
...... Single ...... Divorce .... Name of spouse........................Nationality..........................
Residing in House/Village............No. ......Soi......................Rd. ....Moo...................

Tumbol/Sub-district……………….Amphoe/District……………Province………………
Tel No. ………………..

       4. I would like to declare the cost of property to perform this juristic act in amount of ……………………….Baht…………………Satang.

   5.   I hereby certify that:

(1)   The transfer of property I made is not for foreigner or in foreigner's favors
(2)   The cost of property declared in 4. is true.
(3)   The Superficiary has the right to build Buildings, structures and plantations, upon or under the land for the period of 30 years
(4)   The right of superficies has been granted as a free gift whereby no any remuneration or rental shall be paid to the Land Owner
(5)   ---

On ………(Date/Month/year)………

Signature………………………..Lessor applicant
     Signature………………………..Lessee applicant
         Signature…………………………..Investigator

Remarks: This is a translation from an example of a standard Land Department form. The Right of Superficies is not necessarily free and is mostly granted for a remuneration

- Appendix 18 -
Land Department Form
Rights of Superficies Agreement
- *Unofficial Translation* -

(Tor.Dor.36)

Agreement to Establish the Right of Superficies

Land

Title Deed No. ....Land Plot No. .... Survey Page................…...
Tumbol………………………………... Amphoe…………………………... Province…………………….
This agreement is made on this day .... of Month…………………B.E. ……………....

At Provincial Land Office …………………….

ID.Card No.

Between ....
.... Lessor Age ....
....

Nationality……………………………………………... Child of…………………………………………………….
Residing in House/Village……………... No. ……….. Soi…………………….Rd. ……Moo………….
Tumbol/Sub-district……………..Amphoe/ District…………..Province…………….
Tel No. ………………..

ID Card No.

Between ....
.... Lessee Age ....
....

Nationality……………………………………………... Child of…………………………………………………….
Residing in House/Village……………... No. ……….. Soi…………………….Rd. ……Moo………….
Tumbol/Sub-district……………..Amphoe/ District…………..Province…………….
Tel No. ………………..

The Parties do hereby agree with the terms and conditions as follows:

No. 1 The Land owner agrees to grant the Superficiary the right of Superficies on the land mentioned above, with the right to own, upon or under the land, building, structures or plantations for 3o years from the date of execution this agreement onward.

No. 2 The Superficiary acquired the right of superficies by giving as a free gift, no any remuneration or a rental shall be paid to the Land owner.

This Agreement has been executed by the Parties in triplicated; one copy is kept by Land Office. Each Land Owner and the Superficiary kept another copies. (This copy is for the ....)

The Parties have reviewed and fully understood all content of this agreement do hereby affixed their signatures or fingerprint in the presence of witnesses and land officer.

(Signature of the Lessor)............Signature.......
(Signature of the Lessee)............Signature..................
(Signature of the witness)............Signature..................
(Signature of the witness)............Signature..................

In the presence of
............Signature........... Land Officer   Land Officer's seal
                                ------------------------ Writer
                                ----------------------Checker

Remarks: This is a translation from an example of a standard form for a Right of Superficies agreement from the Land Department. The Right of Superficies is not necessarily free and is mostly granted for a remuneration

- Appendix 19 -
EXAMPLE OF AGREEMENT TO CREATE A RIGHT OF HABITATION
- Unofficial Translation -

October ...., B.E...........

This agreement is made between

Mr. ...., aged ......, nationality of Thai, holding ID. Card No..................., residing at ......
moo...... Tumbol ...., Amphoe..........., hereinafter known as "Host" and
Mr..........................., nationality of ...., aged...... , holding a passport
No..........., hereinafter known as "Habitant"

(1)   Whereas the Host is the owner of a house which locates at .... moo ....,.........
District........, Sub-District............,Province......... including all property in such house,
hereinafter known as "Building"

(2)   Whereas the Host borrowed money from the Habitant in the amount of
...................Baht (...................) according to the loan agreement dated October,
...................................and the Host has already received such amount of money since
the day entering into the loan agreement.

(3)   Whereas the Host mortgaged the land title deed No........., land No..........., surveying
page........, Tumbol......., Amphoe..............., Bangkok, including the structure(house) in the
land-allocated project named "...............Project..........." which locates at.............., Moo
...........District........., Sub-District..........., Bangkok as a guarantee of the loan in the amount
of ....Baht...................) Baht (according to the loan agreement dated October,
...........B.E. ....

The Parties hereby agree as follows:

No 1.   The Host agrees to grant the Habitant the right of habitation in the Building of
the Host. The Habitant agrees to pay the amount of .... (...........)Baht to
the Host.

No.2   The Host has already received the amount of .... (...........)Baht from the
Habitant since the day entering into the agreement.

No 3.   The right of habitation shall last for 30 years. Upon the expiration, both parties
agree to extend the right of habitation for the next 30 years in each time for
the life of the Habitant.

No 4.   The right of habitation in the Building shall include the inhabitance of person
in family. The Habitant cannot transfer the right of habitation to others or the
third party.

No.5   The Host and the Habitant agree to register the creation of the right of habitation at the Land Office, ...Sub-District, Bangkok not exceeding the date of November, ...B.E........

No 6.   The Habitant is bound to take as much care of the Building as a person of ordinary prudence would take of his own property and to do ordinary maintenance and petty repairs. The Habitant shall not make any alterations in or additions to the Building except a written notice to the Host is given.

No.7   The Habitant is liable for any loss or damage caused to the Building habited except loss or damage resulting from proper use.

This agreement is made in duplicate. Both parties have read and understood the entire content of the agreement hereby affix their signatures in th presence of witnesses.

Signature........................the Host Mr..........................
Signature........................the Habitant Mr......................
Signature........................the Witness ....
Signature........................the Witness ....

Remarks: This sample of a Right to Habitation agreement represents a very specific transaction. A Right to Habitation may be established without a loan or mortgage agreement between the host and the habitant. Also note that a Right to Habitation requires a 30-day period of publication.

- Appendix 20 -
Building Construction, Modification and Removal License
- *Unofficial Translation* -

Original Form Or.
[ooo]/2546

Building Construction, Modification and Removal License
No. Yor. [0000]./2003

Authorization is granted to [0000]. By Mr. [0000]. the owner of the building, residing at [0000]. Bangkok -----------------------------------

No. 1 For the construction of the building No. – [0000]. Bangkok on title deeds No. [0000]. Land No. [0000]. The land belongs to [0000].

No. 2 For the utilization as building

(1) Type x storey Number   x   purpose   residence
--------------------Area   xxxxxx   square meters Parking, u-turn area, entrance and exit area for - cars, Area _____ square meters
(2) Type drain pipe   Number   1   purpose   drainage
Length   80   meters   Parking, u-turn area, entrance and exit area for   -
cars, Area _____ square meters
(3) Type_____- Number _____-_____ purpose ____-_____

Area/ Lenght _____-_____   Parking, u-turn area, entrance and exit area for -
cars, Area _____ square meters

according to the layout plan, the plan, subscription of the plan and the calculation No. -_____ attached to this license.

No. 3. Mr. [0000]. Por Yor. [0000].   and Mr. [0000]. SorSorTor. [0000]. -------------------------- are operators.

No.4 The Licensee shall fulfill the following conditions.

(1) The licensee shall perform in accordance with the rules, measures, and conditions indicated in the ministerial regulation or local legislation that was issued according to the section 8(11) section 9 or section 10 of the Building Control Act B.E. 2522 . *License fee 20 Baht. Plan review fee 6,880.00 Baht. Total 6,900.00 Baht (Six thousand nine hundred baht only)*

This license shall be valid until December xx, 2004

Issued on December xx, 2003

Signed

(...)

- Appendix 21 –

Remarks: It might happen that a buyers purchases a land pursuant to an agreement that provide the payment in several installments over one or two year period. What happen if the Seller decides to breach the agreement and to sell and transfer the land to a third party before the completion of the sale and purchase agreement with the first buyer and the transfer of the land at the Land Department? One of the options available to a buyer in such circumstances would be to file an application to block the land at the Land Department as shown below.

Application for Blocking Land
- *Unofficial Translation* -

(Tor.Dor. 9)

The **Application** for blocking the land in a number of 6 Title Deeds **No.**................

**Land
Position**.................... **Thumbol**...................................
No. ....**Survey**..**Page**................
Ampher ....Title Deed No ....Province.....................

Date....Month   B.E.

I, hereby,   Age........Year Nationality..........................
................Race..Son of.......
....
Residing At ....**No** ....**Moo**....**Thumbol**
Ampher ....**Province**...,
would like to submit the application to the provincial land officer ......Branch.....
.... with the truth that:-

Clause1. Mr [0000000] who is the owner of the land mentioned above, and has executed the agreement to sale such land to [XXX] Co.,Ltd. more details as described in Sale Agreement dated   . During September,   up to   December [XXX] Co.,Ltd has paid 4 installments of a total amount of Baht   .- for deposit according to clause 3.1 of the Sale Agreement. The terms of payment of the land price and the schedule to transfer the ownership of the land was specified in clause 2.1 and

2.2 respectively. Upon receipt of the first payments the agreement stipulated that the owner should transfer 38-3-5.2 Rais and the buyer paid another amount of   .-
But on the date of the transfer the owner informed the buyer that he could not transfer the land with the area as agreed because some parcels of land have been mortgaged with Financial Institutes, therefore, he asked to transfer instead other lands also sold pursuant to the agreement but of a lesser area. Whereas, under clause 1.5 of the Sale Agreement the parties agreed that the amount of the payment due and payable on the appointed date of transfer shall be adjusted accordingly by reference to the unit price of Baht   per Rai. Then, the buyer paid for the land another 8 installments of a total amount of Baht   .- Baht All payments have been made on the due date scheduled into the agreement. While the transfer was not scheduled for another 3 months according to the agreement the owner has transferred the land with title deeds No and   respectively to a new buyer. Thus, it shall be deemed that the seller breached the agreement and with his conduct relating to remove and distribute property, therefore, the buyer is a person of interest and may file a lawsuit to execute the registration or change of the registration for those lands. As such, the buyer will file a lawsuit to the court asking for court order to terminate the juristic acts of sale between the seller and the new buyer. As for the remaining not transferred title deeds, the buyer will file a lawsuit to force the seller to perform his obligation under the agreement and also to claim for damage which incurred from his failure to comply with the agreement. Whereas, some of parcel of land has been transferred to the third person, the buyer will file a lawsuit against third party with the issue that they are jointly defraud to transfer and remove property that it might cause damage to the buyer.

The buyer attached evidence as follow to this application as follows;

Clause 2. Therefore, I would like to ask the competent officer to execute and block as directed in the application.

-Signature of -   Representative according to power of attorney dated

- Appendix 22-
Acceptation of Application for Blocking Land
- *Unofficial Translation* -

Memorandum
Division of Official: Registration Division
No: **Date:**
Subject: Application for blocking lands
Attn: The Chef of the Land Office of ………. Province, Branch Office.
                              As for [0000] has submitted the application to block the title
deeds no …………… survey page…………………., Thumbon………., Ampher …………Province
respectively, more details described in application no ……………dated……………., and
claimed that the owner of the above mentioned lands, has breached the Sale and
Purchase Agreement dated …………and having behavior to defraud by way of remove
and distribute the property, therefore, the applicant requested to block the land for
filling a lawsuit asking for court order to dismiss the juristic acts of sale between the
seller and the new buyer and force him to comply with the agreement. Due to some of
lands under this application has been transferred to the third party (new buyer), then,
the applicant will file a lawsuit against the third party with the ground that jointly
defraud to transfer and distribute property.

After consideration the application for blocking the lands, the
committee is of the opinion that the applicant is the interested person to the land and
may file a lawsuit to execute for registration or changing the registration to the land,
therefore, the Committee has an order to block the lands for 30 days from the day of
order to block, and inform the interested person to know. Whereas this order is the
administrative order where it should be proceed under the Administrative Procedure
Act B.E. 2539 or it should process in other manner, please give instruction.

Sign_____-Signature-_____President of Committee
Sign_____-Signature-_____ Committee
Sign_____-Signature-_____ Committee

Remarks: The application to block a land under such circumstances is not the end of the
matter. The blocking order by the Land Department is valid only for a 30-day period.
Therefore, it's necessary to file legal action in a court of law within this period in order
to keep the land blocked. If no legal action is initiated during this period, the land is
freed from blockage.

www.ingramcontent.com/pod-product-compliance
Lightning Source LLC
Chambersburg PA
CBHW060322200326
41519CB00011BA/1806